Revised and Updated Edition

Florida Gardener's Handbook

All You Need to Know to Plan, Plant & Maintain a Florida Garden

Tom MacCubbin and Georgia Tasker with Robert Bowden and Joe Lamp'l

COOL
SPRINGS
PRESS

© 2021Quarto Publishing Group USA Inc.
Text © 2012 Tom MacCubbin, Georgia B. Tasker, Robert Bowden, Joe Lamp'l

First Published in 2012. Second edition published in 2021
by Cool Springs Press, an imprint of The Quarto Group,
100 Cummings Center, Suite 265-D, Beverly, MA 01915, USA.
T (978) 282-9590 F (978) 283-2742 QuartoKnows.com

Cool Springs Presstitles are also available at discount for retail, wholesale, promotional, and bulk purchase. For details, contact the Special Sales Manager by email at specialsales@quarto.com or by mail at The Quarto Group, Attn: Special Sales Manager, 100 Cummings Center, Suite 265-D, Beverly, MA 01915, USA.

25 24 23 22 21   1 2 3 4 5

ISBN: 978-0-7603-7053-7

Digital edition published in 2021

Library of Congress Cataloging-in-Publication Data available

Page Layout: Mattie Wells
Printed in China

PREFACE TO THE 2ND EDITION

This 2021 edition of *The Florida Gardener's Handbook* has been consolidated, reorganized, and updated in several ways. The plant profiles have been updated for consistency and to include the scientific name and the plant family. Also, the native range for the plants has been added for the non-crop plants. Potentially invasive species were removed because they have been shown to damage Florida's native and wild areas. More Florida native plants have been added as individual profiles or as alternatives to related non-native plants.

The recommended reduction of landscape-wide synthetic pesticides, herbicides, and fertilizers has been stressed to help improve the health of our waterways and aquifers. Organic methods for enriching the soil and for pest control are encouraged. The lawn care section focuses on more sustainable lawn care techniques so Floridians can do their part to reduce the huge environmental impacts of highly managed turf grass. It's better for our health and better for our planet.

We hope you enjoy this updated and modernized edition. Happy gardening!

CONTENTS

Welcome to Gardening in Florida 6

Plant Profiles
Annuals 18
Bulbs 36
Fruit & Nuts 54
Herbs & Vegetables 76
Lawns 96
Ornamental Grasses & Ground Covers 106
Perennials 122
Shrubs 142
Trees & Palms 168
Tropical Plants 192
Vines 210

Appendices
Invasive Plants in Florida 224
Florida's Pests 224

Glossary 228
Bibliography 231
Photo Credits 233
Meet the Authors 234
Botanical Index 236
Index of Common Names 239

WELCOME to GARDENING
in Florida

Whether you are new to the state or just new to gardening, you are about to have lots of fun. You'll enjoy colorful flowers and reap harvests from fruit and vegetable plants in your own yard. Even if you already have some local gardening experience, there is always more to learn and new adventures ahead.

Florida is different from most other states. It's a long state, almost 900 miles (1,448 km) from the Pensacola point in the Panhandle to the tip of the Keys. There is frost-free growing in the southern part of the state and there are multiple freezes in the north. Before you begin planting, you can learn a little about some other features of our state:

- Most of the soil is sand; gardeners often call it "beach sand" or "sugar sand."
- There is a 5-month wet season (aka, the hurricane season) from June through October when most parts of Florida receive 60 to 70 percent of their precipitation. The 7-month dry season is when most parts of the state receive only one inch (2.5 cm) or so of rain each month.
- Fall and spring are times for warm-season plantings, winter is devoted to cool-season plantings, and summer is the time for a few plants that don't mind the heat.
- Gardeners on the coast and some isolated inland areas have to deal with salty water.
- Pests are active year-round, but then so are the butterflies and the birds.
- Trees, flowers, and vegetables are often planted at different times than in other states. And in South Florida, you'll want to learn about tropical crops and some new varieties of fruits.

And we have not even mentioned the incredible variety of plants that are available for Florida landscapes. We live in a gardener's paradise.

FLORIDA'S CLIMATE

Most of the state is considered a subtropical climate. Luckily, Florida weather tends to be fairly predictable within its three climatic zones. On average, spring and fall are warm and dry, summer hot and wet, and winter cool and dry.

NORTH FLORIDA
- extends northward from State Road 40.
- has about 60 inches (152 cm) of rainfall per year.
- is sure to get frosts and freezing weather in winter.
- has a first frost in December and last frost during mid-February.
- has 350 to 650 annual hours below 45°F (7°C).
- has summers of similar duration to those in temperate areas.

CENTRAL FLORIDA
- lies between State Roads 40 and 70.
- has about 56 inches (142 cm) of rainfall per year.
- has frosts most years and some light freezes in winter.
- has a first frost by late December and a last frost during early February.
- has 150 to 350 annual hours below 45°F (7°C).
- has extended summerlike, hot, humid weather in late spring and fall.

SOUTH FLORIDA
- extends below State Road 70 across the state.
- has about 56 inches (142 cm) of rainfall per year.
- has infrequent frosts and no freezes.
- has 50 to 150 annual hours below 45°F (7°C).
- has extended, summerlike, hot, humid weather into spring and fall.

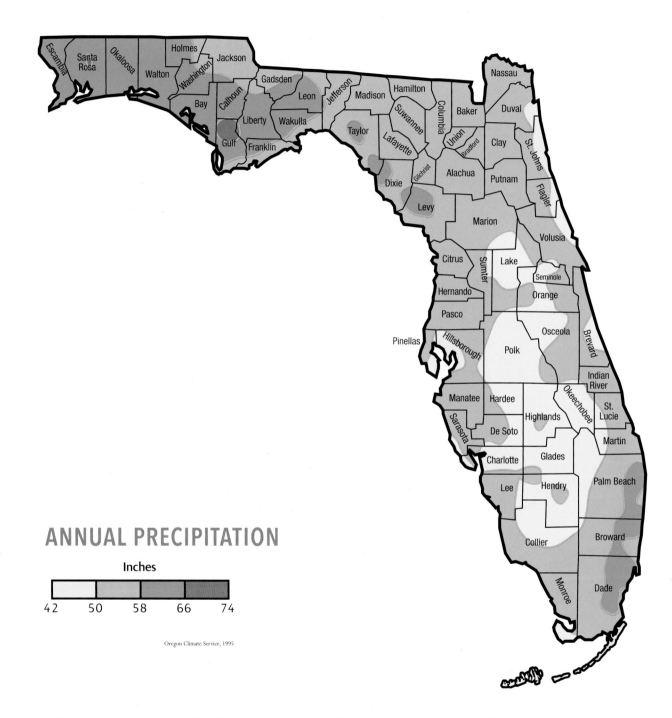

ANNUAL PRECIPITATION

Inches

42   50   58   66   74

Oregon Climate Service, 1995

Florida receives a lot of rain, but 60 to 70 percent of it comes during the 5-month wet season, so Florida gardeners need to be prepared for drought during the rest of the year.

WINTER HARDINESS

There are four USDA plant hardiness zones in Florida: Zones 8 through 11. It would be nice to believe that the listed temperatures are accurate for all areas of each zone. But Florida is full of microclimates where temperatures can be much higher or lower than average during cold weather. Nevertheless, hardiness zones are reasonable guides for determining what will grow in your area, as long as you recognize that there may be exceptions.

WINTER CARE

If your plants are chosen properly and are mostly natives to your area, they will need very little winter care. Most trees, shrubs, vines, and similar plants go dormant when shorter days signal the season's end.

Much of Florida's real plant damage occurs when warm days are followed by sudden freezes that catch plants in active growth.

There are numerous ways to increase the winter survival rate of cold-sensitive plants:

- Keep the plants in pots that can be moved indoors. Or dig the plants just before the freeze and put them in pots or burlap to move into warmer locations.
- Mound up soil over the lower stems to protect the buds from freezing. With some plants the tops can be removed 1 or 2 feet (30–60 cm) above ground, then soil mounded over the stems.
- Cover plants with cloth sheets or quilts draped to the ground. Do not use plastic.
- Outdoor-approved lights can be added to provide heat.
  Perhaps the best advice in planning your landscape is to use cold-hardy plants that are perfect for your region.

FLORIDA HEAT

Gardeners often wonder why tulips, daffodils, forsythia, and lilacs don't grow well locally and why petunias and snapdragons give out by early summer. Much of the problem is the amount of heat received in a warm climate. Another problem is that the cool weather in the winter (even in North Florida) is not consistent enough that the soil stays cold. Before you make a plant selection, check to see if a plant can be grown in your region. Sadly, just because a plant is offered for sale in garden centers, that doesn't guarantee that it's appropriate for your region. Buyer beware!

FLORIDA'S NATIVE PLANTS

Plants that are native to Florida come is all sizes, shapes, and colors, with more than 2,500 species. When selected for the right location, natives in the landscape require less maintenance, water, and fertilizer, and no pesticides. They are easier on the gardener, the pocketbook, and the environment. Planting natives is also a good way to help restore natural communities that have been greatly reduced by decades of development in the state. In this book, the native range is included for all but the edible plants, and when given a choice, natives help landscapes reflect "The Real Florida."

Native plant resources:

- The Florida Native Plant Society has local chapters around the state that hold educational meetings, field trips, and plant sales. The Society has an excellent website with an interactive tool for plant selection that helps you choose the right native for your county. Visit them at www.fnps.org.
- The Florida Association of Native Nurseries has a website where you can search for a supplier of a certain plant or a native nursery near you. www.PlantRealFlorida.org
- Florida Wildflowers Growers Cooperative offers native wildflower seeds. www.floridawildflowers.com
- The Florida Yards and Neighborhoods Program manages a website with information and interactive options to help you choose the right plants for your needs. www.FloridaYards.org

POLLINATOR GARDENING

Florida is a state with some of the most diverse wildlife populations in the United States. However, as its natural wildlife habitat gets replaced by human development, the environment suitable for animals and birds decreases in size and diversity. With careful planning, it is possible to provide a landscape that is attractive to both people and wildlife by building habitat to host the birds and the butterflies.

To attract butterflies, birds, and animals to your yard, first stop all landscape-wide pesticide applications. The reason not to use broad-spectrum insecticides in your garden or lawn is that they kill many butterflies and other beneficial insects. Make sure that any plants you purchase have not been treated with systemic insecticides such as neonicotinoids, because these poisons will kill the pollinators and the caterpillars (larval stage of butterflies and moths), which are essential food for birds. House pets, especially cats, that run loose in the yard are one of the biggest deterrents for birds and other wildlife.

Then three essential features must be provided for insects and birds—food, water, and cover. The more plant diversity you can provide, the more types of wildlife will visit your property. So, while a large, neatly mowed lawn might appear attractive on the surface, it contains only a single kind of plant reliant on lots of herbicides and pesticides. That isn't very appealing to wildlife.

FOOD

Food can be provided by plants that bear seeds, produce nectar, or provide food for caterpillars. When deciding what to plant in your landscape, choose plants that will be a food source for the type of wildlife you would like to attract. Butterflies need both sources of nectar as well as food supplies for caterpillars after eggs hatch. If nothing is eating your plants, then they are not playing a vital role in your yard's working ecosystem

WATER

Water can be as simple as a birdbath that is kept full or something more elaborate like a creek or ornamental pond. To prevent mosquitoes from breeding, standing water must be kept fresh or contain fish that will eat the larva. The sound of moving water is like a beacon for wildlife and also sounds wonderful in the yard.

COVER

Cover for wildlife means areas in which they feel safe to nest, hide, sleep, eat, and travel. Build layers of foliage from the ground to the canopy. Leave snags (dead trees) in the landscape.

Birds may be year-round residents, migrants, or winter visitors. Check the type of food and preferred nesting sites that various birds like and plant accordingly. Hummingbirds favor nectar-rich plants with bright orange or red flowers into which they can insert their long beaks. The blossoms generally need to be at least 2 feet (60 cm) above the ground. They may also visit feeders designed specifically for them.

It's a fun family project to make your landscape friendlier to wildlife.

Zebra longwing butterfly larvae on a native passionvine. The adult zebra longwing is the Florida state insect.

PLAN AND DESIGN

This is the first step whether you are creating a new garden or updating your current landscape. Start with your property plan to create a master drawing. There are also several landscape software programs available. Identify trees, planting areas, topography, structures (house, garage, shed), and the hardscape (driveways, patios, pools, fences, paths). Inventory specific growing conditions, such as shade, sun, drainage, flooding, and wind direction.

Check for any municipal codes, easements, deed restrictions, and overhead and underground utilities. Call 811 or go to www.sunshine811.com to have the lines for sewer, electric, telephone, and cable TV companies marked so you won't cut wires and interrupt service. Keep trees 20 or more feet (6 m) away from underground infrastructure.

Decide how you and your family want to use the yard. Plan which spaces should be private and which should be public. Decide where you want sun and where would you like to create a shady area. Consider surrounding views to block or ones you would like to incorporate into your design. Be sure to plan for the full year, since plants and your needs change season by season. Another important consideration is to design for both the young and full-grown plants, especially for trees and larger plants.

CONSERVING WATER IN THE LANDSCAPE

If we weren't the Sunshine State, Florida might well be called the Aquatic State. We have almost 1,200 miles (1,930 km) of coastline, more than 4,000 lakes, 11,000 miles (17,700 km) of waterways, the second largest lake in the United States, and the world's largest concentration of first-magnitude springs. We are directly tied to our aquatic resources.

Unfortunately for gardeners, as these limited water resources become more precious because of drought and development, outdoor usage has been restricted by local agencies and water management districts. The time of day and frequency that water can be used on lawns and plantings is limited, depending upon the time of year and size of the current reserves. Some counties now have year-round restrictions. Others make reclaimed water available.

Some experts estimate that more than 50 percent of landscape water use is wasted due to evaporation, runoff, and unnecessary watering. And that runoff from our properties is polluting our waterways with fertilizers and organic matter. As a result, we need to design our landscapes to absorb more water with rain gardens and rain barrels.

INSTALL RAIN BARRELS

Install a series of rain barrels to collect water from your roof and to reduce the strain on our municipal water systems. They are now available in decorator styles. Some municipalities make them available to residents for a very low cost. Rain barrel systems are designed with screening covering the intake to keep out mosquitoes and tree debris.

Using rain barrel water reduces our general use of tap water and has a number of other advantages, but the most important for gardeners is that it has no purifiers added, so it's better for the soil's microorganisms. Use it for all your container gardens, to wet your compost piles, and for vegetable gardens. (Yes, rain barrel water is safe for all your crops.)

XERISCAPING: USING THE RIGHT PLANT IN THE RIGHT PLACE

Xeriscape (pronounced zera-scape): The word comes from xeros, meaning dry, with landscape. Technically, Florida's too wet to be a true xeriscape, but we can adapt the concept of using plants whose natural requirements are appropriate to the local climate and natural rainfall. This reduces the need for irrigation, maintenance, and other resources. This concept also includes grouping plants according to their water needs and using plants that are better adapted to the local area–specifically choosing native plants whenever possible.

Ninety percent of the state's public water supply comes from underground sources, primarily our aquifers. Unfortunately, these sources are not large enough to support all the needs of our population during rainy years, and in dry times they are depleted even faster. The results of over-pumping to fill the public water requirements are lowered lake levels, sinkhole formations, and saltwater intrusion into some regions of the state's aquifer.

As an outcome of these problems, Florida's five regional water-management districts restrict when we can use our landscape-wide irrigation systems. They also support xeriscaping principles that help conserve the state's unique aquatic resources. The districts produce numerous resources (printed and electronic) to help gardeners understand and implement gardens that work for both them and for nature.

The following are summaries of xeriscape gardening's seven principles.

1. Water deeply and less often

If all moisture needed is right near the surface, plants won't use extra energy and nutrients to grow roots deeper into the soil. Deep watering encourages deep roots, which makes plants more drought tolerant.

At the same time, don't over-water, because once the surface layer of most soils becomes saturated, all the water applied from that point on is wasted.

2. Water at the right time of day

The hotter and windier it is, the more water is lost to evaporation before it even reaches the ground. Depending on your irrigation system and the timing of when you water, as much as half the water can be lost to drift and evaporation.

Water very early in the morning when temperatures are cooler and winds are calmer. The coolness and darkness, along with calm skies, allow soil to soak up the maximum amount of water.

3. Program your irrigation system

How much water is enough to keep our lawns and landscapes healthy without overdoing it? Experts estimate that lawns need an average of 1 inch (2.5 cm) of water per week from all sources (irrigation and rain) to stay green. Lawns that are allowed to go dormant and native landscapes rarely need any irrigation though.

To find out how much water your sprinklers (automatic or manual) are delivering, place straight-sided cans around the yard and check how long it takes to get 1 inch (2.5 cm) of water. Also note if your irrigation system needs to have some heads adjusted. Your goal is to have it deliver even coverage to the desired areas. Watering driveways and streets is a big waste of water.

Include a rain sensor in your automatic system. Studies have shown that installing a rain-sensing device in areas with frequent rains can reduce water usage by as much as 30 percent.

4. Convert to soaker hoses and micro sprinklers

Watering directly at the soil level is more efficient. There is no drift or evaporation, and by watering at the soil level, the foliage stays dry. Keeping foliage dry is an important step in minimizing plant diseases.

Micro sprinkler systems are also called drip irrigation, micro-irrigation, and trickle irrigation, and they are easy to install. These systems are readily available as kits or individual components. They can be set up temporarily to irrigate newly planted trees or shrubs until the roots are established.

5. Mulch, mulch, mulch

Mulch is one of the most versatile additions to any garden. It has many uses, with one of the most important being to conserve water. A layer of mulch up to 4 inches (10 cm) thick will provide an insulating blanket that reduces evaporation, slows runoff, and moderates soil temperature on hot days. It also dramatically reduces weed growth, which also conserves water.

Mulch should be organic matter, such as leaves, straw, compost, pine needles, bark, or wood chips. Using mulch can reduce water usage by 5 to 10 percent. In dry climates, rocks are often used as mulch, but they don't usually work well in Florida for several reasons: they get too hot, weeds readily grow in rocks, and there's too much general leaf fall, which is a chore to keep clear of the rocks.

6. Choose proper plants

Select plants that match the conditions in various spots around your yard. Whenever possible, preserve existing native vegetation. Those trees and shrubs have learned how to successfully grow in the conditions you have, without extensive water, fertilizer, or maintenance. Native plants are important components to xeriscape gardens because of those characteristics.

Group plants into areas according to how much moisture they require. This concept is central to the effectiveness and popularity of xeriscaping and is often summarized by the phrase, "right plant in the right place."

7. Use turf wisely

Reducing turf area results in a savings of water usage and reduction of the amount of time and expense that homeowners have to spend cutting, edging, fertilizing, weed killing, and preventing pests. Start reducing turf by enlarging the beds that surround it. Some beautiful home landscapes don't have any turf grass at all.

One of the easiest and most beneficial ways to use turf wisely is to reduce fertilizing and irrigation, because the less the grass grows, the less water is needed and the fewer times it has to be mowed. Some people convert their monoculture turf to diverse "Freedom Lawns." These actions will greatly reduce water usage, improve the health of Florida's aquifer and waterways, save time and money, and reduce noise pollution in your neighborhood. More details are in the Lawns chapter, page 96.

SOILS

The first step to understanding the soil in your yard is to determine its composition, from sand to clay. Then test the pH (acidity) of several samples around your yard. Test kits are available at most garden centers and assistance may be available at your local Extension Service.

Most plants prefer neutral or slightly acidic soil. However, some prefer either alkaline soils or more acidic levels. Amendments can be added to adjust pH levels, although they do not permanently alter the pH. If you have acidic soil, it's best to choose acid-loving plants like gardenias, azaleas, blueberries, and camellias.

Most Florida landscapes have sandy soil. But you can grow great plants in sandy soils if you add organic matter. Florida also has some pockets of clay, areas with high organic matter, and rocky soils. Wherever possible, amend your soils with organic matter, especially compost. These additions help the soil hold moisture, supply some nutrients for plant growth, and add microbes to activate the soil's ecosystem.

Synthetic fertilizers can push plant growth, but they do not help the soil. They easily wash away and end up polluting our waterways. So we recommend taking care of the soil with organic amendments and supplementing this when necessary with organic fertilizers such as fish or seaweed emulsions. Either way, keep a fertilizer-free zone at least 20 feet (6 m) wide around lakes and waterways.

You will notice in the planting instructions below that no fertilizer or compost is added to the planting hole. It's best to let the tree, shrub, vine, or ground cover plantings get a start on establishment for 4 to 6 weeks, and then apply a topdressing of compost in a circle at the edge of the original planting hole. This enriches the soil and increases the water retention.

Most shrubs, vines, and ground covers can use another compost application the following March. For trees, add compost for 2 or 3 more years every March.

Annuals and perennials require a feeding program that is a little different: they are immediately put on a regular maintenance program. Give annuals and perennials a feeding with fish emulsion every 6 weeks or so if needed.

Some of the organic amendments available for use:

- **COMPOST:** Make your own at home or pick it up at county landfills. Work 4 to 6 inches (10 to 15 cm) into most planting sites, including both sand or clay soils.
- **COCONUT COIR:** Made from coconut husks, this sustainable product absorbs as much water as peat moss. Work 4 to 6 inches (10 to 15 cm) into sandy or clay soils before planting. Unlike peat moss, coir is not acidic and offers more nutrients. Peat moss can never be sustainably harvested because bogs, where it's produced, add less than 1/10 of an inch (2.5 mm cm) per year.
- **MANURES:** Chicken, cow, and horse manure are all readily available. For edible beds, use about 25 pounds (11 kg) for each 100 square feet (30 m) of bed area to be planted, or follow package instructions. Composted manure can be applied to the soil surface. Fresh manure should be added to the soil 90 to 120 days before planting edibles. For the rest of the landscape, manures are rarely needed.
- **POTTING SOILS:** A potting soil can be used as an amendment for small garden spots, but it can be costly to use in large beds.
- **TOPSOIL:** Florida does not have standards for topsoil. Be careful when ordering to make sure it's not the same sandy soil found in your yard, and that it is free of weeds.

PLANTING SUGGESTIONS

Container-grown plants come from small cell-packs to 30-gallon (113.5 L) or larger pots and are easy to transport and plant in a new location. It's a good idea to check the root balls to make sure they are not potbound at purchase time. If plants have very tightly wrapped root systems, they may not grow out into the surrounding soil and will be short-lived.

Here are a few tips to get container-grown plants quickly established:

- Find a site where the plant will have ample room to grow above and below ground.
- Soak the root ball of the plant and break up the root ball to spread roots out. For trees, this is especially important so you can remedy coiling roots and find the root flare.
- Dig the hole twice as wide as but no deeper than the root ball.
- Position the plant in the center of the hole and at the same depth it was growing or with the top of the root ball 1 to 2 inches (2.5 to 5 cm) above the ground.
- Fill in around the root ball with local soil, adding water as you plant.
- Create a 4- to 6-inch- (10- to 15-cm-) high soil berm at the edge of the root ball around the plant to hold water.
- Spread a 3- to 4-inch (7.5- to 10-cm) layer of mulch up to the edge of the root ball of trees and shrubs. Add a light mulch layer over the root system.
- If tall plants are not steady, add temporary stakes or guy wires.
- Water the plant. Thoroughly wet the soil. Don't rely on irrigation systems to water new plantings—do it by hand. Irrigate during the early-morning hours to conserve water. Where possible, install temporary drip irrigation systems or use soaker hoses for new plantings.
- Control weeds and keep a mulch layer in place up to the edge of the root ball and a light layer over the roots.
- Do not prune trees and shrubs for shape until a year or more after planting, and then prune no more than 20 percent of the tree each year.

HOW TO USE THIS BOOK

Each entry in this guide provides you with information about a plant's particular characteristics, habits, and basic requirements for active growth as well as our personal experiences and knowledge of the plant. We have included the information you need to help you realize each plant's potential. You will find such pertinent information as native range, mature height and spread, bloom period and seasonal colors (if any), sun and soil preferences, water requirements, fertilizing needs, pruning and care, and specific pest information. (Detailed information on Florida's pests is in the appendix.)

SUN PREFERENCES

Symbols represent the range of sunlight suitable for each plant. The icon representing "Full Sun" means the plant needs to be sited in a full-sun (8 to 10 hours of sun daily) location. "Part Sun" means the plant likes full sun, but will appreciate a few hours of protection from harsh, late-afternoon sun. "Part Shade" means the plant can be situated where it receives partial sun all day, or morning sun, or dappled shade. "Full Shade" means the plant needs a shady location protected from direct sunlight. Some plants can be grown in more than one range of sunlight, so you will sometimes see more than one sun symbol.

 Full Sun

 Part Sun

 Part Shade

 Shade/Deep Shade

ADDITIONAL BENEFITS

Many plants offer benefits that further enhance their appeal. The following symbols indicate some of the more important additional benefits:

 Attracts Butterflies

 Has Fragrance

 Attracts Pollinators

 Attracts Hummingbirds

 Suitable for Cut Flowers or Arrangements

 Provides Food or Shelter for Wildlife

 Provides Edible Fruit

 Long Bloom Period

 Good Fall Color

 Provides Attractive Fruit

 Native Plant

 Drought Resistant

 Good for Containers

 Tropical or Tropical Looking

 Tolerates Seaside Conditions

 Award Winner

HARDINESS ZONES

Cold-hardiness zone designations were developed by the United States Department of Agriculture (USDA) to indicate the minimum average temperature for an area. A zone assigned to an individual plant indicates the lowest temperature at which the plant can be expected to survive over the winter. Florida has zones ranging from 8A to 11. And the hardiness zones are indicated in most of the plant profiles. Though a plant may grow in zones other than its recommended cold-hardiness zone, it is a good indication of which plants to consider for your landscape.

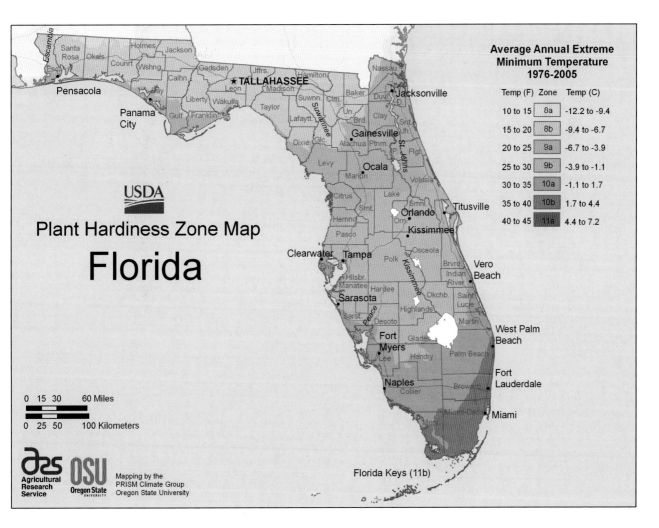

USDA Plant Hardiness Zone Map, 2012. Agricultural Research Service, U.S. Department of Agriculture. Accessed from https://planthardiness.ars.usda.gov/.

ANNUALS
for Florida

Florida gardeners have learned that a quick way to add color to the landscape is to use annual flowers. Many can be purchased in bloom at local garden centers to bring home and create an instant garden, but don't buy plants that have been grown using systemic insecticides, because they may harm pollinators and butterfly caterpillars. As the name annual implies, the plants last only one season or maybe longer in South Florida. However, they offer plenty of color for 6 to 8 weeks or more. A few, including geraniums, impatiens, and coleus, continue growing until seasonal changes in temperature cause decline.

CONSIDERATIONS BEFORE PLANTING

In Florida there are two main types of annuals: the warm-season and the cool-season plants. Warm-season annuals usually grow well between March and November. Then as the days shorten and temperatures dip into the 40s (4°C to 9°C) or lower at night, it's time to add the cool-season types. They are usually planted November through February in most areas of Florida. Consult the annuals chart (pages 32 and 34) before planting the garden.

Most annuals prefer mostly sunny locations. When picking a planting location, remember the shifting pattern of the sun throughout the year. During the winter, the sun dips down in the horizon to create more shade in many locations.

Gardeners have the option of sowing annual seeds directly into the ground or into flats or pots. You can also seed into individual cells of market packs and keep them where the tending and irrigation is easy. You can transplant the seedlings to the beds once they have sprouted.

Planting annuals in containers is easy, but be sure to start with a well-drained potting soil. You can buy it or make your own by combining equal parts of coconut coir, perlite, and compost.

IN-GROUND ANNUALS

WATERING

Newly germinated or newly planted seedlings are vulnerable to drying out. Water annuals daily for the first week or two until the roots begin to grow out into the surrounding soil. Reduce watering frequency gradually until the plants are established enough to survive with the landscape-wide irrigation and rainfall. Choose drought-tolerant annuals to save water.

FERTILIZING

If you prepared the soil with compost when you planted the annuals, most will not need additional fertilizing. But you could apply an organic fertilizer such as fish or seaweed emulsion after the seedlings are well established.

GROOMING

Traditional gardening used to include deadheading (the removal of fading flowers) to keep the plants neat and to encourage additional blooms. But now the trend is to let the plants grow into their natural forms so the birds can come in to eat the seeds. Of course, you can trim plants back when they lean into paths, but less formal and looser flower beds mean less work for you.

CONTAINER ANNUALS

Container gardens can be devoted to one type of annual, or you can create the wildflower look by mixing several together. If you use more than one type, make sure their irrigation needs are the same and keep the tall flowers to the center or back of the container. You may want to use cascading types around the edges.

WATERING

Check containers daily and water when surface soil feels dry to the touch. When plants begin to fill their pots, they may need water once or twice a day. Setting up drip irrigation for your containers will make a big difference in the tending time.

FERTILIZING

Use a top-dressing of compost every 6 weeks or so to keep the soil alive in your container. If the plants need more nutrients, supplement this with fish emulsion.

GROOMING

Remove declining individuals and replant as needed.

PEST CONTROL

Annual flowers have very few pests, but check your plantings frequently to prevent major problems. Holes in leaves, yellow spots, and browning plant parts can all mean pests are active. You may notice some of the following problems: caterpillars, mites, aphids, or slugs. See the appendix, page 224 for more on pests and what actions to take.

AGERATUM

Ageratum houstonianum
Daisy family: Asteraceae

HARDINESS– Zones 8–11. Any freezing weather can cause major damage.

NATIVE RANGE–Mexico and Central America

COLOR(S)– White or blue flowers

PEAK SEASON–Blooms spring to summer

MATURE SIZE–8 inches to over 2 feet tall (20 to 60 cm)

WATER NEEDS–Thoroughly moisten soil before and after planting. Water frequently for first few weeks. In sandy soils and containers, water when surface feels dry.

CARE–Space 12 to 18 inches (30 to 45 cm) apart to allow for spread.

PROBLEMS–None.

USES AND SELECTIONS–Ageratum provides a carpet of blue or pure-white blossoms above spreading foliage. It is ideal for compact plantings along walkways or a blanket of border color in front of taller plants. Goes well with backdrops of bush daisy, dusty miller, or petunias. Can be planted in beds, container gardens, or hanging baskets. The blue mistflower (*Conoclinium coelestinum*) looks like ageratum, but it's native to all of Florida and would be a better choice for butterfly gardens.

BABY'S BREATH

Gypsophila paniculata
Carnation family: Caryophyllaceae

HARDINESS–Zones 8–10

NATIVE RANGE–Eurasia

COLOR(S)– Tiny white flowers

PEAK SEASON–Blooms in summer

MATURE SIZE–1½ to 4 feet x 3 to 4 feet (45 to 122 cm x 91 to 122 cm)

WATER NEEDS–Allow to dry out between waterings.

CARE–Prefers slightly alkaline soil and thrives in lean, well-drained soils. It is also somewhat salt tolerant. It is full and billowing, so allow it sufficient elbow room. Can also be grown as a perennial.

PROBLEMS–If kept too wet, it may get rot.

USES AND SELECTIONS–The little white blooms are often used as accents in bouquets. It can also be used for bedding, borders, containers, and hanging baskets. Improved versions with plusher double flowers are now common, as well as pink or violet-tinged varieties.

BUTTER DAISIES

Melampodium divaricatum
Daisy family: Asteraceae

HARDINESS– Zones 8–11. Grows best during warmer months. Damaged by freezes.

NATIVE RANGE–Mexico, Central & South America

COLOR(S)– Yellow flowers

PEAK SEASON–Blooms summer through fall

MATURE SIZE–10 to 36 inches x 15 to 48 inches (25 to 90 cm x 38 to 122 cm

WATER NEEDS–Drought tolerant once established

CARE–Plant in well-drained soil. This carefree plant loves heat and blooms prolifically. The bushy mounds are filled with self-cleaning flowers, so deadheading isn't required; it is self-branching, so trimming isn't needed either. It readily self-seeds, providing lots of new seedlings.

PROBLEMS–Pest- and disease-free

USES AND SELECTIONS–Plant butter daisies (aka blackfoot daisies) in beds, borders, in mass plantings, and as edging. Use shorter, compact selections as ground covers and in containers. Cultivars include 'Compact Million Gold', 'Lemon Delight', and 'Derby'.

CALENDULA

Calendula officinalis
Daisy family: Asteraceae

HARDINESS–Zones 8-11. Cool-weather annual used throughout Florida. Declines after day temperatures consistently reach 80°F (27°C).

NATIVE RANGE–Western Mediterranean

COLOR(S)– Bright yellow, orange

PEAK SEASON–Fall and winter blooms

MATURE SIZE–8 to 24 inches (20 to 61 cm) tall, flowers over 2 inches (5 cm) in diameter

WATER NEEDS–Thoroughly moisten soil before and after planting. Water frequently for the first few weeks, especially for sandy soil. Check container plantings often; water when the soil surface feels dry.

CARE–Add plenty of organic material to sandy soil. Allow 12- to 18-inch (30- to 46-cm) spacing. Add a light mulch layer. Remove declining blossoms so new ones develop.

PROBLEMS–Planting in well-drained soil prevents most problems.

USES AND SELECTIONS–Mix with greenery such as coleus or dusty miller. Good for bright color masses in flower beds, container gardens, and hanging baskets. Suitable for cut flowers.

CELOSIA

Celosia argentea
Spinach family: Amaranthaceae

HARDINESS–Zones 8-11. Does not tolerate frosts.

NATIVE RANGE–Mexico, Central & South America, Africa, India

COLOR(S)– Yellow, orange, red, pink flowers

PEAK SEASON–Blooms fall to late spring

MATURE SIZE–10 to 18 inches (25 to 46 cm)

WATER NEEDS–Thoroughly moisten soil before and after planting. Water frequently for the first few weeks, especially for sandy soil. Then water when the soil surface feels dry.

CARE–Plant 10 to 12 inches (25 to 30 cm) apart. Remove declining blossoms to keep color coming. Gives about 6 to 8 weeks of good color before fading.

PROBLEMS–Rainy, damp weather causes flowers to rot.

USES AND SELECTIONS–A unique way to add garden color, with brightly colored flowers held high above foliage. There are two flower forms–plume and cockscomb. Plant a bed of mixed colors, combine with other plants, use as a backdrop, or plant in containers. Cut flowers good for bouquets or drying.

COLEUS

Coleus x hybridus
Mint family: Lamiaceae

HARDINESS–Zones 8-11. Does not tolerate frost.

NATIVE RANGE–Africa, India, Asia, Australia

COLOR(S)– Various-shaped leaves have mixtures of pink, green, yellow, bronze, or red

PEAK SEASON–Year-round foliage

MATURE SIZE–1 to 2 feet (30 to 61 cm) tall

WATER NEEDS–Keep new plants moist. Once established, water when soil feels dry. Check container plantings daily.

CARE–Add plenty of organic material to sandy soil. Space 8 to 12 inches (20 to 30 cm) apart. Add light mulch layer. With Florida's long growing season, coleus may grow too tall. Cutting it back will make it bushier, and you can root the trimmings to start new plants.

PROBLEMS–None.

USES AND SELECTIONS–Good for providing color in the shade. Plant with low-growing gingers and liriope. Use in beds or containers. Varieties with greater sun tolerance and ruffled leaves may be available.

COSMOS

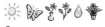

Cosmos spp.
Daisy family: Asteraceae

HARDINESS–Zones 8-10.

NATIVE RANGE–SW states, Mexico, Central & South America

COLOR(S)– Red, white, pink, purple, yellow flowers

PEAK SEASON–Spring and summer

MATURE SIZE–1 to 7 feet (30 to 213 cm) tall

WATER NEEDS–Somewhat drought tolerant once established.

CARE–Easy to grow, thriving even in poor soils, if well-drained. Space 8 to 12 inches (20 to 30 cm) apart. Stake taller varieties or plant in a meadow with bunching grasses. Very easy to grow from seeds and to transplant.

PROBLEMS–Virtually pest resistant. If too much fertilizer is applied, they will grow lots of feathery foliage at the expense of flowers.

USES AND SELECTIONS–Cosmos (also called Mexican aster) is one of the best nectar plants for attracting butterflies. The flowers are also ideal for cut flowers and for pressing. Use taller varieties as background or border plants. Use shorter varieties in front of hedges. They are also good for wildflower, meadow, and butterfly gardens. There are several species and hybrids available, including the dwarf 'Sonata Series', which is ideal for container plantings.

DUSTY MILLER

Jacobaea maritima
Daisy family: Asteraceae

HARDINESS– Zones 8-10. Doesn't do well in Florida's hot, wet summers.

NATIVE RANGE–Mediterranean

COLOR(S)– Fuzzy gray-green leaves look silvery

PEAK SEASON–Fall through spring

MATURE SIZE–12 to 18 inches (30 to 46 cm) tall

WATER NEEDS–After establishing, water when soil feels dry. Container-grown plants may need more frequent watering.

CARE–Add plenty of organic material to sandy soil. Space 8 to 10 inches (20 to 25 cm) apart. Do not plant too deeply. Add light mulch layer.

PROBLEMS–Hot, damp weather causes plants to decline.

USES AND SELECTIONS–The leaves of dusty miller vary from coarsely toothed to lace-like. They add textural interest and are the perfect foil to brightly colored annuals in beds and containers. Use plants with contrasting colors, such as salvia, purple petunias, or red begonias. Good selections are 'Cirrus', 'Silver Dust', and 'Silver Queen'.

GERANIUM

Pelargonium x hortorum
Geranium family: Geraniaceae

HARDINESS– Zones 8-11. Planting can begin in October if winter protection is provid-ed.

NATIVE RANGE–None, because this is a hybrid.

COLOR(S)– Foliage can have zonal marking. Blooms are pink, red, and lavender, plus white and blends.

PEAK SEASON–Fall through spring

MATURE SIZE–18 to 24 inches (46 to 61 cm) tall

WATER NEEDS–After establishing, water when soil feels dry. Container-grown plants may need more frequent watering.

CARE–Add plenty of organic material to sandy soil. Space 12 to 18 inches (30 to 46 cm) apart. Do not plant too deeply. Add light mulch layer. Tolerates some shade, but needs sunny location for best flowering.

PROBLEMS–Summer rains may cause rot and plant decline.

USES AND SELECTIONS–A beloved bedding plant, geranium produces colorful flower clusters above the foliage. Some genus members are perennials. However, in Florida, geraniums are treated as cool-season annuals, to be replaced when the summer rainy season starts. Can be planted in beds or containers.

GLOBE AMARANTH

Gomphrena globosa
Spinach family: Amaranthaceae

HARDINESS– Zones 8–11. Plant during warmer months. It is damaged by frosts and freezes.

NATIVE RANGE–Mexico, Central & South America

COLOR(S)– Yellow, white, pink, purple flowers

PEAK SEASON–Blooms summer through fall

MATURE SIZE–12 to 24 inches x 6 to 12 inches (30 to 61 cm x 15 to 30 cm)

WATER NEEDS–Moderately drought tolerant. Water when very dry and do not overwater.

CARE–This carefree plant tolerates poor soil, heat, and drought. To dry these flowers, cut just before they completely open and hang upside down in a warm, dark place. When planted close together they produce longer stems, which are better for drying.

PROBLEMS–None.

USES AND SELECTIONS–The showy cloverlike flowers of globe amaranth look good in borders, edging, and mass plantings. They are ideal in containers, along walkways, and in drier areas where color is needed. Many hybrids are available in different colors and growth habits, including more compact plants.

HOLLYHOCK

Alcea rosea
Mallow family: Malvaceae

HARDINESS– Zones 8–9. Plant during fall to experience winter cold.

NATIVE RANGE–Eastern Mediterranean

COLOR(S)– Yellow, white, pink, lavender, maroon, red flowers

PEAK SEASON–Blooms spring and summer

MATURE SIZE–5 to 8 feet x 2 to 3 feet (152 to 244 cm x 61 to 91 cm)

WATER NEEDS–Somewhat drought tolerant once established. Water during very dry periods. Do not overwater.

CARE–Easy to grow. Shelter tall varieties from wind or stake them. Hollyhocks self-sow, so site them where they can multiply, or deadhead the flowers to prevent volunteers next season.

PROBLEMS–The heat of summer may cause decline. Leaves may develop rust disease and should not be composted.

USES AND SELECTIONS–Tall, showy hollyhocks are a cottage garden classic. They are great swaying along a fence or wall. They may also be planted at the back of a perennial bed, in mixed borders, in xeriscape gardens, or near an entryway. Not all varieties are suitable for Florida.

IMPATIENS

Impatiens walleriana
Balsam family: Balsaminaceae

HARDINESS– Zones 8–11. Dies back after freezes, but cold-affected impatiens may grow back.

NATIVE RANGE–Eastern Africa

COLOR(S)– All color flowers

PEAK SEASON–Blooms year-round

MATURE SIZE–10 to 24 inches (25 to 61 cm) tall

WATER NEEDS–Impatiens are thirsty and require frequent watering.

CARE–If impatiens become tall and lanky, prune back to within 1 foot (30 cm) of the ground.

PROBLEMS–Extensively planted in Florida, leading to large monocultures that provide few ecosystem services.

USES AND SELECTIONS–Impatiens provide color in the deep shade. Can be planted in beds, containers, and hanging baskets.

LOBELIA

Lobelia erinus
Bellflower family: Campanulaceae

HARDINESS– Zones 8–11. Cold tolerant. Survives all but hard freezes.

NATIVE RANGE–Central and southern Africa

COLOR(S)– Blue, violet, white, purple flowers

PEAK SEASON–Blooms winter and spring

MATURE SIZE–3 to 12 inches x 12 to 24 inches (8 to 30 cm x 30 to 61 cm)

WATER NEEDS–Needs plenty of moisture

CARE–Plant these cool-season annuals in rich, fertile, well-drained soil. In warmer parts of Florida, plant in partial shade. When temperatures get too hot, plants decline. Plants are best obtained as transplants during the later fall and winter.

PROBLEMS–They need lots of moisture, but if kept too damp, the stem or roots may rot.

USES AND SELECTIONS–Use compact varieties for edgings, borders, or mass plantings. Lobelia with trailing habit can be used in containers, raised beds, or cascading over walls. Cultivars include 'Cambridge Blue' (compact), 'Crystal Palace' (bronze-green leaves), 'Paper Moon' (white flowers), and 'Sapphire' (trailing with purple flowers). Cardinal flower (*L. cardinalis*), native to wet places in North and Central Florida, attracts hummingbirds, butterflies, and other pollinators.

MARIGOLD

Tagetes erecta
Daisy family: Asteraceae

HARDINESS–Zones 8–11. Frosts and freezes kill marigolds. In warmer areas they can be grown year-round.

NATIVE RANGE–Mexico

COLOR(S)– Yellow, orange, red, maroon, white flowers

PEAK SEASON–Blooms spring through fall

MATURE SIZE–8 to 12 or more inches (20 to 30 cm)

WATER NEEDS–Space 6 to 12 inches (15 to 30 cm) apart in thoroughly moistened soil. Once they're established, little irrigation will be needed.

CARE–Protect marigold plantings from frosts.

PROBLEMS–None.

USES AND SELECTIONS–Marigolds can be planted in beds and containers. Suitable for flower beds or along walkways. Marigolds can be used as a cover crop in vegetable beds and elsewhere to reduce root-knot nematodes in the soil.

MEXICAN SUNFLOWER

Tithonia rotundifolia
Daisy family: Asteraceae

HARDINESS– Zones 8–11. Damaged by frosts and freezes.

NATIVE RANGE–Mexico, Central America

COLOR(S)– Brilliant red-orange flowers

PEAK SEASON–Blooms spring through fall

MATURE SIZE–5 to 6 feet x 3 to 4 feet (152 to 183 cm x 91 to 122 cm)

WATER NEEDS–Drought tolerant. Water when dry.

CARE–Plant in well-drained soil. Does best in full sun. The stems and leaves are covered with soft fuzz. Heat tolerant and grows quickly. In a single season it can self-seed for a second generation. Allow plenty of room.

PROBLEMS–It self-seeds and could become weedy.

USES AND SELECTIONS–An excellent butterfly plant. Use in borders and beds. Popular cultivars 'Torch' and 'Fiesta del Sol' (dwarf) were All-America Selections. Another dwarf variety, 'Goldfinger', is also ideal for smaller gardens, growing to 3 feet (91 cm) tall. When cutting flowers for arrangements, carefully cut them with a sharp knife to prevent damaging the delicate stem. *Tithonia diversifolia* (also called Mexican sun-flower or shrub sunflower) may also be available.

NICOTIANA

Nicotiana alata
Nightshade family: Solanaceae

HARDINESS– Zones 8–11. In North and Central Florida limit plantings to spring. In South Florida plant both spring and early fall. Nicotiana does not grow well in hot summer or cooler winter months.

NATIVE RANGE–Eastern South America

COLOR(S)– Red, pink, white flowers

PEAK SEASON–Blooms spring and fall

MATURE SIZE–18 to 24 inches (46 to 61 cm)

WATER NEEDS–Space 12 to 18 inches (30 to 46 cm) apart in thoroughly moistened soil. Once established, water when soil feels dry.

CARE–Extend flowering by keeping plant from going to seed. As soon as flowering stalks finish blooming, cut them back.

PROBLEMS–Hot, rainy weather destroys flowers. This tobacco relative is protected against most insects.

USES AND SELECTIONS–Plant this garden tobacco alone or as backdrop for other plants. Mix with warm-season flowers including celosia, marigolds, and zinnias.

ORNAMENTAL PEPPER

Capsicum annuum
Nightshade family: Solanaceae

HARDINESS– Zones 8–11. Damaged by frosts and freezes.

NATIVE RANGE–Mexico and Central America

COLOR(S)– White, yellow, orange, red, purple fruit

PEAK SEASON–Fruiting from late spring to frost

MATURE SIZE–12 to 20 inches x 12 to 18 inches (30 to 51 cm x 30 to 46 cm)

WATER NEEDS–Water regularly.

CARE–Plant in well-drained, enriched soil. Grow in full sun or partial shade. Fruit can be round, short and stubby, or long and narrow.

PROBLEMS–Generally pest-free. Although edible, peppers are far too hot for most to tolerate, so tell children not to eat them.

USES AND SELECTIONS–With peppers remaining on the plant for a long time in varying stages of ripeness, ornamental pepper is often a riot of color. Use in containers, mass plantings, borders, and mixed with flowers in beds. Many cultivars are developed for fruit size, shape, and color. Several have been All-America Selections, including 'Black Pearl' (dark fruit with black-purple leaves), 'Holiday Time', 'Chilly Chili', and 'Candle-light'.

PANSY

Viola x wittrockiana
Violet family: Violaceae

HARDINESS– Zones 8–11. Wait until there is a consistent chill in the air before planting.

NATIVE RANGE–None. This is a hybrid.

COLOR(S)– All color flowers

PEAK SEASON–Blooms fall and winter

MATURE SIZE–10 to 12 inches (25 to 30 cm) tall

WATER NEEDS–Space 6 to 8 inches (15 to 20 cm) apart in thoroughly moistened soil. Pansies fill in slowly.

CARE–Remove old blossoms to keep new flowers forming.

PROBLEMS–May have aphids and slugs as pests. Hand pick or use water to rinse. Decline when hot spring weather arrives.

USES AND SELECTIONS–Can be planted in beds, containers, and hanging baskets. Edge borders or fill entire gardens with mix of pansy colors. Johnny-jump-up (*Viola tricolor*) is another pansy with a smaller flower that might also be useful.

PETUNIA

Petunia x atkinsiana
Nightshade family: Solanaceae

HARDINESS– Zones 8-11. Plant when weather cools. Needs protection from severe freezes.

NATIVE RANGE–None. This is a hybrid.

COLOR(S)– Flowers all colors and blends

PEAK SEASON–Fall through spring blooms

MATURE SIZE–12 to 18 inches (30 to 46 cm) tall

WATER NEEDS–Space 8 to 10 inches (20 to 25 cm) apart in thoroughly moistened soil.

CARE–Often grow lanky and full of old blossoms and seedpods. Periodically prune to remove old portions and encourage new growth.

PROBLEMS–None.

USES AND SELECTIONS–Plant in beds, containers, and hanging baskets. Varieties range from just over 1-inch (2.5-cm) flowers to over 4 inches (10 cm) across. They take light frosts and provide spring color when gardens need it most. Mix with greenery, other cool-season plants, shrubs, or bulb plantings. Good companions include calendula, pinks, and snapdragons. 'Wave' hybrids can last into warmer months.

PINKS

Dianthus spp.
Carnation family: Caryophyllaceae

HARDINESS– Zones 8-9. Northern plantings can survive light freeze with little protection. It doesn't tolerate heat, so southern plants are often shorter-lived.

NATIVE RANGE–Alaska, Eurasia, Africa

COLOR(S)– Pink, white, or red flowers

PEAK SEASON–Blooms fall through spring

MATURE SIZE–8 to 18 inches (20 to 46 cm)

WATER NEEDS–After established, water when soil feels dry. Container-grown plants may need more frequent watering.

CARE–Add plenty of organic material to sandy soil. Space 8 to 10 inches (20 to 25 cm) apart. Do not plant too deeply. Add light mulch layer. May live for more than one growing season.

PROBLEMS–Not heat tolerant

USES AND SELECTIONS–Use for large color masses in flower beds or color splashes along walkways or in containers. Good selections are 'Baby Doll', 'Carpet', 'Charms', 'Flash', 'Floral Lace', 'Ideal', 'Magic Charm', and 'Telstar'.

PORTULACA

Portulaca grandiflora
Portulaca family: Portulacaceae

HARDINESS–Zones 8-11. Provides color in sun-drenched areas when Florida's summer sun withers other plants. Cool weather causes decline.

NATIVE RANGE–South America

COLOR(S)– Brilliant reds, pinks, oranges, yellows, creams, white flowers

PEAK SEASON–Blooms spring through summer

MATURE SIZE–3 to 6 inches (7.5 to 15 cm) tall

WATER NEEDS–Space 8 to 10 inches (20 to 25 cm) apart in thoroughly moistened soil.

CARE–Portulaca is drought tolerant. Portulacas will flower (in sunny locations) for 6 to 8 weeks before gradually declining.

PROBLEMS–Excessive moisture causes rot.

USES AND SELECTIONS–Also called moss rose. Plant in beds, containers, and hanging baskets. Portulaca is best used as a border, to highlight beds of greenery, or in hanging baskets with taller plants. Also suitable for rock gardens or xeriscape plantings.

SALVIA

Salvia splendens
Mint family: Lamiaceae

HARDINESS– Zones 8-11. Provides almost year-round color throughout Florida. In southern regions salvia can be grown as a perennial. It will be damaged by frosts.

NATIVE RANGE–South America

COLOR(S)– Bright red, salmon, pink, purple, and white flowers

PEAK SEASON–Blooms year-round in frost-free zones.

MATURE SIZE–8 to 18 inches (20 to 46 cm) tall

WATER NEEDS–Space 10 to 16 inches (25 to 41 cm) apart in thoroughly moistened soil. Once established, wait until soil surface feels dry, then soak.

CARE–It could be trimmed if necessary. May reseed.

PROBLEMS–None.

USES AND SELECTIONS–Plant beds or containers. A mix of colors displays well, as do clusters planted with dusty miller, petunia, and snapdragon.

SNAPDRAGON

Antirrhinum majus
Plantain family: Plantaginaceae

HARDINESS–Zones 8-10. Tolerant of frost and light freezes. In North and Central Florida, provide protection for more severe cold. In South Florida, wait for cooler fall weather to plant.

NATIVE RANGE–Western Mediterranean

COLOR(S)– All color flowers

PEAK SEASON–Blooms fall through spring

MATURE SIZE–8 to 36 inches (20 to 91 cm)

WATER NEEDS–Space 8 to 12 inches (20 to 30 cm) apart in thoroughly moistened soil. Drought tolerant once established.

CARE–Removal of flower and seed heads encourages new shoots and prevents rapid decline of plantings.

PROBLEMS–Prevent wind damage with stakes or garden wire.

USES AND SELECTIONS–Can be planted in beds or containers using a single color or mixture. A good planting combination is to surround hollyhocks or petunias. New hybrids are more compact, but taller varieties (like 'Rocket' hybrids) make excellent bouquets.

SUNFLOWERS

Helianthus spp.
Daisy family: Asteraceae

HARDINESS– Zones 4-9. Plant during warmer months in North Florida, year-round in Central and South Florida.

NATIVE RANGE–The Americas

COLOR(S)– Yellow, orange, red flowers

PEAK SEASON–Blooms best spring through fall

MATURE SIZE–2 to 15 feet (61 cm to 4.5 m)

WATER NEEDS–Drought tolerant

CARE–Plant in enriched soil with adequate potassium for strong stems. To harvest seeds, cut flower after it dries. Hang upside down in well-ventilated place. When completely dry, remove seeds for eating by you or local wildlife.

PROBLEMS–Bugs may damage foliage and flowers. Hand pick to control. Sunflowers are allelopathic, so they may prevent germination or damage nearby plants.

USES AND SELECTIONS–Sunflowers are a native American crop of global importance, grown for oil, snack seed, birdseed, garden flowers, and cut flowers. Several are native to Florida. Plant for borders, screening, and along fences. They are also good in wildlife and children's gardens. Some new cultivars have shorter heights and different colors. All-America Selection winners include 'Soraya' and 'Ring of Fire' (bi-colored petals).

TORENIA

Torenia fournieri
Lindernia family: Linderniaceae

HARDINESS– Zones 8–10. Also called summer pansy and wishbone flower, start planting torenia as soon as cold weather is over.

NATIVE RANGE–India and Southeast Asia

COLOR(S)– Lavender, white, blue, and pink combinations

PEAK SEASON–Blooms spring through fall

MATURE SIZE–Sprawling plants 6 to 12 inches (15 to 30 cm) tall

WATER NEEDS–Space 8 to 12 inches (20 to 30 cm) apart in thoroughly moistened soil. Drought tolerant.

CARE–A vigorous grower that tolerates heat, rain, and light shade. Torenia produces cycles of blooms for the entire warm season.

PROBLEMS–None.

USES AND SELECTIONS–Can be planted in beds, containers, or hanging baskets. Torenia can be used as a ground cover or as edging with celosia, marigolds, or nicotiana.

TROPICAL SAGE

Salvia coccinea
Mint family: Lamiaceae

HARDINESS–Zones 8–11. Provides almost year-round color throughout Florida. In South Florida, it can be grown as a perennial. It will be damaged, but not killed, by frosts.

NATIVE RANGE–Florida and other southeastern states

COLOR(S)– Bright-red or pink flowers

PEAK SEASON–Blooms from early spring to early winter in North Florida. It blooms year-round in frost-free zones.

MATURE SIZE–10 to 30 inches (25 to 76 cm) tall

WATER NEEDS–Space 8 to 12 inches (20 to 30 cm) apart in thoroughly moistened soil.

CARE–It can be trimmed if necessary. Freely reseeds.

PROBLEMS–None.

USES AND SELECTIONS–Also called scarlet sage, it's an excellent addition to pollinator gardens. Hummingbirds love it. It reseeds, so expect more once you have it.

VERBENA

Verbena x hybrida
Verbena family: Verbenaceae

HARDINESS– Zones 8–11. Cold sensitive and may be damaged by frosts and freezes in North and Central Florida. Grows best in spring and fall.

NATIVE RANGE–None because this is a hybrid. However, there are several verbena species that are native to Florida.

COLOR(S)– Deep-green leaves with blue, purple, red, white, and cream flowers

PEAK SEASON–Spring through early winter blooms

MATURE SIZE–Wide-spreading plants 10 to 12 inches (25 to 30 cm) tall

WATER NEEDS–Space 10 to 14 inches (25 to 36 cm) apart in thoroughly moistened soil.

CARE–Most selections give 6 to 8 weeks of good flowering before needing to be replaced.

PROBLEMS–Blooms may be damaged by summer heat and rains.

USES AND SELECTIONS–Use in beds, containers, or hanging baskets. It makes attractive edging for borders or to spill over sides of hanging baskets. Plant with celosia, dusty miller, geraniums, or snapdragons.

ZINNIA

Zinnia elegans
Daisy family: Asteraceae

HARDINESS–Zones 8–11. Plant before weather gets too hot and humid. The North Florida season is longer. Early plantings in Central and South Florida give 6 to 8 weeks of flowering.

NATIVE RANGE–Mexico and Central America

COLOR(S)– Pink, red, orange, plum, white flowers

PEAK SEASON–Blooms from spring into summer

MATURE SIZE–8 to 36 inches (20 to 91 cm) tall

WATER NEEDS–Space 8 to 15 inches (20 to 38 cm) apart in thoroughly moistened soil.

CARE–A carefree plant with big, long-lasting blossoms. Extend flowering period by removing declining blossoms.

PROBLEMS–Plant in spring to avoid fungal diseases.

USES AND SELECTIONS–Use both tall and short varieties in beds or containers. Plant smaller selections as edging and taller types as focal points. Newer varieties better tolerate summer heat and rains. Excellent as cut flowers.

ANNUALS

VARIETY	FLOWER COLOR	HEIGHT (INCHES)	SPACING (INCHES)	COLD HARDINESS	LIGHT LEVEL
Ageratum	White, blue, pink	6-18	10-12	Tender	Sun to light shade
Alyssum	White, pink, purple	6-12	10-12	Tender	Sun to light shade
Amaranthus	Red	36-48	12-18	Tender	Sun
Aster	White, pink, blue	18-24	12-18	Tender	Sun to light shade
Baby's Breath	White, pink	18-36	18-24	Hardy	Sun
Balsam	White, red, purple	18-24	12-18	Tender	Sun to light shade
Browallia	White, purple	12-18	10-12	Tender	Sun to light shade
Calendula	Orange, yellow	12-18	10-12	Hardy	Sun
California Poppy	Yellow, orange	18-24	12-18	Hardy	Sun
Celosia	Orange, red, yellow	8-24	10-12	Tender	Sun
Cleome	White, pink	36-48	18-24	Hardy	Sun
Coleus	Insignificant	12-30	12-18	Tender	Sun to light shade
Cosmos	White, pink, yellow	18-36	12-18	Tender	Sun
Dahlberg Daisy	Yellow	6-8	8-12	Tender	Sun
Delphinium	White, pink, purple	24-36	12-18	Hardy	Sun
Dianthus	White, pink, red	12-18	8-12	Hardy	Sun to light shade
Dusty Miller	Yellow	12-24	10-12	Hardy	Sun to light shade
Foxglove	White, pink, purple	24-36	12-18	Hardy	Sun to light shade
Gazania	Orange, red, yellow	12-18	8-12	Tender	Sun
Geranium	White, red, lavender	18-24	12-24	Tender	Sun
Globe Amaranth	Pink, purple	12-24	12-18	Tender	Sun
Hollyhock	White, pink, purple	48-60	18-24	Hardy	Sun
Impatiens	White, pink, purple	12-24	12-18	Tender	Shade
Johnny-Jump-Up	Yellow, pink, blue, purple	8-12	8-12	Hardy	Sun
Lobelia	White, blue, purple	8-12	8-12	Tender	Sun to light shade
Marigold	Yellow, orange	10-36	12-18	Tender	Sun
Melampodium	Yellow	18-24	12-18	Tender	Sun
Mexican Sunflower	Orange	36-48	18-24	Tender	Sun

* = Inconspicuous Flower Color   N = North Florida   C = Central Florida   S = South Florida

ANNUALS

VARIETY	FLOWER COLOR	HEIGHT (INCHES)	SPACING (INCHES)	COLD HARDINESS	LIGHT LEVEL
Nasturtium	White, yellow, orange	36–48	12–18	Tender	Sun
Nicotiana	White, pink, red	12–24	12–18	Tender	Sun
Nierembergia	White, purple	8–12	10–12	Tender	Sun to light shade
Ornamental Kale or Cabbage	Yellow	10–12	12–18	Hardy	Sun
Ornamental Pepper	Cream	12–18	10–12	Tender	Sun
Pansy	Yellow, orange, purple	6–8	8–10	Hardy	Sun
Periwinkle	White, pink, purple	12–18	12–24	Tender	Sun
Petunia	White, pink, red, purple	8–16	12–18	Hardy	Sun to light shade
Phlox (Annual)	White, pink, purple	12–18	12–18	Hardy	Sun
Purslane	White, yellow, pink	8–12	12–18	Tender	Sun
Moss Rose	White, yellow, pink, orange	6–10	8–12	Tender	Sun
Scarlet Sage	White, red, pink, purple	12–24	12–18	Tender	Sun to light shade
Silk Flower	Pink, red	18–24	12–18	Tender	Sun
Snapdragon	White, pink, yellow, red	10–36	10–12	Hardy	Sun to light shade
Stock	White, pink, purple	12–24	10–12	Hardy	Sun
Strawflower	Red, yellow, orange	18–24	10–12	Tender	Sun
Sunflower	Yellow, orange	12–124	12–24	Tender	Sun
Sweet Pea	White, pink, red, purple	18–72	8–12	Hardy	Sun
Torenia	White, pink, blue, purple	10–18	12–18	Tender	Sun to light shade
Verbena	White, red, purple	8–12	12–18	Tender	Sun
Zinnia	White, yellow, orange, red	12–36	12–24	Tender	Sun

* = Inconspicuous Flower Color   N = North Florida   C = Central Florida   S = South Florida

ANNUALS PLANTING TIMES BY REGION

VARIETY	NORTH	CENTRAL	SOUTH
Ageratum	March–May September–November	February–May	November–March
Alyssum	February–March September–November	February–April	October–March
Amaranthus	March–May	March–May	October–March
Aster	March–April	February–April	October–March
Baby's Breath	February–March October–December	February–March	August–December
Balsam	March–June	February–June	February–May
Browallia	March–May	March–April	February–March
Calendula	February–April	November–March	November–March
California Poppy	November–January	November–February	November–February
Celosia	March–May	8–24	10–12
September–November	March–May	36–48	18–24
September–November	March–May	12–30	12–18
Cleome	March–June September–November	March–May	February–May
Coleus	April–May	March–September	March–October
Cosmos	April–May	March–April	November–March
Dahlberg Daisy	April–June	March–June	March–June
Delphinium	February–March	November–January	November–February
Dianthus	November–March	November–March	November–February
Dusty Miller	February–May	November–May	November–April
Foxglove	February–March	December–March	December–February
Gazania	March–May September–November	March–May	November–May
Geranium	March–May	November–April	November–March
Globe Amaranth	March–September September–October	March–May September–November	March–May
Hollyhock	March–April	November–December	Not recommended
Impatiens	March–September	March–November	March–November
Johnny-Jump-Up	November–February	November–February	November–January

* = Inconspicuous Flower Color   N = North Florida   C = Central Florida   S = South Florida

ANNUALS PLANTING TIMES BY REGION

VARIETY	NORTH	CENTRAL	SOUTH
Lobelia	March–April	November–March	November–February
Marigold	April–June September–October	March–June	October–March
Melampodium	March–July	March–July	February–August
Mexican Sunflower	April–July	March–June	February–June
Nasturtium	March–April	November–March	November–March
Nicotiana	March–May September–October	March–April September–October	February–April
Nierembergia	April–July	March–July	March–July
Ornamental Kale or Cabbage	November–February	November–March	November–February
Ornamental Pepper	March–June	March–May	September–April
Pansy	November–February	November–February	November–January
Periwinkle	March–June	March–October	March–October
Petunia	November–March	November–April	November–March
Phlox (Annual)	October–November	October–December	October–December
Purslane	April–July	April–June	April–June
Moss Rose	April–July	March–May	March–May
Scarlet Sage	March–June September–November	March–May September–November	February–May
Silk Flower	April–July	April–July	March–July
Snapdragon	October–March	November–March	November–March
Stock	March–April	November–March	November–March
Strawflower	March–May	March–April	November–March
Sunflower	February–May September–October	February–May	November–April
Sweet Pea	October–February	November–February	November–February
Torenia	March–June September–October	March–June September–October	February–March
Verbena	March–May October–November	March–April October–November	February–March
Zinnia	March–May September–October	March–April September–October	February–March

* = Inconspicuous Flower Color   N = North Florida   C = Central Florida   S = South Florida

FLORIDA ANNUALS CARE: BY THE MONTH

JANUARY

❏ It's great planting weather. It will soon be too late for some cool-season annuals like pansies.

❏ When warm-season annuals start to fade, add cool-season color. If frosts and freezing weather have damaged some plants, replace them.

❏ Annuals grow a little more slowly during cooler months, but check at least once a week for pests and water needs. Cold weather could appear at any time, so be prepared to protect plants that need it.

❏ Plants that have been growing for a few months may be getting lanky or forming seed heads. Stretch their life by pruning faded flowers, cutting spindly stems, and applying compost. Or enjoy the winter texture of the seed heads and the birds that eat the seeds.

❏ January is one of the driest months, so provide extra irrigation if necessary.

FEBRUARY

❏ This is rejuvenation month for most annual flower beds. As you remove old plants, try to determine if they had any problems, such as weeds, nematodes, or insects. Careful preparation of new beds can help prevent some problems. Consider adding perennials to reduce this seasonal chore.

❏ With longer and warmer days, annual flowers should start making more active growth. Good care is needed now to help old beds keep blooming and new beds to fill in quickly.

❏ This is still the cool-but-dry season. Plants use moisture slowly, but will need some extra water when soil surface begins to dry.

❏ Check for pests weekly, especially cutworms.

MARCH

❏ Like crop rotation, don't use the same plants in the same spot every year. This encourages pests specific to one plant.

❏ Water new plantings daily for a week or two. Don't count on an irrigation system. Reduce watering to an as-needed schedule when plants grow into surrounding soil. Overwatering causes root and stem rots.

❏ As weather becomes warmer, pest problems will become more intense. Hand remove leaves affected by mites, aphids, leafminers, caterpillars, slugs, and snails.

APRIL

❏ Now is a good time to start sunflower seeds. They are favorites of many, especially kids. Use normal planting techniques for other flower beds and container gardens.

❏ Check for any plants that need staking. Renew mulch that is too thin and keep it a few inches from the base of annuals.

❏ If the rain doesn't last enough to soak into the soil, look for signs of wilting and water if the surface inch is dry.

❏ Keep an eye out for aphids, garden flea hoppers, mites, whiteflies, slugs, and snails.

MAY

❏ Most annuals last only a few months, set seed, and then decline. Remove spent plants and prepare soil by working in organic matter. Set new plants at the proper spacing, then water. In order to break the cycle of seasonal plantings, consider adding perennials and small shrubs to the mix.

❏ To sow from seed, press big seeds into pots or cell-packs of germination mix and sprinkle small seeds on surface. Keep moist, in bright light. Fertilize weekly with half-strength solution. Transplant when seedlings are 4 to 6 inches (10 to 15 cm) tall, about 4 to 6 weeks.

❏ Stake tall plants. Replace severely damaged plants.

❏ Don't overwater, which might cause flower damage and stem and root rots.

❏ This month could start the rainy season and reduce the mite problem. Aphids, garden flea hoppers, grasshoppers, whiteflies, slugs, and snails like hotter weather.

JUNE

❏ Record annuals' performance and your preferences as a guide for choosing plants next year.

❏ Replant during summer months to correct problems and replace dying flowers. When filling in bare spots, remove declining plant stems, leaves, and roots.

❏ Weed after watering. Hand pulling is a good, quick method. Other control methods are mulch, newspaper, and pre-emergence herbicide.

❏ If plants' growth slows or foliage yellows, lay in some rich compost to invigorate the soil.

❏ Leaf spots increase with the rains. Especially susceptible are impatiens and salvias. Reduce watering to an as-needed schedule, and keep foliage as dry as possible.

JULY

❏ In this rainy season some annuals, like petunia and celosia, fade. More rain-tolerant hot-weather annuals include: coleus, globe amaranth, impatiens, and butter daisies.

❏ Watch for summer annuals' moisture needs and for any damage that requires pruning or replanting.

❏ This is the wet season, so stop all landscape-wide fertilizers.

❏ Rot problems are big summer concerns. Few annuals can stand wet feet. Note problem areas so future plantings can be modified. Look for flea hoppers, grasshoppers, nematodes, whiteflies, slugs, and snails.

AUGUST

❏ Many gardeners take a break this hot time of year and allow annuals to gradually decline. Others continue with full replacement. After mid-August is a good time to start the first fall warm-season flowers, like marigolds, salvia, nicotiana, verbena, and sunflowers.

❏ Some long-lived annuals, including impatiens and coleus, may become lanky and overgrown. Trim back a foot or more to let new shoots sprout from the base.

❏ August can be the wettest month. Turn off irrigation systems and let nature do the watering. Closely watch moisture levels of hanging baskets and containers.

❏ Newly planted annuals or those in containers may need special feedings.

❏ Leaf spots and stem disease continue to be a problem. Consider changing to other selections in problem areas or use soaker hoses for watering (they are less likely to wet the foliage).

❏ Watch for garden flea hoppers, grasshoppers, nematodes, whiteflies, slugs, and snails.

SEPTEMBER

❏ Many flowers can be added to the early-fall annual gardens.

❏ Container gardens may begin to decline after a long summer growing season. Many have run out of room and set seed. Replant as soon as they begin to decline.

❏ Now is the time for major bed renovation. The beginning of the month is also a good time to start seeds of quick-growing warm-season annuals.

❏ Keep existing plants growing until new beds can be planted. Weeding, staking, pruning, and feeding can keep the plants attractive for longer.

❏ The wet season will be ending—make sure your irrigation system will be ready when needed.

❏ Expect leaf spot and stem disease to continue until rains subside. Watch for garden flea hoppers, grasshoppers, nematodes, slugs, snails, and whiteflies.

OCTOBER

❏ Cooler weather starts arriving, marking the in-between time of warm- and cool-season flowers. The transition can be handled four ways: 1) Continue planting warm-season annuals during early October, then gradually work in cool-season plants. 2) After warm-season flowers finish, let beds lie fallow until after mid-October, when you can plant cool-season plants. 3) Take a chance on the month being cool and jump directly into planting cool-season annuals. 4) Continue planting warm-season annuals and wait until November or December to change.

❏ This is an easy month to care for new plantings. Keep weeds out and check for moisture levels and pests.

❏ The dry season may begin early, so watch moisture levels.

❏ As weather turns cool, plants will not use as many nutrients. Feed less frequently.

❏ Mites are back with the drier weather. However, root rot and leaf spot should decrease, and nematodes are less active. Watch for garden flea hoppers, grasshoppers, white-flies, slugs, and snails.

NOVEMBER

❏ Most cool-season annuals are frost-resistant. These plants need coolness to flower, but not freezing weather. If in doubt, provide frost protection, such as a tempo-rary blanket or hay covering. Don't use plastic.

❏ Cooler temperatures mean annuals will not use as much water. However, during this drier season, check all flower beds and container gardens for moisture levels.

❏ Insect populations decline during cooler months. Keep up frequent garden visits to check for pests and other problems. Check for root rots, garden flea hoppers, grasshoppers, nematodes, slugs, snails, and whiteflies.

DECEMBER

❏ Create some festive holiday-season plantings. Red and white combinations work well, including petunias and dianthus. Also combine silvery dusty miller with red flowered annuals or poinsettias.

❏ Start early to fill empty flower spots. Garden centers concentrate on holiday plants and forget about annual flowers. Annuals may be purchased even though they aren't needed right away. Keep them healthy by placing in appropriate light level, feeding weekly with balanced fertilizer, keeping no more than a month before planting, and checking water needs daily.

❏ Be on guard for cold weather. Frosts are common in North Florida this month. Control winter weeds and stake taller-growing plants if needed.

BULBS
for Florida

C lose your eyes and think of some plants that grow from bulbs. What immediately comes to mind? Admit it: you see tulips, daffodils, crocus, and hyacinths.

Now erase that image, because most northern bulbs don't grow well in Florida. You can force a few, but forcing is a chore. Happily, you will find that some of our Florida favorites rival their northern relatives. Some can be in bloom at just about any time of year. Many have extended flowering seasons, so you might see them in bloom several times a year.

We use a broad definition of bulb in this chapter. A true bulb resembles an onion–it has some residual roots, a small stem portion, and lots of leaves packed closely together. (Some true Florida bulbs are amaryllis, crinum, and rain lilies.) Many other plants that we call bulbs are technically classified as stems and include corms, tubers, tuberous roots, and rhizomes. All these plants grow in a similar manner, forming a clump or cluster from which arise attractive foliage and, often, colorful flowers.

You can plant entire beds of bulbs or use them for small spots of color. Some grow well in containers and can be moved into the home or to patios, porches, or balconies when in bloom. Only a few lend themselves to naturalization. If you want them to naturalize, do not mow the areas until flowering and foliage growth is over.

PLANTING

Most Florida bulbs can stay in the ground for several years before being divided. Check to make sure the bulbs will receive appropriate light. While some grow well in sandy soils, all seem to prefer an improved planting site. A few like damp, poorly drained soil, but most do not like soggy soil.

You should also select a planting site that is free of deep-rooted noxious weeds such as torpedo grass. It is difficult to pull weeds out of the planting site year after year. They can be hand dug, but you're unlikely to get all of the underground shoots this way. Some people use a nonselective herbicide that allows replanting after the weeds decline.

Once the weeds are under control, you are ready to prepare the bed for your next bulb planting. Enrich sandy and clay soils with liberal quantities of organic matter. Some good sources are compost, coconut coir, and composted manures. Some gardeners add bone meal, a traditional product for bulb plantings. It contains some nitrogen, calcium, and phosphorus.

The best planting recommendation is to follow the instructions on the label that comes with the bulbs–or consult our planting chart on pages 50 and 52. Proper spacing and planting depth is important. Some bulbs do not flower or multiply well if planted too deep. Don't irrigate when planting dormant bulbs with no leaves.

CARE

It's easy to care for most bulbs. Add a top dressing of compost before they start their growth cycle each season.

WATERING

Some bulbs—such as our native irises and cannas—like wet feet, but many other bulbs rot if they're too wet for long periods. Landscape-wide irrigation should be adequate for those upland bulbs.

FERTILIZING

Most bulbs are not heavy feeders. Perhaps the real secret of Florida bulb care is to add compost to the soil when the bulbs are making active growth and can use the nutrients.

SPRING-FLOWERING BULBS AND THOSE THAT LOSE THEIR FOLIAGE AFTER FLOWERING: Add compost once in March.

TROPICAL BULBS THAT GROW SPRING THROUGH FALL: Add compost every couple of months.

CONTAINER PLANTINGS DURING PERIODS OF ACTIVE GROWTH: Add compost to the top of the soil to renew the soil organisms. You could supplement this with organic products including fish or seaweed emulsions or compost tea.

PEST CONTROL

Bulbs have only a few pests. The bulbaceous plants seem particularly susceptible to grasshoppers, snails, and slugs, but luckily, most are large and easily hand picked.

AFRICAN IRIS

Dietes spp.
Iris family: Iridaceae

HARDINESS–Zones 8B–10. Hardier than other tropical bulbs, can be grown in pots to overwinter inside in North Florida.

NATIVE RANGE–Eastern Africa

COLOR(S)–White, cream, yellow flowers

PEAK SEASON–Blooms spring and summer; foliage evergreen

MATURE SIZE–2 to 4 feet (61 to 122 cm) tall, 1 to 3 feet (30 to 91 cm) spread

WATER NEEDS–Although it will grow in sandy soils, they flower best in rich, moist soil.

CARE–Can be planted any time during the year, spaced 18 to 24 inches (46 to 61 cm) apart. Need soil with good drainage. Very carefree and only requires a light fertilization once or twice a year.

PROBLEMS–None.

USES AND SELECTIONS–Use this versatile perennial as an edging or border plant, in mass plantings, or in containers. The stiff leaves radiate in a dense fan pattern and make the plant attractive as an accent or ground cover.

AFRICAN LILY

Agapanthus africanus
Amaryllis family: Amaryllidaceae

HARDINESS–Zones 8–10. Grows best in North and Central Florida. Protect from severe freezes. Plantings in South Florida are usually short-lived.

NATIVE RANGE–South Africa

COLOR(S)–Blue, white flowers

PEAK SEASON–Blooms spring and summer; strap-like leaves evergreen

MATURE SIZE–3 feet (91 cm) tall; 1 to 2 feet (30 to 61 cm) spread

WATER NEEDS–Will grow in sandy soils but needs plenty of water and nutrients. Enrich and mulch soil to maintain moisture and make more drought-tolerant plantings.

CARE–Rhizomes best planted from October through March, spaced 12 inches (30 cm) apart. Does best in areas with morning sun and afternoon shade. Needs well-drained soil. Add compost in March, May, and September. After flowering, cut old stalks near ground.

PROBLEMS–None.

USES AND SELECTIONS–Also called lily-of-the-Nile. Excellent as an accent plant or a backdrop in perennial beds, for spot color throughout landscape, or in containers.

AMARYLLIS

Hippeastrum spp.
Amaryllis family: Amaryllidaceae

HARDINESS–Zones 8–10. Protect from freezing.

NATIVE RANGE–South America

COLOR(S)–Red, pink, orange, salmon, white flowers

PEAK SEASON–Blooms winter and spring

MATURE SIZE–2 feet (61 cm) tall

WATER NEEDS–Use enriched soil and mulch to maintain moisture. Withhold water during resting stage.

CARE–Plant in fall to early spring, spaced 12 inches (30 cm) or more apart. To maintain energy in the bulb, after flowering, cut old stalks near ground before seeds form. Refresh planting bed or container with compost.

PROBLEMS–None.

USES AND SELECTIONS–A favorite Christmas present for Florida gardeners, Amaryllis can be planted as border plants, in a bed of their own, or in containers.

AMAZON LILY

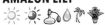

Urceolina × grandiflora
Amaryllis family: Amaryllidaceae

HARDINESS–Zones 9–11. Restrict plantings to containers in colder Florida gardens.

NATIVE RANGE–Northern South America

COLOR(S)–White flowers

PEAK SEASON–Sporadic winter and early spring blooms; large green leaves evergreen

MATURE SIZE–1 foot (30 cm) tall

WATER NEEDS–Use enriched soil and mulch to maintain moisture.

CARE–Plant bulbs any time of year, spaced 3 to 4 inches (7.5 to 10 cm) apart. In an 8-inch (20-cm) pot, add 3 to 4 bulbs. Add compost a couple of times a year. Encourage flowering by alternating moist and dry periods for about a month, followed by a feeding to start growth and flowers. After flowering, cut old stalks near ground.

PROBLEMS–None.

USES AND SELECTIONS–Amazon lily can be used in beds or pots. Plant with caladiums, gingers, impatiens, and begonias or use it as a ground cover in front of other greenery. Can be used as a substitute for hostas.

AZTEC LILY

Sprekelia formosissima
Amaryllis family: Amaryllidaceae

HARDINESS–Zones 8–11. In areas with frost, protect Aztec lily bulbs with heavy mulch.

NATIVE RANGE–Mexico

COLOR(S)–Scarlet red flowers; green leaves

PEAK SEASON–Spring and summer blooms

MATURE SIZE–Flower about 5 inches (12.5 cm) across on 15-inch (38-cm) stalk. Strap-like leaves grow to 20 inches (51 cm).

WATER NEEDS–Provide extra water when growing new leaves and blooming. Keep dry when dormant.

CARE–Plant container-grown plants any time. Divide and plant bulbs in fall, with top of bulb just above ground level. Add compost to the soil in March and September. When crowded and allowed to occasionally dry out, it may bloom several times during summer.

PROBLEMS–None.

USES AND SELECTIONS–Aztec lily blooms look like a cross between an amaryllis and an orchid. It has several common names: Jacobean lily, St. James lily, and orchid lily. This is the only species in the genus, with several cultivars. It can also grow in containers.

BLOOD LILY

Scadoxus multiflorus
Amaryllis family: Amaryllidaceae

HARDINESS–Zones 8–11. Use extra mulch in northern regions for cold protection.

NATIVE RANGE–Africa & Arabia

COLOR(S)–Red flowers

PEAK SEASON–Spring and early summer blooms; leaves dormant in winter

MATURE SIZE–18 to 24 inches (46 to 61 cm) tall; flower ball 6 inches (15 cm) or larger

WATER NEEDS–Will tolerate sandy soils, but mulched and amended soils retain moisture better.

CARE–Plant from January through March, spaced 6 to 8 inches (15 to 20 cm) apart. Add compost in March and August. After flowering, cut old stalks near ground.

PROBLEMS–None.

USES AND SELECTIONS–Blood lily can be used in beds or pots. Plant with other bulbs and perennials, in front of shrubs, or as a specimen where it can be viewed up close. Combine with amaryllis, crinum, impatiens, gingers, and African iris. Grows best with filtered sun but can also grow in more intense shade under trees.

BUGLE LILY

Watsonia spp.
Iris family: Iridaceae

HARDINESS–Zones 9-10

NATIVE RANGE–South Africa

COLOR(S)–Intense pink, mauve, red, orange, white flowers

PEAK SEASON–Blooms late spring and summer; evergreen foliage in some species

MATURE SIZE–3 to 5 feet x 2 to 3 feet (91 to 152 cm x 61 to 91 cm)

WATER NEEDS–Drought tolerant once established

CARE–Plant corms September through May in well-drained soil. These tough plants do not need much care. Do not divide until they become crowded.

PROBLEMS–None.

USES AND SELECTIONS–This tall, clump-forming plant has thin upright foliage with long flower spikes to 5 feet (152 cm), each with up to forty tubular blooms. Like its cousin gladiolus, it's ideal for cut flowers. The blooms are fragrant. Use these showy plants as specimens, as borders, at the back of perennial beds, or in xeriscape plantings. There are many species and cultivars.

CALADIUM

Caladium x hortulanum
Arum family: Araceae

HARDINESS–Zones 9-11

NATIVE RANGE–None. This is a hybrid, but the caladium species are native to Central & South America.

COLOR(S)–Red, rose, pink, white, silver, bronze, green leaves

PEAK SEASON–Summer foliage

MATURE SIZE–18 to 24 inches (46 to 61 cm)

WATER NEEDS–Plant 1 to 2 inches (2.5 to 5 cm) deep in late winter or spring using enriched soil. Water sparingly until leaves emerge, then keep it moist.

CARE–Caladiums tolerate Florida's summer heat and humidity. They look best with some shade from midday heat and some irrigation. After the leaves die back each fall, keep bulbs in the ground or dig up and dry them for replanting in April. Under poor growing conditions, may need replacing after about 3 years.

PROBLEMS–None.

USES AND SELECTIONS–Caladiums' complex color forms look best in masses. They can be used in beds, around the base of trees, or in containers. The long-lasting leaves are good for flower arranging.

CALLA LILY

Zantedeschia spp.
Arum family: Araceae

HARDINESS–Zones 9-10. Container culture best for South Florida.

NATIVE RANGE–Southern Africa

COLOR(S)–White, pink, yellow, cream, lavender, purple, and almost-black flowers; green and variegated leaves

PEAK SEASON–Blooms in spring; foliage dormant fall and winter

MATURE SIZE–6 to 36 inches (15 to 91 cm)

WATER NEEDS–Will grow in sandy soils with plenty of water and nutrients. Enhance the soil and use mulch to retain moisture. In containers use loose potting mix. Some species can be grown at the edges of ponds; keep at surface level.

CARE–Plant 1 to 2 inches (2.5 to 5 cm) deep in enriched soil from September through January. Add compost in March and August. After flowering, cut old stalks near ground.

PROBLEMS–Spider mites and thrips may be pests. Rinse off with water.

USES AND SELECTIONS–Create a tropical look with clusters of calla lilies among warm-climate plants, such as philodendrons, caladiums, anthuriums, gingers, canna, and bananas. Use cut flowers and leaves for bouquets.

CANNA

Canna spp.
Canna family: Cannaceae

HARDINESS–Zones 9-11. *C. flaccida* to Zone 8.

NATIVE RANGE–Southeastern states, Mexico, Central & South America

COLOR(S)–Green, bronze, and striped leaves; red, orange, yellow, pink, cream, white, and bicolored flowers

PEAK SEASON–Blooms spring and summer

MATURE SIZE–2 to 4 feet (61 to 122 cm)

WATER NEEDS–Cannas love rich, moist soil. The native *C. flaccida* is an aquatic. Many hybrids can be acclimatized to grow in ponds.

CARE–To be vigorous they require good rich soil.

PROBLEMS–Leaf rollers, moth larva, spider mites, and rust may be problems, especially in South Florida. Inspect regularly and hand pick.

USES AND SELECTIONS–There are various species and multiple hybrids used in Florida. The tropical leaves and bright flowers of canna are often used as a focal point in beds and containers. In water gardens they are used as tall background plantings. Golden canna (*C. flaccida*) is native to most of Florida.

CRINUM LILY

Crinum spp.
Amaryllis family: Amaryllidaceae

HARDINESS–Zones 8-11. Recover quickly from killing frosts in northern regions.

NATIVE RANGE–Southeastern states, including Florida. Also Mexico, Central & South America, Africa, India, Asia, and Australia.

COLOR(S)–White, pink, rose, or striped flowers; green or burgundy foliage

PEAK SEASON–Blooms spring; leaves evergreen

MATURE SIZE–To 5 feet tall x to 5 feet wide (1.5 m x 1.5 m)

WATER NEEDS–Tolerant of most conditions, from wetland to dry areas. Somewhat drought tolerant.

CARE–Leave plenty of space between the large bulbs. Plant any time, but winter is best. Those in high shade look nicer. Add compost in spring. Moderately salt tolerant.

PROBLEMS–None.

USES AND SELECTIONS–Crinum lilies thrive in water garden accents and in dry areas. Use in groupings to accent their large fragrant flowers. There are several species and popular selections with rose and striped flowers, plus the white Florida native (*C. americanum*). They look good with ferns or as large specimen plants. Also use as a cut flower.

DAYLILY

Hemerocallis spp.
Asphodelus family: Asphodelaceae

HARDINESS–Zones 8-9a. In South Florida, check local garden centers for best selections.

NATIVE RANGE–Asia

COLOR(S)–Flowers in yellow, orange, pink, red, lavender, and blends

PEAK SEASON–Blooms spring and summer

MATURE SIZE–To 2 feet (61 cm)

WATER NEEDS–Grows in sandy soils, but does better with enriched soil and mulch to conserve moisture.

CARE–Add at any time of year. Set with base of foliage at or above soil level. Add compost in March and September.

PROBLEMS–None.

USES AND SELECTIONS–Although blossoms last one day, numerous buds result in continual blossoms throughout the season. Use in beds, rock gardens, perennial borders, and containers. Fill entire beds with daylilies or mix with annuals, perennials, and shrubs. Flowers, buds, and tubers are edible. The best daylilies for Florida are evergreen and semi-evergreen types. Florida has some of the nation's most popular breeders and growers.

GLADIOLUS

Gladiolus spp.
Iris family: Iridaceae

HARDINESS–Zones 8–11. Plant any time in South Florida. In North and Central Florida, plant spring and summer.

NATIVE RANGE–Eurasia, Africa

COLOR(S)–Flowers in all colors and blends

PEAK SEASON–Blooms spring and summer

MATURE SIZE–To 2 feet (61 cm)

WATER NEEDS–Enriched soil with good drainage. Will grow in sandy soils with plenty of water and nutrients. Add mulch to conserve moisture.

CARE–Plant corms 2 to 3 inches (5 to 7.5 cm) deep and 4 to 6 inches (10 to 15 cm) apart. Add compost top dressing while growing. After stalks develop, stake to prevent wind damage. Plants gradually decline for rest period after a few months of flowering, before starting new growth.

PROBLEMS–Glads will last only a few years in Florida.

USES AND SELECTIONS–Plant in groupings alone or with other bulbs, perennials, and shrubs. Mix with canna, crinum, or rain lilies. Excellent as cut flowers, lasting up to a week. Both tall and short forms are available.

GLORIOSA LILY

Gloriosa spp.
Colchicum family: Colchicaceae

HARDINESS–Zones 8–11. Goes dormant in cooler regions when affected by cold.

NATIVE RANGE–Africa, India, Southeast Asia

COLOR(S)–Flowers are crimson-banded and yellow.

PEAK SEASON–Blooms spring through summer

MATURE SIZE–To 6 feet (183 cm)

WATER NEEDS–Likes enriched, well-drained soil. Grow in sandy soils with plenty of water and nutrients. Mulch to conserve moisture.

CARE–Plant V-shaped tubers 2 to 4 inches (5 to 10 cm) deep and 12 to 18 inches (30 to 46 cm) apart. Trim vines to keep in bounds. After flowering, cold, or drought, the plants die back. Trim dead vines and wait for new growth.

PROBLEMS–It's poisonous if ingested.

USES AND SELECTIONS–The gloriosa lily is well named, because the blooms are indeed glorious. Also called climbing lily, it's best trained to a trellis. Plant as accent near patio or home entrance. Use as backdrop, along fence or wall, or among perennials that decline during winter. Plant with shorter-growing African iris, crinums, and gingers.

HURRICANE LILY

Lycoris spp.
Amaryllis family: Amaryllidaceae

HARDINESS–Zones 8–10

NATIVE RANGE–Southeastern Asia to Japan

COLOR(S)–Red flowers; blue-green foliage

PEAK SEASON–Blooms August and September; foliage fall and winter

MATURE SIZE–Blooming stalk to 24 inches (61 cm); flower cluster to 8 inches (20 cm) across

WATER NEEDS–Prefers moist soil, but doesn't need regular watering

CARE–Plant dormant bulbs in late summer and autumn. Growing lilies can be planted any time. Not picky about soil, but prefers enriched soil. Let leaves die completely in spring, do not cut off. This is the time to divide if needed. Delicate flowers last longer if protected from wind and sun.

PROBLEMS–The bulbs are slightly toxic.

USES AND SELECTIONS–Sometimes called surprise lilies because flowers appear suddenly (before foliage) after heavy rains. Plant under trees, in mixed borders, or in front of shrubs. Use in clusters for fall color. There are several species and hybrids. The most common for Florida is *L. radiata var. radiata*, with red-orange flowers.

KAFFIR LILY

Clivia miniata
Amaryllis family: Amaryllidaceae

HARDINESS–Zones 9-11. Grow in containers in North Florida. Protect all plantings from freezing.

NATIVE RANGE–South Africa

COLOR(S)–Bright orange, yellow flowers

PEAK SEASON–Blooms spring; deep-green foliage evergreen

MATURE SIZE–18 to 24 inches (46 to 61 cm)

WATER NEEDS–Likes enriched coarse soil with excellent drainage. Does not like to be soggy. Keep plants drier during winter months.

CARE–Plant bulbs just below soil surface, 14 to 20 inches (36 to 51 cm) apart. Add compost in March and September. After flowering, cut old stalk near ground. New plants multiply rapidly, but take 3 years to flower.

PROBLEMS–None.

USES AND SELECTIONS–Does well in lower light where flowering plant sections are limited. Best in clusters for perennial beds, among shrubs, in containers for showy displays, or indoors. Combine with caladium or impatiens.

LOUISIANA IRIS

Iris spp. (This is a group of several species and cultivars. Some are native to Florida.)
Iris family: Iridaceae

HARDINESS–Zones 8-9

NATIVE RANGE–Southeastern states

COLOR(S)–Yellow, blue, red, reddish/brown, white, and purple flowers

PEAK SEASON–Spring blooms; strap-like leaves evergreen

MATURE SIZE–To 3 feet (91 cm) tall

WATER NEEDS–Best planted in or near standing water. Will also grow in drier conditions if kept moist, using enriched soil and mulch.

CARE–Plant spring through summer in rich soil. Space 8 to 12 inches (20 to 30 cm) apart with roots in the ground. Feed in March, May, and September. Cut old stalks back to ground after flowering.

PROBLEMS–Rhizomes in ponds should be kept slightly above the water surface.

USES AND SELECTIONS–Thrives in wetland conditions but also does well in terrestrial plantings if kept moist. Use along pond edges or plant in containers. Mass plantings make dramatic statements. Both flowers and leaves are often used in flower arrangements. Blue flag iris (*I. virginica*), one of the most commonly available, is native to most of North Florida.

PERUVIAN LILY

Alstroemeria spp.
Alstroemeria Family: Alstroemeriaceae

HARDINESS–Zones 8-10. Check with local sources to get hardiest types for South Florida.

NATIVE RANGE–South America

COLOR(S)–Green/red, pink, yellow, white, lavender flowers

PEAK SEASON–Blooms spring and early summer

MATURE SIZE–18 to 24 inches (46 to 61 cm) tall

WATER NEEDS–Will grow well in sandy soil with plenty of water and nutrients. Enrich soil and use mulch to retain moisture. Less water is needed during winter months.

CARE–Best planted from later winter through spring, 6 to 9 inches (15 to 23 cm) deep and 1 foot (30 cm) apart. Need light feeding in March and May. Cut old stalks back to ground after flowering or allow seeds to develop.

PROBLEMS–May be affected by slugs and cutworms. Hand pick or use recommended pest control.

USES AND SELECTIONS–Use in areas with filtered light, in mixed beds or by themselves. It also does well in containers. When used as a cut flower, it has a long vase life.

RAIN LILY

Zephyranthes spp.
Amaryllis family: Amaryllidaceae

HARDINESS–Zones 8–11

NATIVE RANGE–The Americas (Some are native to Florida.)

COLOR(S)–White, yellow, pink flowers

PEAK SEASON–Blooms spring to early fall; thin leaves usually evergreen

MATURE SIZE–To 12 inches (30 cm) tall

WATER NEEDS–Drought tolerant, although foliage may die back without adequate water. Grows best in moist soil. Less water is needed during winter.

CARE–Flowering for rain lily (also called zephyr lily) begins with the rainy season. Plant 1 to 2 inches (2.5 to 5 cm) deep, spaced 3 to 4 inches (7.5 to 10 cm) apart. Need light feeding in March, May, and September. Seeds germinate quickly when sown in loose potting mix.

PROBLEMS–None.

USES AND SELECTIONS–Best planted in clusters as if naturalized in flower and perennial beds. Also use along walkways, as ground cover, in containers, and in water gardens. Native rain lilies may pop up in meadows and yards after a rain event. Atamasco rain lily (*Z. atamasca)* and Simpson's zephyr lily (*Z. simpsonii*) are Florida natives.

SNOWFLAKE

Leucojum aestivum
Amaryllis family: Amaryllidaceae

HARDINESS–Zones 8–9

NATIVE RANGE–Europe

COLOR(S)–Flower white with colored tips

PEAK SEASON–February to March blooms; dormant in summer

MATURE SIZE–1 to 2 feet (30 to 61 cm) high

WATER NEEDS–Water during spring growth and flowering. Tolerates drought during summer dormancy. Also tolerates soggy soils.

CARE–Plant these carefree bulbs in organic enriched soil from September through November. You may leave in the ground for about 10 years before digging and dividing.

PROBLEMS–None.

USES AND SELECTIONS–Snowflake is easy to grow and multiples freely. The arching thin leaves and delicate nodding flowers look best in large clumps. The blooms usually appear in late winter or early spring. (In Zone 9, it may bloom in fall and winter.) The flowers have a faint fragrance. There are about ten species, but *L. aestivum* is one that's more likely to grow well in Florida.

SOCIETY GARLIC

Tulbaghia violacea
Amaryllis family: Amaryllidaceae

HARDINESS–Zones 9–11

NATIVE RANGE–South Africa

COLOR(S)–Lilac, pink, white flowers

PEAK SEASON–Peak blooms spring and summer

MATURE SIZE–1 to 2 feet (30 to 61 cm) x equal spread

WATER NEEDS–Keep moist to get started.

CARE–Plant close to surface in bed with good drainage and organic matter. Add a little bone meal in bottom of the hole. Use slow-release fertilizer in spring, summer, and fall. The plant forms clumps, and tubers can be separated in winter.

PROBLEMS–If overwatered or kept in shade, can succumb to fungus. Also attracts aphids and whiteflies. Some people object to the odor.

USES AND SELECTIONS–These tropical bulbs are better in groups. Use as a medium-level backdrop to smaller-growing plants or en masse in front of shrubs. Try society garlic among culinary herbs. This is in the onion family and was thought to be less offensive than true garlic, hence the name.

SPIDER LILY

Hymenocallis latifolia
Amaryllis family: Amaryllidaceae

HARDINESS–Zones 9–11

NATIVE RANGE–Florida, Cuba, Bahamas

COLOR(S)–White flowers

PEAK SEASON–Summer

MATURE SIZE–2 to 3 feet (61 to 91 cm) tall and wide

WATER NEEDS–Provide some irrigation upon planting. Occurs in coastal zones.

CARE–Use compost when planting, but no other care will be needed.

PROBLEMS–Grasshoppers. Hand pick.

USES AND SELECTIONS–The large strap-like leaves add texture to the garden. There are several other species of spider lily native to Florida, but this one is the most likely to be available.

WALKING IRIS

Trimezia spp.
Iris family: Iridaceae

HARDINESS–Zones 10b–11. Grow in pots in North Florida. In Central Florida will die back if damaged by freezes, but regrow in spring.

NATIVE RANGE–Central & South America

COLOR(S)–White, yellow, blue, brown blossoms

PEAK SEASON–Year-round blooms in South Florida

MATURE SIZE–To 3 feet (91 cm) tall

WATER NEEDS–Walking iris is not drought tolerant, so use enriched soil, water regularly, and apply mulch.

CARE–Plant any time of year in partial shade. Apply compost in spring. To hasten the rooting of small plantlets, bend over flower stalks and anchor them in place. Occasionally clean out old stolons and leaves from beds to allow new plantlets to root.

PROBLEMS–None.

USES AND SELECTIONS–Use this as a tallish ground cover around trees or palms, or in a Japanese garden where the fan shape of the flat leaves can be highlighted. It also does well in foundation planters or a shrub bed where a vertical element is desired.

BULBS

VARIETY	AREA	WHEN TO PLANT	DEPTH (INCHES)	SPACING (INCHES)	LIGHT NEEDS	BLOOMS
Achimenes	NC	Feb.–April	1	2–3	Light shade	June–Sept.
African Lily	NCS	Year-round	Tip at soil	12–14	Sun to light shade	May–July
Alstroemeria	NCS	Jan.–Mar.	4–6	10–12	Sun to light shade	June–July
Amaryllis	NCS	Year-round	Tip at soil	12–14	Sun to light shade	Mar.–June
Amazon Lily	CS	Feb.–June	Tip at soil	10–12	Light shade	Dec.–Mar.
Anemone	NC	Oct.–Dec.	1	6–8	Sun to light shade	Mar.–April
Aztec Lily	NCS	Year-round	3–4	8–10	Sun	April–Aug.
Blackberry Lily	NCS	Feb.–Oct.	1	6–8	Sun	May–July
Blood Lily	NCS	Mar.–May	Tip at soil	8–10	Light shade	June–July
Blue Flag Iris	NCS	Sep.–Nov.	1–2	8–10	Sun to light shade	Mar.–May
Caladium	NCS	Feb.–May	2–3	12–14	Sun to light shade	Insignificant
Calla Lily	NC	Sept.–Mar.	3–4	12–24	Sun to light shade	Mar.–May
Canna	NCS	Feb.–Aug.	1–2	12–18	Sun to light shade	April–Nov.
Costus	S	Feb.–April	2–4	12–24	Light shade	June–Sep.
Crinum	NCS	Year-round	Neck at soil	18–24	Sun to light shade	Mar.–Nov.
Crocosmia	NCS	Feb.–Oct.	1–2	3–4	Sun	May–Sept.
Dahlia	NC	Feb.–May	4–6	12–24	Sun	May–Aug.
Daylily	NCS	Year-round	Stem at soil	12–24	Sun to light shade	April–June
Elephant Ear	NCS	Mar.–Nov.	3–4	24–48	Sun to light shade	Insignificant
Ginger	CS	May–Aug.	2–4	12–24	Light shade	May–Oct.
Ginger Lily	CS	Feb.–April	1–3	12–24	Sun to shade	May–Oct.
Gladiolus	NCS	Year-round	2–3	4–6	Sun	In 3 months
Gloriosa Lily	NCS	Feb.–April	2–4	12–18	Sun to light shade	April–Sept.
Heliconia	S	May–Oct.	Stem at soil	12–18	Sun to light shade	April-Oct.
Hurricane Lily	NC	Dec.–Feb.	3–4	8–10	Sun to light shade	Sept.–Oct.
Kaffir Lily	NCS	Year-round	Tip at soil	12–18	Light shade	Mar.–May
Lapeirousia	NCS	Oct.–Dec.	1	3–4	Sun to light shade	Feb.–Mar.
Lily	NC	Feb.–April	4–6	10–12	Sun to light shade	April–July

N = North Florida C = Central Florida S = South Florida

BULBS

VARIETY	AREA	WHEN TO PLANT	DEPTH (INCHES)	SPACING (INCHES)	LIGHT NEEDS	BLOOMS
Louisiana Iris	NC	Year-round	1–2	10–12	Sun to light shade	April–June
Moraea	NCS	Year-round	1–2	6–8	Sun	April–Aug
Narcissus	NC	Sept.–Dec.	2–4	6–8	Sun to light shade	Mar.–April
Pineapple Lily	NCS	Oct.–Nov.	5–6	10–12	Sun	June–July
Pride of Burma	CS	Feb.–April	2–3	8–12	Light shade	April–June
Rain Lily	NCS	Feb.–Sept.	1–2	4–6	Sun to light shade	May–Sept.
Shell Ginger	CS	Year-round	1	12–24	Sun to light shade	April–Oct.
Snowflake	NC	Sept.–Nov.	3–4	4–6	Sun to light shade	Feb.–Mar.
Society Garlic	CS	Year-round	1–2	6–8	Sun	Mar.–Nov.
Spider Lily	NCS	Year-round	3–5	12–18	Sun	April–Aug.
Tiger Flower	NC	Feb.–Mar.	3–4	4–8	Sun to light shade	June–Aug.
Tritonia	NCS	Jan.–Mar.	2–3	2–3	Sun	April–Aug.
Tuberose	NC	Jan.–Mar.	1–2	10–12	Sun	April–Aug.
Tuberous Begonia	NC	Jan.–Mar.	1–2	10–12	Light shade	May–July
Voodoo Lily	NCS	Jan.–Mar.	4–6	12–24	Sun to light shade	May–June
Walking Iris	NCS	Year-round	Stem at soil	12–14	Light shade	April–Oct.
Watsonia	NCS	Oct.–May	3–4	6–8	Sun to light shade	In 3 months

N = North Florida C = Central Florida S = South Florida

FLORIDA BULBS CARE: BY THE MONTH

JANUARY

❏ Prepare bulb beds. Dig out or spot-kill all perennial weeds. Till deeply, adding organic matter to sandy and clay soils. Also add some bone meal.

❏ Be ready to move container-grown and less-hardy bulbs inside. Most others may have their foliage damaged by severe cold but can be left in the ground and expected to survive in most parts of the state.

❏ Freeze damage to in-ground plantings may be prevented by covering the plants with blankets.

❏ Moisten soil when it feels dry. Renew mulch to a 2- to 3-inch (5- to 7.5-cm) layer.

❏ To get a jump start on the growing season, start some bulbs in pots, such as canna, caladiums, or blood lily. Keep them moist and warm. Move into garden when weather is suitable.

FEBRUARY

❏ Plant new bulbs and those relocated from the landscape. If growing plants are added, provide staking if needed.

❏ Prune out declining and winter-damaged foliage.

❏ Refresh 2 to 3 inches (5 to 7.5 cm) of mulch.

❏ When growth begins, start spring feeding. Use compost or organic emulsions.

❏ Pests may start to appear. Hand pick or rinse with water only.

MARCH

❏ Early this month is the best time to transplant canna, caladiums, and blood lilies so they will be ready to bloom on time.

❏ Spring-blooming bulbs (including amaryllis and swamp lily) will go to seed after flower. Unless you want to collect seeds, cut off seedpods to conserve energy for the bulbs.

❏ Keep the soil moist now to ensure good blooms.

❏ Some pests are hatching, like lubber grasshoppers. After hatching they are black with yellow and red lines. They are also very hungry and easier to control than adults. Other pests are aphids, mites, and thrips. Hand pick or rinse away with water.

APRIL

❏ Container-grown bulbs give a quicker start than bulbs in the dormant stage. Plant the same as normal bulb planting, although increased distance between plants may be possible. Keep soil moist until roots grow out. Remove any faded flowers or damaged foliage. Stake if needed.

❏ Remove flower stalks after blossoms fade. When foliage fades, cut old leaves (which may encourage pests) to main stem or ground.

❏ Most bulbs are drought resistant, but if they wilt, irrigate. Container plantings will need more frequent waterings.

❏ Apply compost or bone meal to warm-season bulbs.

❏ Slugs and snails can be a major problem, as evidenced by early-morning slime trails. Hand pick, use shallow trays of beer, or apply slug and snail baits. Also watch for aphids, grasshoppers, and mites.

MAY

❏ Divide and replant bugle lilies, daylilies, gladiolus, Louisiana iris, Kaffir lilies, shell ginger, society garlic, and walking iris. Keep growing bulbs moist.

❏ If weather turns windy, tall flowering stalks may blow over during a storm. Keep stakes and tape handy for their support. When stems are severely damaged, use them as lovely cut flowers.

❏ Red blotch disease may appear on amaryllis and crinums. Infected foliage should be pruned. Watch for aphids, grasshoppers, mites, and thrips.

JUNE

❏ Add clumps of daylilies to the landscape. Plant in mostly sunny areas. Keep moist for best growth and flowering, even though they tolerate drought.

❏ As other flowering bulbs die back, divide and replant gladiolus and watsonia.

❏ Cut bouquets to display in the home. It's a good way to enjoy the blooms without having to remove the spent flowers later on.

❏ You won't have to water as often with the frequent summer rains. Most bulbs don't mind extra water, but a few can drown without well-drained soil.

❏ Watch for grasshoppers, mites, thrips, slugs, and snails. Aphids are a special problem for daylilies. Red blotch disease may occur on amaryllis, swamp lily, and other bulbs.JULY

❏ If bulbs are in the way or need to be divided, summer is a good time. Most make rapid growth afterward.

❏ Help your gloriosa lily climb, but keep it off nearby shrubs and trees since it can get out of control. Gingers grow very rapidly and may crowd other plantings. Prune out new shoots, or dig some to share.

❏ Summer rains should do most of the watering, but there may be dry times. Keep beds mulched and check soil frequently for dry spots.

❏ During summer rains, some bulbs may need to be moved or they will rot from excess moisture.

❏ Watch for red blotch, aphids, grasshoppers, mites, thrips, slugs and snails.

AUGUST

❏ Container bulbs may need transplanting, especially if rootbound. Do not transplant bulbs that may be going dormant. Allow calla lilies to go dormant by withholding water and fertilizer. Keep potted calla lilies on the dry side during dormancy, until growth resumes.

❏ Remove older, yellowing leaves to make plants more attractive and keep down diseases. Remove faded flowers and old stalks. If you are not saving seeds, remove old seedpods.

❏ A few bulbs, like canna, suffer from rust. Also watch for red blotch and trim out affected plant parts. Hand pick or rinse with water to control aphids, grasshoppers, mites, thrips, slugs, and snails. The leaf roller caterpillar can damage canna leaves.

SEPTEMBER

❏ Fall normally starts with amaryllis and zephyr lily for early plantings. Continue transplanting as needed. If bulbs are wounded during digging, allow the spots to dry before replanting.

❏ If bulb plantings are overgrown, do some rejuvenation pruning.

❏ Dry season is coming. If you have an irrigation system, make sure it is working properly.

❏ Apply the final topdressing of compost for the year.

❏ Stay alert and keep checking for damage on foliage and flowers. With drier weather ahead, expect mites to become more active. The most prevalent problems are red blotch, aphids, caterpillars, grasshoppers, thrips, slugs, and snails.

OCTOBER

❏ A few true daffodils grow and flower in Central and North Florida. Add them (and others that need just a short period of cold) during fall months, starting in October.

❏ Check other bulb plantings. Many may have filled beds and can be divided or transplanted. Outdoor temperatures are much more comfortable at this time of year.

❏ As many bulbs decline, remove old stems. Mark the bed areas so you will not disturb them. These areas can be planted with annual flowers for temporary color.

❏ Most pests start to decline in the fall.

NOVEMBER

❏ Some bulbs that can be planted at this time of year are swamp lily, daylily, Kaffir lily, and Louisiana iris. Almost any bulb growing a clump of foliage can be divided and moved.

❏ If amaryllis did not flower well in spring, it may be due to continuous growth of bulbs. Withholding water during fall is one technique to encourage late-winter flowering.

❏ Clean up declining bulb growth. Bring container plantings of caladiums and similar bulbs inside to a shady, well-ventilated spot.

❏ Hand pick any of the few insects that may still be active.

DECEMBER

❏ Happy holidays! It's a great time to share your love of bulbs. A bulb-planting kit– complete with container, soil, fertilizer, and bulbs or starter plants–makes a great holiday gift.

❏ Begin new beds while the weather is cool. Till the soil, add organic matter, and let rest until planting.

❏ Check the bulb beds for declining plant portions and pests. Check bulbs in storage. Keep caladiums at about 70°F (21°C). Other bulbs can be stored between 40°F to 60°F (4°C to 16°C) .

FRUIT & NUTS
for Florida

You can really make your Florida landscape pay by adding fruiting trees and shrubs that provide food. It's easy to replace some or all of the ornamental plants in any design. Just look for fruiting plants with similar growth habits.

PLANNING

To make your fruiting trees and shrubs worth the effort, select most of the plants to produce a bumper crop each year. Consider sharing excess harvests with a local soup kitchen. Some offer harvesting help for large trees. (www. feedingamerica.org)

When choosing plants:

- Consider the hardiness and heat tolerance of the plants. Choose only those that will do well in your location.
- Look at pest problems associated with the crop.
- Make sure you have the needed room. Some, like avocados, grapefruits, and oranges, can grow quite large.
- Realize there may be pruning, thinning, and other chores required. If your time is limited, pick the plants that need the least amount of extra care. Many gardeners select only one or two favorites with good production.

Find the harvest times on the fruiting plant list (pages 70 to 71) and plan for year-round fruit harvests.

PLANTING

Normal planting procedures are used. (See page 15 for tree planting instructions in the introduction.) Specific instructions are provided for each crop in this section. Most fruiting plants, especially citrus, grow fine in any well-drained Florida soil.

If the site is not immediately ready for your new plant, it can be held for a week or two in the nursery container. It is best if the wait is not too long.

Some fruiting plants are received bare root (with no soil on their roots). These should be timed to arrive during the winter months so they can become established before hot spring weather. Planting is similar to that of container plants, except the roots are spread out over a mound of soil as the plant is positioned so it sets at the same level it grew in the nursery.

CARE

Citrus trees need very little pruning to maintain their natural rounded shape, with lower limbs growing to the ground. Dead limbs or sprouts growing from below the grafted area should be removed. Some other fruiting plants have very specific pruning needs. The yearly "as needed" trimming is usually performed to improve fruit production and keep the crop within reach. Get familiar with each crop to know the care needed to provide the best yields.

Keep the weeds and grass away from the base by 1 to 2 feet (30 to 61 cm). Except for citrus, trees and shrubs should be mulched.

WATERING

Young plantings need a good start, and this includes plenty of water. For the first few weeks, water daily. Then gradually taper off the waterings but keep the soil moist until the plantings are well established.

Most fruiting plants are drought tolerant. However, care is needed for younger plantings during drier times, and most trees produce the most fruit with an even moisture supply. A problem known as fruit splitting is often increased by intermittent periods of moisture.

FERTILIZING

Fruiting plants vary as to fertilizer needs. You can develop special schedules or stick to a general feeding program. All appear to grow best when fed more than once a year.

- Apply a 6-6-6, 8-8-8, or similar fertilizer that also contains minor nutrients. If desired, citrus fertilizers may be used for citrus trees, mangos, and avocados.
- Feed new fruit tree plantings lightly every 6 to 8 weeks from March through September. Use ¼ pound (113 g) of fertilizer per plant, scattered under the spread of the branches, but make sure excess cannot wash away into the storm drain system, especially during the wet season.
- This may be gradually increased to ½ pound (227 g) as the plants begin to grow. Citrus tree feedings should be increased to provide 1½ pounds (680 g) at the end of the first year, 2½ pounds (1 kg) at the end of year two, and 4 pounds (1.8 kg) at the end of year three.
- Feed established non-citrus fruit trees in March at the rate of 1 pound (454 g) for each 100 square feet (30 square m) of area.
- Apply the fertilizer over mulches.

Lemon

Lime

CITRUS
Citrus spp.
Rue family: Rutaceae

WHEN TO PLANT–Add container-grown plants any time, although cooler times are best.

WHERE TO PLANT–In full sun, Zones 9-11. In northern range, plant in southern exposure to protect from cold winds. Kumquat is the most cold-tolerant citrus; the small kumquat tree can be grown in areas that freeze. Lemons and limes are more cold-sensitive than other citrus. Grow below a line from Daytona Beach to Crystal River. Plant in full sun. Some can be grown in containers.

HOW TO PLANT–Plant in hole about two times wider than root ball (but no deeper), at same depth as in container.

WATER NEEDS–Requires good drainage; grows well in Florida's sandy soils. New trees need frequent watering for a few months.

CARE–Fertilize new trees frequently (four or five times March to October) for first 2 years. Beginning in fourth year, feed with citrus fertilizer in March and early October with ¼ pound (113 g) per inch (2.5 cm) of trunk circumference. Prune lower limbs to make maintenance and harvesting easier. Citrus sometimes suffers cold damage in Central Florida. Mound soil around trunk to protect grafted portions from freezing. Quickly prune away any growth from the root stock, which will originate below the graft. Do not use mulch of any type for citrus–keep soil bare.

PROBLEMS–Citrus greening is an incurable bacterial disease that can affect any citrus crop. It's carried by the Asian citrus psyllid, a sucking insect that was first found in Florida in 1998. For information on symptoms of this disease and what to do about it, see this Florida Agriculture Extension Service webpage: https://edis. ifas.ufl.edu/topic_citrus_greening Control caterpillars by hand picking or applying *Bacillus thuringiensis* (Bt) spray. For serious infestations, spray aphids and whiteflies with oil spray or other recommended controls.

HARVEST– When grown from seed, citrus may take 6 to 10 years to fruit. Citrus ripens fall to spring, depending upon species and variety. Pick limes when starting to change color. Tahitian limes mature from June to September, key limes almost year-round.

GRAPEFRUIT SELECTIONS–'Duncan', 'Flame', 'Marsh', 'Redblush' (new name for 'Ruby'), 'Thompson'

KUMQUAT SELECTIONS–Several species and hybrids are available, including limequats and orangequats.

LEMON SELECTIONS–'Avon', 'Bearss', 'Eureka'. 'Ponderosa' is large and grown for show.

LIME SELECTIONS–Tahitian (Persian) limes tolerate more cold than key (Mexican) limes.

ORANGE SELECTIONS–All varieties bloom in the spring. Small orange trees are suitable for townhouses or apartment patios, and can be grown in large containers.

TANGERINE SELECTIONS–Often called mandarin. 'Sunburst', 'Dancy'

Kumquat

Tangerine

Orange

SELECTED CITRUS PLANTINGS

NAME	AREA	HARVEST TIME	SPACING (INCHES)	HEIGHT(FEET)	BEST USE OF FRUITS
ORANGES					
Ambersweet	CS	Oct.–Dec.	0–15	3–3½	Easy to peel, good juice quality
Cara Cara	CS	Oct.–Jan.	0–6	3–3½	A red-fleshed navel selection
Gardner	CS	Jan.–Mar.	6–24	2½–3	Good juice quality
Hamlin	CS	Oct.–Jan.	0–6	2¾–3	Early juice orange
Midsweet	CS	Jan.–Mar.	6–24	2½–3	Good juice quality
Navel	CS	Oct.–Jan.	0–6	3–3½	Very popular, eat fresh or juice
Parson Brown	CS	Oct.–Jan.	10–20	2½–2¾	Low fruit yields but early
Pineapple	CS	Dec.–Feb.	15–25	2¾–3	Excellent juice but seedy
Rhode Red	CS	Mar.–June	0–6	2¾–3	A red-fleshed Valencia selection
Sunstar	CS	Jan.–Mar.	6–20	2½–3	Good juice quality
Valencia	CS	Mar.–June	0–6	2¾–3	Excellent juice quality
GRAPEFRUIT AND RELATED FRUITS					
Duncan	CS	Nov.–May	30–70	3½–5	An old variety, white flesh
Flame	CS	Nov.–May	0–6	3¾–4½	Most popular, dark red flesh
Foster	CS	Nov.–May	30–50	3½–5	Good older variety, pink flesh
Marsh	CS	Nov.–May	0–6	3½–4½	Very popular, white flesh
Pink Marsh	CS	Dec.–May	0–6	3¾–4½	Also called Thompson, pink flesh
Pummelo	CS	Nov.–Feb.	50	5–7	May be a parent of the grapefruit
Ray Ruby	CS	Nov.–May	0–6	3½–4	Dark red flesh
Redblush	CS	Nov.–May	0–6	3½–4½	Also called Ruby Red, red flesh
Star Ruby	CS	Dec.–May	0–6	3½–4	Dark red flesh

* = Inconspicuous Flower Color   N = North Florida   C = Central Florida   S = South Florida

SELECTED CITRUS PLANTINGS

NAME	AREA	HARVEST TIME	SPACING (INCHES)	HEIGHT(FEET)	BEST USE OF FRUITS
MANDARINS AND HYBRIDS					
Dancy	CS	Dec.–Jan.	6–20	2¼–2½	Easy-to-peel-and-section tangerine
Fallglo	CS	Oct.–Nov.	30–40	3–3½	Easy-peeling Temple hybrid
Minneola	CS	Dec.–Jan.	7–12	3–3½	A tangelo, often called Honeybell
Murcott	CS	Jan.–Mar.	10–20	2½–2¾	A hybrid with a unique flavor
Nova	CS	Nov.–Dec.	1–30	2¾–3	A hybrid with good flavor
Lee	CS	Nov.–Dec.	10–25	2¾–3	A hybrid with good flavor
Orlando	CS	Nov.–Jan.	0–35	2¾–3	A heavy producing tangelo
Osceola	CS	Oct.–Nov.	15–25	2¼–2¾	A hybrid with good flavor
Ponkan	CS	Dec.–Jan.	3–7	2¾–3½	Good flavor, easy-to-peel tangerine
Robinson	CS	Oct.–Dec.	1–20	2½–2¾	Good flavor, tangerine
Satsuma	NCS	Sept.–Nov.	0–6	2¼–2½	A hybrid with sweet taste
Sunburst	CS	Nov.–Dec.	1–20	2½–3	A tangerine with sweet taste
Temple	CS	Jan.–Mar.	15–20	2¼–3	Sweet, easy to peel
ACID CITRUS					
Calamondin	CS	Year-round	6–10	1–1½	A heavy producing small tree
Key Lime	CS	Year-round	12–20	1–1½	A small tree with good production
Kumquat	NCS	Year-round	6–10	¾–1	A small tree, several varieties
Lemon	S	July–Dec.	1–6	2–2½	Numerous varieties
Limequat	CS	Year-round	0–16	1–1½	Hybrid of key lime and kumquat
Meyer Lemon	CS	Nov.–Mar.	10	2½–3	Grows as a bush
Ponderosa	S	Year-round	20–30	4–5	A hybrid to grow as a small tree
Tahiti Lime	S	June–Sept.	0	1¾–2½	A hybrid also called Persian lime

* = Inconspicuous Flower Color   N = North Florida   C = Central Florida   S = South Florida

APPLE
Malus domestica
Rose family: Rosaceae

WHEN TO PLANT–Apple trees that are grown in 3- to 5-gallon containers can be planted any time of year.

WHERE TO PLANT–Plant in North Florida in full sun with well-prepared, well-drained soil.

HOW TO PLANT–Place the root ball 1 to 2 inches (2.5 to 5 cm) higher than the soil level to compensate for settling. Create a saucer with remaining soil and water every other day for 4 to 5 weeks or until well-rooted.

WATER NEEDS–Apple tree prefers moist, well-drained soil. Drought can cause leaf drop and premature fruit drop.

CARE–Apples are traditionally grown in cooler climates, so growing apples in Florida is not an easy task. Keep well watered and fertilize with a general 6-6-6-2 (NPKMg) fertilizer four times a year.

PROBLEMS–Watch for apple scab (looks like blotches on fruit with leaves that are gnarled and twisted) and fire blight (a serious disease that can be spread from tree to tree).

HARVEST–Apples can be harvested when they separate from the tree when gently pulled.

SELECTIONS–For Florida gardens try 'Anna', 'Dorsett Golden', and tropic 'Sweet'.

AVOCADO
Persea Americana
Laurel family: Lauraceae

WHEN TO PLANT–Plant at any time.

WHERE TO PLANT–In frost-free zones. Needs well-drained soil in full sun. Position 15 to 20 feet (4.5 to 6 m) from buildings, sidewalks, and streets. Also used as landscape tree.

HOW TO PLANT–Place 1 inch (2.5 cm) above the soil line. In areas prone to flooding, plant on mounds.

WATER NEEDS–Established trees require watering only during severe drought–but for best production, water weekly.

CARE–Feed new trees every other month. Fertilize established trees in February and September with Avocado-type fertilizer.

PROBLEMS–Pick fruit before squirrels get them. The laurel wilt disease can kill trees. It is a fungal disease carried by a beetle, which has been moving south. Ask your local Extension Service agent if it is a problem in your area.

HARVEST–Avocados do not ripen on the tree. They are picked at maximum size, ripening about a week later. They don't have to be picked at the same time. Harvest seasons range from May to March, depending on variety.

SELECTIONS–There are numerous varieties developed for Florida, some with moderate cold hardiness. They have different ripening seasons and sizes. Check with local gardeners or your Extension Service to find out which work best in your area.

BANANA
Musa spp.
Banana family: Musaceae

WHEN TO PLANT–In South and Central Florida plant March through May. Where heavy freezes occur, plants will die back to the ground. Once established, harvesting is possible. Small varieties planted in pots can be brought indoors for cold protection.

WHERE TO PLANT–Plant in full sun (best for fruit production) to part shade in well-drained, compost-enriched soils. Protect from strong winds. Also plant for tropical foliage.

HOW TO PLANT–Place root ball 1 to 2 inches (2.5 to 5 cm) above soil line to compensate for settling. Mulch to maintain moisture.

WATER NEEDS–Bananas like plenty of water but not standing water.

CARE–Fertilize lightly every 2 months, increasing amount as plant grows. Annual micronutrient spray is helpful.

PROBLEMS–Without enough fertilizer, the fruit weight may cause stalk to buckle. For best fruiting, thin the stand to 1 foot (30 cm) between trunks.

HARVEST–Blooms after 10 to 18 months. Fruit ripens about 5 months later. After bananas form and the first hand that formed begins to turn yellow, cut entire bunch from the main stalk.

SELECTIONS–'Goldfinger', 'Lady Finger', 'Manzano', 'Mysore', 'Rajapuri'. Dwarf: 'Dwarf Cavendish', 'Dwarf Orinoco', 'Dwarf Red'.

BLACKBERRY
Rubus spp.
Rose family: Rosaceae

WHEN TO PLANT–Plant bare root in December to February, immediately after purchase. Plant containerized any time.

WHERE TO PLANT–Prefers mildly acidic, well-drained soil in full sun or light shade.

HOW TO PLANT–Clip roots of bare-root plants to about 6 inches (15 cm) and plant with crown just above soil level. Container-grown plants should also be set slightly above soil level. Provide ample growing room.

WATER NEEDS–Always mulch to retain moisture and reduce weeds.

CARE–After the first year, prune main canes down to 36 inches (91 cm). Fruit is produced on year-old canes–more pruning results in more berries. Don't prune more than 1/3 of the canes down to the ground each season. Erect-type blackberries are easier to grow than trailing, which need support. Apply light fertilizer (with micronutrients) in spring, 18 inches (46 cm) away from plant centers to protect shallow roots.

PROBLEMS–Plants can withstand very cold temperatures, but flowers are very susceptible to cold.

HARVEST–Blackberries fruit in summer. Trailing types, often called dewberries, ripen earlier, with smaller berries.

SELECTIONS–'Brazos' is most popular selection. Thornless varieties: 'Apache', 'Choctaw', and 'Ouachita'.

BLUEBERRY
Vaccinium spp.
Heath family: Ericaceae

WHEN TO PLANT–During late fall or winter.

WHERE TO PLANT–In acidic (pH 4.5 to 5.2), well-drained soil high in organic matter. Need full sun, with plenty of room.

HOW TO PLANT–Add lots of acidic organic materials. Plant a few inches (about 5 cm) above soil level. To improve soil condition and acidity, place bands of pine bark (2 feet [61 cm] wide) around every plant and renew regularly.

WATER NEEDS–Needs 45 inches (114 cm) of rain each year, but it may die if roots are flooded or stand in water for more than just a short time.

CARE–Once established, apply 2 ounces (57 g) per plant of azalea-camellia fertilizer, in 2-foot (61-cm) circle in the spring and again in the fall. Gradually increase dose to 4 ounces (113 g) per year and spreading circle to 4 feet (122 cm).

PROBLEMS–Improper pH leads to plant decline. If planted near hardwood trees or within 20 feet (6 m) of structures with alkaline cement foundations, will produce less fruit.

HARVEST–Late spring and early summer

SELECTIONS–Only use varieties specifically for Florida: southern highbush (good for Central and South Florida) and rabbiteye. Southern highbush: 'Emerald', 'Gulf Coast', and 'Sharpblue'. Rabbiteye: 'Beckyblue', 'Bonita', and 'Woodruff'.

COCONUT PALM
Cocos nucifera
Palm family: Arecaceae

WHEN TO PLANT–Plant from sprouted nuts in early summer. Plant container-grown trees any time.

WHERE TO PLANT–In full sun, Zones 10 and 11. Plant in good drainage, where large crown won't be crowded.

HOW TO PLANT–Bury the sprouted nut about halfway, placed sideways in thick, damp layer of mulch.

WATER NEEDS–Keep new tree moist. Tolerates drought once established.

CARE–Water in about 3 pounds (1.3 kg) of fertilizer every 4 months for the first year. After that, feed annually in the spring.

PROBLEMS–Very sensitive to cold weather. New varieties are resistant to lethal yellowing disease.

HARVEST–Once old enough to fruit (7 to 10 years), coconuts are produced throughout the year. Fruits take approximately 1 year to ripen, but green coconuts are sometimes harvested for coconut water after 6 or 7 months. Production is 50 to 200 coconuts per year, depending upon cultivar and climate.

SELECTIONS–The coconut palm is used to provide a tropical look to landscapes. 'Dwarf Green', 'Golden Malayan', 'Mayan', 'Red Spectate'.

FIG
Ficus carica plus other species
Mulberry family: Moraceae

WHEN TO PLANT—Plant bare-root figs in fall, container-grown figs any time.

WHERE TO PLANT—In full to part sun, with plenty of room to grow. Needs well-drained soil. Keep away from standing water or soggy soils.

HOW TO PLANT—Dig a hole twice as wide and deep as the root mass. Place a few inches above the soil line. Water thoroughly and add a good mulch layer.

WATER NEEDS—Water daily for first 2 weeks after planting. Gradually reduce frequency to once or twice weekly during hot weather.

CARE—Figs have a healthy fibrous root system, so deep cultivation is not recommended. Maintain mulch layer that does not touch the trunk. Fertilize monthly during growing season. Pruning is generally not required. Figs produce better with an annual dose of calcium once established. Apply 1 cup (237 ml) of calcium nitrate under the canopy, increasing the amount as the plant gets larger.

PROBLEMS—There are no insect pests to speak of, but figs are highly prized by birds.

HARVEST—July and August ('Celeste') or July through fall ('Brown Turkey')

SELECTIONS—'Celeste' is the most frequently planted, but 'Brown Turkey' is also popular.

GRAPE
Vitis vinifera, the common grape, plus other species
Grape family: Vitaceae

WHEN TO PLANT—Any time of year

WHERE TO PLANT—In full sun in well-drained soil with a clay base

HOW TO PLANT—Place individual plants 8 feet (244 cm) apart in rows at least 6 feet (183 cm) apart. Plant a few inches above the soil line. Rows on a north-south axis maximize sunlight.

WATER NEEDS—Water every few days after planting. Gradually reduce frequency. Then provide plenty of water before harvest.

CARE—Grapes produce fruit on new wood. However, too much new wood and grapes will be small in size and quantity. Special trellises and year-round pruning ensure good fruit production and easy harvesting. In the first year, apply ¼ pound (113 g) of 8-8-8 fertilizer per plant. Increase amount annually to 4 pounds (1.8 kg).

PROBLEMS—Bunch grapes may need a fungicide spray program for anthracnose.

HARVEST—June through September, depending on variety.

SELECTIONS—Scuppernong, muscadine, and bunch grapes are all Florida grapes. They can be eaten fresh or used for wine. Purple: 'Conquistador', 'Blue Lake', 'Black Spanish'. Green: 'Stover', 'Blanc Du Bois', 'Suwannee'. Red: 'Daytona'.

JABOTICABA
Plinia cauliflora
Myrtle family: Myrtaceae

WHEN TO PLANT—Can be planted any time. Don't grow where freezing temperatures are common.

WHERE TO PLANT—Plant in full to part sun (part sun reduces number of fruits) in well-drained, deep, sandy soil. May also be planted as a specimen tree.

HOW TO PLANT—Place 1 inch (2.5 cm) above the soil line (to compensate for settling). Plant in mounds if holes are difficult to dig.

WATER NEEDS—Roots are quite shallow, so supplement rainfall and use mulch.

CARE—Apply general 8-8-8-2 (NPKMg) fertilizer annually. Pruning is rarely needed, but plants can be trimmed into a hedge without significant fruit reduction. In alkaline soils add mulch and semi-annual chelated iron drench.

PROBLEMS—Deer may eat new foliage. Squirrels and raccoons enjoy the fruit.

HARVEST—Harvest when fruits are dark purple or black, and soft.

SELECTIONS—Jaboticaba or Brazilian grapetree produces fruit the size of large grapes that erupt from the main trunk, which has unique flaking bark. 'Paulista' has large, sweet fruit, 'Rajada' has green skin, and 'Sabra' produces up to four crops in South Florida.

JACKFRUIT
Artocarpus heterophyllus
Mulberry family: Moraceae

WHEN TO PLANT–Any time of year in South Florida. This is a tropical fruit.

WHERE TO PLANT–Plant in full sun in well-drained soil where flooding is not a problem. Plant at least 30 feet (9 m) from houses and trees.

HOW TO PLANT–Place 1 or 2 inches (2.5 to 5 cm) higher than the soil level.

WATER NEEDS–Does not like soggy soil

CARE–Trees can reach 40 feet (12 m) tall but can be pruned to 10 or 15 feet (3 to 4.5 m) without significant fruit reduction. During first year apply 1 pound (454 g) of fertilizer (8-8-8 with micronutrients) five times. Afterward apply 5 pounds (2.3 kg) annually. In alkaline soils apply chelated iron once per year.

PROBLEMS–Virtually pest-free, although scale can affect leaves and stems. The latex-like sap can stain clothes and may cause skin irritation in some people.

HARVEST–Jackfruits are very large (up to 60 pounds [27 kg]), with two parts, one of which is inedible. Harvest when fruit develops a pungent odor. It will ripen in 4 to 7 days.

SELECTIONS–Varieties good for Florida gardens include 'Black Gold', 'Cheena', 'Chompa Gob', 'Honey Gold', and 'Lemon Gold'.

LOQUAT
Eriobotrya japonica
Rose family: Rosaceae

WHEN TO PLANT–At any time

WHERE TO PLANT–Produce most fruit in full sun. Not finicky as to soil type and are even somewhat salt tolerant. However, they do not like wet or water-logged soils.

HOW TO PLANT–Place root ball a few inches (5 cm) above the soil (to compensate for settling).

WATER NEEDS–Water young trees frequently, then gradually reduce waterings.

CARE–Loquat trees do not require pruning. Feed one-year-old plants 1 pound (454 g) general fertilizer 8-8-8-2 (NPKMg) annually in the spring. Increase to 5 pounds (2.3 kg) as tree gets bigger. If grown in alkaline soil, apply chelated iron soil drench twice per year.

PROBLEMS–Fire blight may be a problem. Cut out damaged portions and spray with fungicide.

HARVEST–Generally bloom in the late fall or early winter and produce fruit in spring; in warmer areas, may have two or three crops. Fruit ripens in approximately 120 days. Let the fruit ripen on the tree.

SELECTIONS–Also popular as a small shade tree. 'Advance', 'Champagne', 'Emanuel', 'Golitch', 'Juda', 'Judith', 'Oliver', 'Thales', 'Thursby', 'Wolfe'

LYCHEE
Litchi chinensis
Soapberry family: Sapindaceae.

WHEN TO PLANT–Plant any time of year. More mature trees better withstand freezes, so plant in early spring in North Florida.

WHERE TO PLANT–Grow best in full sun, with well-drained, well-composted soil and plenty of room. Also planted as landscape tree.

HOW TO PLANT–Place top of root ball 1 to 3 inches (2.5 to 7.5 cm) above soil line. More lychees have been killed by planting too deep than for any other reason.

WATER NEEDS–Water daily for first 3 weeks after planting. Established trees are somewhat drought tolerant, but for best fruit production, water weekly. Cannot tolerate standing water.

CARE–Feed 4 to 6 weeks after planting and continue alternate months for first year. Then fertilize in March, May, and early October. In limestone soils, add minor nutrient foliar spray two or three times annually.

PROBLEMS–Lychees are not strong enough for ladder picking (like citrus). Use long poles with sharp clippers.

HARVEST–The entire cluster of lychees is harvested when bright red in late spring through summer. Individual fruits are clipped from the cluster.

SELECTIONS–'Mauritius', 'Brewster'

MACADAMIA
Macadamia spp.
Protea family: Proteaceae

WHEN TO PLANT–Macadamia trees are sold in 3- to 5-gallon (11.4 to 19 L) containers and can be planted at any time of the year.

WHERE TO PLANT–Plant in full sun with well-prepared, well-drained soil in areas of Florida where hard freezes are not reoccurring.

HOW TO PLANT–Place the root ball 1 or 2 inches (2.5 to 5 cm) higher than the native soil level to compensate for settling. Create a saucer with remaining soil and water every other day for 4 to 5 weeks or until well rooted.

WATER NEEDS–Prefers moist soil. Although drought tolerant, extended periods of drought will cause premature nut drop.

CARE–Macadamia trees are long-lived rainforest trees from Australia that require high humidity and high temperatures. Young trees may be killed during cold periods, but adult trees may withstand temperatures to 28°F (-2°C) without damage. Requires no special care.

PROBLEMS–The nuts are toxic to dogs.

HARVEST–Fruits mature in fall. The nuts are protected by a thick sheath that falls off when mature, exposing a very hard, brown shell.

SELECTIONS–Plant any of the four different species in Florida.

MANGO
Mangifera indica
Cashew family: Anacardiaceae

WHEN TO PLANT–Plant at beginning of rainy season, in frost-free zones.

WHERE TO PLANT–Plant in full sun with well-drained soil, at least 30 feet (9 m) from buildings. Allow plenty of room for the tree's height (30 to 50 feet [9 to 15 m]), as well as for its extensive root system. Often planted as beautiful evergreen shade trees, with new leaves showing a red flush.

HOW TO PLANT–Place with top of root ball 1 or 2 inches (2.5 to 5 cm) above the soil line. Keep mulched.

WATER NEEDS–Water daily for 2 weeks after planting and taper off as plant becomes established. Established trees can withstand drought. However, for best fruit production, water periodically during its development.

CARE–Avoid planting expensive or rare plants beneath it because of fruit and leaf drop. Use fertilizer with extra magnesium and an iron drench once in the spring.

PROBLEMS–Although anthracnose may be a problem, no harm is usually done to the fruit.

HARVEST–Fruits (hanging on long stalks) mature May to September, depending upon type.

SELECTIONS–'Carrie', 'Carrie Atkins', 'Dunkin', 'Edward', 'Florigon', 'Keitt', 'Parvin'. 'Lancetilla' has the largest fruit: 5 or 6 pounds (about 2.5 kg).

PAPAYA
Carica papaya
Papaya family: Caricaceae

WHEN TO PLANT–Start seeds in fall. Plant container-grown papayas or transplants in spring.

WHERE TO PLANT–In full sun with average soil where there is no danger of frost. Can also grow in large containers.

HOW TO PLANT–Plant in average soil. Purchase plants no taller than 2 to 3 feet (61 to 91 cm). Larger plants are frequently rootbound. They quickly grow to 8 feet (2.5 m) and produce in about 10 months.

WATER NEEDS–Needs plenty of water

CARE–Plants can be male, female, or bisexual. Females produce the best fruit, bisexuals' fruits are smaller, and male plants are good for cross pollination. You need at least one male tree in the area. Apply ¼ pound (113 g) of general fertilizer while young. Increase to 1 to 2 pounds (454 to 907 g) annually as plants get larger.

PROBLEMS–Susceptible to nematodes and several other pests, including papaya fruit fly, papaya webworms, spider mites, papaya whitefly, two-spotted mite, papaya ring spot, and powdery mildew.

HARVEST–Produced throughout the year.

SELECTIONS–'Sunrise Solo', 'Red Lady', 'Maradol'

PEACH & NECTARINE
Prunus persica (Peaches and nectarines are different varieties of the same species.)
Rose family: Rosaceae

WHEN TO PLANT–Plant any time

WHERE TO PLANT–In full sun and well-drained soil. Allow plenty of room.

HOW TO PLANT–Set root ball a few inches (5 cm) above soil level.

WATER NEEDS–Water daily for 3 weeks, then gradually taper off.

CARE–The tree must be open in the middle with upward growth. It takes discipline, but for good fruit quality and quantity some initial hard pruning is recommended. Cut the primary single upright leader about 36 inches (91 cm) above the ground to encourage side branching. As tree matures, remove sprouts and branches in the center. New fruit grows on one-year-old wood, so annual pruning is recommended.

PROBLEMS–Alkaline or marl soils can cause poor overall growth, leaf drop, and insect infestations. Use elevated beds of good soil and liberal sprinkling of granulated sulfur each spring in alkaline areas.

HARVEST–Ripen early to mid-May

SELECTIONS–Growing peaches and nectarines in Florida had been possible only for northern areas. New varieties enable gardeners everywhere to grow peaches with only 150 hours of cold chill. Low chill: 'FloridaGlo', 'FloridaPrince', 'UF Beauty'. A new nectarine variety, good for fruit and ornamental characteristics, 'Sunhome' can be grown everywhere in the state and its new growth is purple.

PECAN
Carya illinoinensis
Walnut family: Juglandaceae

WHEN TO PLANT–Plant in fall

WHERE TO PLANT–Pecans, which can grow to 70 feet (21 m), need plenty of room, well-drained soil, and full sun. Plant at least 30 feet (9 m) away from structures. Grows best in North Florida.

HOW TO PLANT–Plant either bare-root or container-grown plants. Some commercial growers apply a single application of diluted white latex paint to the trunk 4 feet (122 cm) high to reduce bark sunscald.

WATER NEEDS–After planting, water at least three times weekly for 2 months. Once established, irrigation is not needed.

CARE–Apply 1 pound (454 g) fertilizer (10-10-10-3 NPKMg) after planting. Apply 1 pound (454 g) fertilizer per 1 inch (2.5 cm) of trunk diameter in early March. Once nut production begins, apply 2 to 4 pounds (1 to 1.8 kg) in February. If planted as a single leader, reduce by 2/3 and train to have symmetrical branches. Mature trees are seldom pruned.

PROBLEMS–None.

HARVEST–Takes 4 to 12 years for nuts, depending on variety.

SELECTIONS–'Cape Fear', 'Elliott', 'Moreland'

PERSIMMON
Diospyros virginiana and Asian persimmon: D. kaki
Ebony family: Ebenaceae
Typically, persimmon is dioecious, which means that trees are either male or female. You will need at least one male tree in the area to have fruit form on the female trees.

WHEN TO PLANT–Plant at any time.

WHERE TO PLANT–Needs well-drained soil. Plant in full sun or slightly dappled shade. Native persimmons grow to 30 feet (9 m) tall, Asian to 8 feet (2.5 m).

HOW TO PLANT–Plant in a hole twice as wide and deep as the containerized root ball.

WATER NEEDS–Water three times a week for first month after planting. Reduce the amount as tree becomes established.

CARE–Keep weeds and turf at least 3 feet (91 cm) away. Do not fertilize during first year. Apply 10 pounds (4.5 kg) of 10-10-10-3 (NPKMg) fertilizer to mature trees once a year in the spring.

PROBLEMS–Blemishes on foliage and fruit don't usually affect fruit quality and can be ignored.

HARVEST–There are astringent and non-astringent varieties. In Florida, astringent varieties are picked, peeled, skewered, and dried. The dried fruit is sweet and delicious. Non-astringent account for most Florida trees. Pick in fall when hard or soft and eat fresh.

SELECTIONS–Persimmons make nice landscape plants.

PINEAPPLE
Ananas comosus
Pineapple family: Bromeliaceae

WHEN TO PLANT–Plant at any time.

WHERE TO PLANT–Plant in any soil in full sun. Pineapples can grow in containers, and in North Florida this is necessary to protect from frost.

HOW TO PLANT–Cut pineapple 1 inch (2.5 cm) below the very top and let air dry for a few days. Many plant directly into the garden, but it's recommended to plant into a con-tainer first. Plant in good potting soil so only the spiky top is sticking out. After 45 to 60 days, plant into the garden in frost-free areas. Further north, leave in the container and bring it indoors when nighttime temperatures reach 40°F (4°C).

WATER NEEDS–Water daily for first month or two.

CARE–Fertilize with 1 to 2 ounces (28 to 57 g) of 6-6-6-4 (NPKMg) every 8 weeks. Gradually increase to 6 ounces (170 g) as the plant grows. Stake the fruit stalk if neces-sary.

PROBLEMS–Root rot can be deterred by not overwatering and planting in well-drained sandy soil. Some growers fashion wire cages around the fruit to keep squirrels and oth-er critters at bay.

HARVEST–Harvest when bottom starts to change from green to yellow. If you're grow-ing it in the ground, the plant will produce new flower heads for several years.

PLUM
Prunus spp.
Rose family: Rosaceae

WHEN TO PLANT–Plant at any time.

WHERE TO PLANT–In full sun and well-drained soil. Trees can reach 10 to 12 feet (3 to 3.5 m) tall and 12 feet (3.5 m) wide, so give them plenty of room.

HOW TO PLANT–Plant a few inches above soil level to allow for settling. In areas where pH is high, plant in elevated beds made of good garden soil. A liberal sprinkling of granulated sulfur once each spring will help lower the pH as well.

WATER NEEDS–Water daily for 3 weeks after planting, then gradually taper off.

CARE–Prune to encourage a central leader.

PROBLEMS–Alkaline or marl soils can cause poor overall growth, leaf drop, and insect infestations. Use raised beds in alkaline areas.

HARVEST–Ripens early to mid-May

SELECTIONS–Growing plums in Florida once was only possible in northern areas. How-ever, new varieties are now available that can be grown throughout the state. They only need 150 hours of cold chill with temperatures below 50°F (10°C). 'Gulfbeauty', 'Gulfblaze', 'Gulfrose', 'Gulfgold', 'Gulfruby'

POMEGRANATE
Punica granatum
Loosestrife family: Lythraceae

WHEN TO PLANT–Plant at any time.

WHERE TO PLANT–In full sun in moist, deep, well-drained soils. They can be grown as shrubs or trees.

HOW TO PLANT–Place root ball slightly higher than soil line.

WATER NEEDS–Needs moist soil, irrigate every 7 to 10 days during dry periods in the growing season. Tolerant of minor, short-term flooding.

CARE–Easy to grow. Fruits are borne on new growth, so lightly trim branch ends before July 1 to create buds for next year. In the spring, apply 1 cup (237 ml) of fertilizer. Use 8-8-8-4 (NPKMg) with micronutrients. As the tree matures, increase the fertilizer somewhat, but be careful because too many nutrients can cause fruit drop.

PROBLEMS–Pomegranates are virtually pest free.

HARVEST–Fruits range from 2 to 5 inches (5 to 12.5 cm) in diameter, and in North and Central Florida, they mature from July to November. In South Florida they may produce year-round.

SELECTIONS–This shrub makes a welcome addition to any landscape. 'Purple Seed', 'Spanish Ruby', 'Wonderful'

STAR FRUIT
Averrhoa carambola
Wood sorrel family: Oxalidaceae

WHEN TO PLANT–Plant at any time

WHERE TO PLANT–In full sun with well-drained soil. Although the small tree withstands some cool weather, it prefers hot and humid Central and South Florida.

HOW TO PLANT–Plant root ball with top slightly above soil level. Water well and add mulch. If you live where flooding occurs, plant in a mound.

WATER NEEDS–While too much water hinders fruit production, star fruit is not tolerant of drought. Provide at least 1 inch (2.5 cm) of water per week. If leaves begin to wilt, it's not getting enough water.

CARE–Fertilize young trees with ½ pound (227 g) of complete 10-10-10-2 (NPKMg) fertilizer in the spring. Spray trees in alkaline soils with micronutrient spray containing manganese and zinc.

PROBLEMS–Virtually trouble free. Use stream of water to wash off occasional aphids. Keep fruit picked to avoid fruit flies. Star fruits are high in oxalic acid, so moderate your intake and don't consume if you have kidney problems.

HARVEST–Depending on variety, may produce several crops per year.

SELECTIONS–'Arkin', 'Fuang Tung', 'Kari', 'Sri Kembangan', 'Thai Knight'

STRAWBERRY
Fragaria × ananassa
Rose family: Rosaceae

WHEN TO PLANT–Plant bare-root plants in fall for up to three production cycles.

WHERE TO PLANT–In full sun in rich, very well-composted, well-drained soil

HOW TO PLANT–Grow in raised linear beds about 8 inches (20 cm) high with irrigation just below the surface, and covered with opaque plastic. Insert plants through slits in the plastic, which is necessary to prevent weeds during entire season. Alternatively, plant in mounds covered with newspaper and hay, with or without soaker hoses. There are also hydroponic systems for growing strawberries with cascading containers that hang on a pole.

WATER NEEDS–Keep soil moist.

CARE–Incorporate fertilizer with ½ slow-release nitrogen and micronutrients into the bed before planting. Protect fruit and flowers from freezing.

PROBLEMS–Try growing strawberries. However, buying them may be easier and cheaper. Use fine mesh netting to keep out birds and animals. Use beer traps for the common slugs. For spider mites and insects, apply neem oil.

HARVEST–Pick frequently, especially during spring, to defeat insects and birds. A plant can produce 1 to 2 pints per season.

SELECTIONS–'Camarosa' (best for North Florida), 'Festival', 'Sweet Charlie' (best for Central Florida)

TAMARIND
Tamarindus indica
Legume family: Fabaceae

WHEN TO PLANT–Container-grown tamarind trees can be planted any time of year.

WHERE TO PLANT–Plant in full sun with well-prepared, well-drained soil. Tamarind trees are tropical and should only be planted in frost-free areas.

HOW TO PLANT–Place the top of the root ball 1 inch (2.5 cm) higher than the soil level to compensate for settling.

WATER NEEDS–Water every other day for 4 to 5 weeks, or until well rooted. Tamarind trees prefer moist, but well-drained soil.

CARE–These slow-growing, long-lived tropical trees require high humidity and high temperatures. Young trees may be killed during cold periods, but adult trees may withstand temperatures down to 28°F (–2°C) without damage.

PROBLEMS–Generally free of pests and diseases.

HARVEST–Fruits mature in late spring to early summer. Ripe fruit is sometimes attacked by beetles and fungi, so harvest mature fruit and refrigerate. Tamarinds may be eaten fresh, but they are most commonly used to make a cooling drink or to flavor preserves and chutney.

SELECTIONS–'Manilla Sweet', 'Markham Waan'

SELECTED FRUIT CROP PLANTINGS

NAME	GROWTH HABIT	HEIGHT (FEET)	AREA	HARVEST TIME	BEST USE OF FRUITS
Apple	Small tree	20–25	NC	May–June	Fresh, juice, baking
Atemoya	Small tree	15–20	S	Aug.–Oct, Nov.–Jan.	Fresh, drinks, ice cream
Avocado	Large tree	40–50	CS	May–Mar.	Fresh, salads, sauces
Banana	Large perennial	12–15	CS	Year-round	Fresh, baking, ice cream
Barbados Cherry	Shrub	15–20	S	April–Oct.	Fresh, juice, jelly
Blackberry	Perennial	4–6	NCS	April–May	Fresh, jelly, baking
Black Sapote	Large tree	40–50	S	Dec.–Mar.	Fresh, desserts
Blueberry	Large shrub	5–15	NC	May–June	Fresh, salads, baking
Canistel	Small tree	15–25	S	Year-round	Fresh, baking
Carambola	Medium tree	25–35	CS	June–Oct., Nov.–Feb.	Fresh, salads, juice
Carissa	Shrub	8–10	CS	Year-round	Jelly, juice
Cattley Guava	Large shrub	15–20	CS	July–Aug.	Fresh, juice, jelly
Coconut	Palm	50–60	S	Year-round	Fresh, baking
Feijoa	Large shrub	12–15	NCS	July–Aug.	Fresh, preserves
Fig	Small tree	10–15	NCS	June–Aug.	Fresh, salads, baking
Grape	Vine	15–20	NCS	June–Aug.	Fresh, juice, jelly, wine
Jaboticaba	Medium tree	20–30	CS	Year-round	Fresh, jelly, wine
Jackfruit	Large tree	40–50	S	Year-round	Fresh
Longan	Large tree	40–50	S	July–Aug.	Fresh, dried
Lychee	Large tree	35–45	S	June–July	Fresh, salads
Macadamia	Large tree	40–50	CS	Aug.–Oct.	As nuts, baking
Mamey Sapote	Large tree	40–50	S	May–July	Fresh, jelly, ice cream

N = North Florida C = Central Florida S = South Florida

SELECTED FRUIT CROP PLANTINGS

NAME	GROWTH HABIT	HEIGHT (FEET)	AREA	HARVEST TIME	BEST USE OF FRUITS
Mango	Large tree	40–50	S	May–Oct.	Fresh, salads
Miracle Fruit	Shrub	4–6	S	Year-round	Fresh
Monstera	Vine	15–20	CS	Aug.–Oct.	Fresh, salads
Nectarine	Small tree	15–20	NC	May–June	Fresh, salads
Papaya	Tree-like	15–20	CS	Year-round	Fresh, salads, juice
Passion Fruit	Vine	15–20	CS	June–Dec.	Fresh, juice
Peach	Small tree	15–20	NCS	May–June	Fresh, salads, baking
Pear	Medium tree	20–30	NC	July–Aug.	Fresh, canned, cooked
Pecan	Large tree	50–60	NC	Oct.–Nov.	As nuts, baking
Persimmon	Small tree	15–20	NC	Sept.–Oct.	Fresh, baking
Pineapple	Perennial	2–3	CS	Year-round	Fresh, salads, baking
Plum	Small tree	15–20	NC	May–June	Fresh, baking
Pomegranate	Large shrub	10–15	NCS	Year-round	Fresh, juice, jelly
Prickly Pear	Cactus	4–6	NCS	Aug.–Sept.	Fresh
Sapodilla	Large tree	40–50	S	Feb.–June	Fresh, juice, jelly
Sea Grape	Large shrub	15–20	CS	July–Aug.	Fresh, jelly
Star Apple	Large tree	40–50	S	Feb.–May	Fresh
Sugar Apple	Small tree	15–20	S	July–Sept., Nov.–Jan.	Fresh, ice cream
Surinam Cherry	Large shrub	10–15	CS	May–Aug.	Fresh, salads, jelly
Tamarind	Large tree	40–50	S	April–June	Drinks, sauce, chutney
Wampee	Small tree	15–20	S	June–Aug.	Fresh, pie
White Sapote	Medium tree	25–30	S	May–Aug.	Fresh

N = North Florida C = Central Florida S = South Florida

JANUARY

❏ This is the height of the citrus harvest season.

❏ January and February are the coldest months of the year. Be prepared to protect cold-sensitive fruit plants. Lemons and limes are the most vulnerable citrus. Mound 1 foot (30 cm) of soil around the base to protect the tree, but not the upper portions, which will later regrow.

❏ Bare-root trees can be planted. Planting container-grown fruits is best delayed until later, unless in warmer regions.

❏ Prune deciduous plants during dormancy. In warmer parts of the state, peaches and nectarines are beginning to bud and need pruning. Delay trimming citrus for another month.

❏ Mature trees need limited watering.

❏ Check for scale insects and sooty mold. If needed, apply an oil spray. Follow all instructions.

FEBRUARY

❏ Citrus trees are cold sensitive and may need protection this month. Many citrus are ready to harvest, although they can be stored on the tree for extended periods.

❏ Some fruit trees need cold weather to produce fruit. When selecting trees, make sure the varieties will fruit in your area. Other fruits need special pollinators.

❏ When purchasing container-grown plants, select ones where the ball is starting to develop a web of roots around the soil. Citrus can be planted once temperatures reach 70°F (21°C). Protect from freezing when necessary.

❏ Prune grapes before the vines sprout new buds. Prune citrus before spring growth begins.

❏ Begin fertilizing in late February or March. Use a special fertilizer for your fruit instead of general garden product.

MARCH

❏ Harvest grapefruit now, when they get sweet.

❏ This is a good time to plant citrus, which don't need amended soil or mulch. When planting other fruits, add organic material as a topdressing outside of the planting hole. Some crops have special needs. For example, blueberries require acidic soil.

❏ Trim figs if needed. Most gardeners grow them as multi-trunk trees. To produce large peaches and nectarines, thin fruit when the size of a quarter.

❏ March is dry and watering is important to mature the crops.

Keep the soil moist for new plantings until roots grow into the surrounding soil. For established plantings, water when the surface soil feels dry to the touch. Bananas and figs need extra moisture.

❏ Feed new plantings lightly every 6 to 8 weeks March through September. Feed established plantings in March, June, and September. Fertilize citrus this month.

❏ Begin insect and disease spray programs using products specifically for home fruit trees.

APRIL

❏ Continue planting container-grown stock. Discontinue bare-root plantings until winter. In northern areas, plant citrus in moveable containers for winter protection.

❏ It's a dry month, and water is important now. Make sure the irrigation system is working. Use soaker hoses and micro sprinklers where possible. Water only during early morning hours.

❏ Some evergreen trees drop much of their foliage in spring, but new leaves quickly follow. Some of the leaves may have spots or pests, but no control is needed.

❏ Bunch grapes may need a spray program. Pests like aphids and caterpillars may start to appear on other fruits. Control only as needed. Keep up any spray programs that have been started for apple, peach, and nectarine plantings.

MAY

❏ Continue planting trees, shrubs, and citrus from containers. Hurry for a good selection.

❏ Some plants send up suckers that should be removed. Check your citrus, lychee, mangoes, and similar plants for shoots from beneath the graft union. Trim these root-stock suckers flush with the trunk.

❏ May can be dry and hot. Pay special attention to water needs of all plantings, especially new ones.

❏ Except for citrus, wait 1 more month for a major fertilizing. New plantings should continue an every-other-month schedule. All fruits growing in containers need every-other-week to monthly feedings, unless using a slow-release fertilizer.

❏ Lace bugs may appear on avocado foliage, with yellow spots then leaves that turn brown. Some damage may be ignored. When needed, oil spray will provide control. Caterpillars may be chewing holes in leaves of many plantings. Damage is unsightly but often minimal. If needed, use a natural spray containing *Bacillus thuringiensis*.

JUNE

❏ All containerized fruiting plants may be planted now.

❏ Citrus fruits may drop. It's a normal process to thin fruit and will reoccur in June and September.

❏ Many plantings have finished fruiting and have produced new growth. Prune as needed.

❏ Apply fertilizer. Use a balanced fertilizer with minor nutrients or a special product for your fruit. Feed new plantings lightly every 6 to 8 weeks with food scattered under the branches. Feed established plants under and out past the branches. Apply fertilizer over mulch. If the May citrus feeding was missed, apply it now.

❏ When peach, nectarine, and plum crops are harvested and general spraying stops, stay alert for borers. Many other fruiting plants may be infested with caterpillars. Most gardeners ignore them since treatment in large trees is difficult. If treatment is done for citrus problems, be sure to use sprays labeled for use with citrus.

JULY

❏ All container-grown fruiting plants can be planted in summer, although fruits may be lost or damaged because of transplant shock.

❏ Finish pruning this month so stems can mature during remainder of season. Harvest fruits as they ripen and remove those on the ground.

❏ Get props ready to support heavy-bearing citrus trees to lighten the load on limbs (if unable to pick extra fruits).

❏ Feed container plants monthly using liquid fertilizer. Only container-grown citrus need feeding this month.

❏ Ripening nectarines and peaches may attract the Caribbean fruit fly, as well as the papaya fruit fly. Watch for leaf spots, aphids, scales, lace bugs, caterpillars, and trunk borers. Control only as needed to prevent major plant decline. Rounded brown spots in citrus fruit may be caused by pecking birds. The fruits usually ripen normally.

AUGUST

❏ Plant citrus and vining fruits this month. Choose vining plants that are not heavily entwined, or prune them back and wait for new shoots to develop.

❏ Immediately after fruiting, blackberries and blueberries need pruning. All pruning should be finished early this month. Other plantings may need pruning too. Remove citrus limbs that might interfere with maintenance or foot traffic. Support young citrus limbs that are loaded with fruit to prevent breaking.

❏ Only container and new plantings receive feeding now, except for citrus. This is a regular month to fertilize citrus.

❏ Caterpillars may be noticeable in the taller trees, although it's almost impossible to reach the tops with sprays. Check for grasshoppers, katydids, lace bugs, scales, and trunk borers. On citrus, most damage can be ignored unless the tree is small or unhealthy.

SEPTEMBER

❏ New fruit trees can still be planted. Avoid trees susceptible to cold damage, but hardy plants can become well established. Plant papaya seeds now for next year. Sow two or more per container, and when they germinate, thin to one.

❏ If desired, prune back large trees immediately after fruiting. Selectively remove limbs. Expect a lower yield next season, but easier-to-harvest fruits. Prop up citrus limbs overladen with fruits. If needed, remove some of the fruits.

❏ Now is the time to apply the last fertilizing of the year, so new growth can mature before cooler winter weather.

❏ Watch for papaya fruit flies. Many fruits are making the final growth of the year. Look for caterpillars, grasshoppers, scale, and mites. Apply pesticides only as needed. Blemishes on citrus usually affect appearance, not flavor. It's too late to apply a chemical control.

OCTOBER

❏ Most fruiting plants can still be added, but not if they are cold sensitive. Container-grown citrus can be planted then protected during cold, or it can be kept in the container until late winter.

❏ Remove cool-season weeds from near the fruit trees.

❏ The dry season often begins halfway through the month. Luckily, temperatures are a little lower and days are shorter, reducing moisture needs; but container-grown fruits still need daily waterings.

❏ Fertilizing is over for most fruits unless you forgot the fall feeding, which should be applied early in the month. Also feed citrus early in the month. Continue to feed all plants in containers.

❏ Twigs on the ground may be caused by the twig girdler. Damage is minimal. However, destroy the twigs. Many deciduous trees will have leaves with spots. This is normal. Citrus pests should be tolerated, since it's best not to spray while you are consuming the fruit.

NOVEMBER

❏ Continue planting the cold-tolerant fruits in central and northern portions of the state. Add cold-sensitive plants only in southern locations. Bare-root citrus can be planted.

❏ Besides harvesting fruits still ripening, especially citrus, limited work is required as plants head into dormant season. You should still take weekly walks among plants to determine any needs. Remove damaged limbs. To discourage pests, remove any fruits on the ground. Control weeds and renew mulches.

❏ As plants become dormant they need less water. Still, if soil becomes dry in upper inch, apply water. Watering of container plants will also become less frequent.

❏ Feeding time is over for all but the container plantings. And if these are dormant or making little growth, fertilizing is over for them too.

❏ Pests are less active in the cooler portions of the state, but you might find aphids, lace bugs, and similar pests feeding where temperatures are warm.

DECEMBER

❏ Except for citrus and a few fruits ripening in cooler locations, fruiting is over. Plan to protect cold-sensitive trees. Move container plants when cold warnings are sounded. Mound up soil around tree trunk bases to protect graft unions from freezing. Add cold-tolerant plants.

❏ Remove broken limbs. Some deciduous fruit trees may start to bloom. Delay their pruning until January.

❏ It's dry, but luckily it's cool. Check soil by touch to see if plants need watering. Do not water during freeze conditions. Make sure the soil is moist before freezing weather. Also water as plants recover from freezes.

❏ Feeding is over for the year. Even container plants are dormant. Some growth may continue in the southernmost portions of the state, and plants will benefit from light feedings.

❏ A few insects still found in the warmer areas are aphids, lace bugs, and scales. Where needed, apply pesticide. Most spraying can be discontinued until spring.

HERBS & VEGETABLES
for Florida

Most gardeners will say there is no better tomato than the one you eat fresh from your garden. And that is true of just about all vegetables, because fresh is better! Corn is never sweeter than when it is picked from the stalk and dunked immediately in boiling water. The same is true of herbs. Stems, with their spicy flavors, are best when gathered right from your own patch.

Most plantings need a sunny location. The general rule: if the plant produces a fruit, pod, or similar edible portion, it needs 6 to 8 hours of sun a day. Herbs, leaf vegetables, and root vegetables can do well with 4 to 6 hours of sun, or a day of lightly filtered sun.

PLANTING

Florida has a year-round season, but you have to select the proper times to plant various crops. Look at our planting chart on pages 88 to 91 before deciding what to plant.

1. Make beds 6 inches (15 cm) above the ground or higher with lumber, plastic beams, concrete blocks, or similar materials. In Florida, use materials that are resistant to rot and termites. A convenient size is 4 feet (122 cm) wide and as long as you like.

2. Fill the beds with soil. You can use existing landscape soil or mix organic matter–including compost, coconut coir, and composted manure–with sand and clay soils. Many gardeners fill small beds with potting soils that are pest-free.

3. To avoid compaction and the introduction of pests, don't step on the soils.

For in-ground plantings:

1. Select a predominantly sunny site. Check for possible shade at different times of the year. In Florida, the sun dips way to the south by midwinter.

2. It's traditional to till the soil deeply and work in liberal quantities of organic matter with sand and clay soils, but building rich gardening soil on top of weeded, but un-tilled soil is a better option that preserves the soil ecosystem.

3. Test the soil acidity and adjust the pH with lime or soil sulfur if needed.

If you are using containers, make a list of what you want to grow and when. Then follow these steps:

1. Select a container big enough to accommodate the root system of the plants. Small herbs can grow in 4- to 5-inch (10- to 12.5-cm) pots, but most vegetables need gallon containers. The containers can be fairly shallow, as most roots only grow 6 to 8 inches (15 to 20 cm) deep, but there will be better drainage with taller pots. Do not use gravel or potsherds in the bottom of the pot. Just use one rock, a screen, or leaves to block soil from moving through the drainage hole(s).

2. Filling the containers with a sterile potting soil means that you won't risk bringing in soilborne pests. On the other hand, filling them with compost or compost mixed with sandy soil means that the soil will be alive with organisms that can help the plants in these small gardens to grow better with little or no added fertilizer.

Use our table as a guide for spacing and planting techniques. If you are cramped for space, use the closer spacing.

WATERING

Edible gardens need plenty of water, and the irrigation schedule should be different than the rest of the landscape for the best crop production. But that doesn't mean you should not conserve. Enriching sandy soil with organic matter prior to planting increases the moisture retention. Keeping a good mulch over the soil also helps. Here are some tips to stretch the time between waterings:

- Water deeply at each irrigation. Feel the soil below the surface.
- Use micro sprinklers and soaker hoses where possible.
- Control weeds, which use water and compete with the crops.
- Adjust your watering schedule to the time of the year.

Hot, dry spring and fall months require more water than the cooler winter and rainy summer months. Water during the early-morning hours to prevent loss due to evaporation and winds and also to allow plant leaves to dry out during the day to reduce fungal blights.

FERTILIZING

Productive gardens need adequate nutrients to produce lots of foliage, fruits, and root crops. Yellowing leaves and slowing growth indicate a nutrient shortage. Take note and adjust for the next season's crop.

LIQUID FERTILIZERS provide instant food for the plantings. Most need to be reapplied every 2 to 3 weeks. Fish or seaweed emulsions and compost tea are organic choices.

GRANULAR FEEDINGS can offer both quick- and slow-release nutrients. Most general garden fertilizers are applied every 3 to 4 weeks. Slow-release products may last for months.

COMPOST is the best all-around soil conditioner. It adds nutrients, humus for water retention, and soil microbes. When you take care of your soil, your soil takes care of your plants.

MANURES have both slow- and quick-release qualities. They are of a low analysis and must be applied frequently in large quantities to be effective. Composted manures can be applied to the surface or made into a tea for drenching around plants. Fresh manure should be laid onto the soil 90 days before planting a crop where the edible portion is not in constant contact with the soil, and 120 days before planting for root-based crops.

PESTS

Florida vegetable and herb plantings have the same types of pests found in most other areas of the world. Here they remain active for longer periods and the numbers can be greater than those found in a cooler climate. They tend to be most active during warmer times of the year. More information on pests on page 224.

One pest that is new to many gardeners is the root knot nematode, a microscopic roundworm that lives in the soil. There are many types of nematodes and most are beneficial, but the root knot nematode causes roots to swell and become less effective at absorbing water and nutrients. Some controls include planting resistant varieties, using sterile soils, planting nematode-retarding cover crops such as marigolds in the summer, or practicing soil solarization during the summer.

BASIL

Sweet basil: Ocimum basilicum; lime basil: O. americanum; lemon basil: O. × africanum
Mint family: Lamiaceae

WHEN TO PLANT–Basil is a warm-weather crop. Plant in successive plantings, 2 to 3 weeks apart, spring through fall.

WHERE TO PLANT–Plant basil in full sun, in well-prepared, well-drained, compost-rich soil.

HOW TO PLANT–Basil seeds can be direct sown in garden rows and thinned to 6 to 14 inches (15 to 36 cm) apart, or transplants can be used with the same spacing.

WATER NEEDS–Basil prefers moist but not wet soil. Although it is drought tolerant, leaf edges may turn brown after wilting. It's still good enough for cooking–it just doesn't look as nice.

CARE–Remove stems with flowers as they appear–this will encourage new growth. On the other hand, leaving some of those flowers will make the pollinators happy.

PROBLEMS–Sweet basil is susceptible to fungal infestations in our hot, wet summers, so grow it early in the season. Lime basil thrives during our wet summers, and if you allow the flowers to stay, it will reseed. Lemon basil, which is a hybrid between sweet and lime basil, also does well during the summer.

HARVEST–Basil leaves can be harvested at any time.

SELECTIONS–Good varieties for Florida include 'Dark Opal', 'Genovese', 'Lettuce Leaf', 'Siam Queen', 'Spicy Globe', and 'Sweet'.

BEANS

Phaseolus spp.
Legume family: Fabaceae

WHEN TO PLANT–In North Florida grow March through November. In Central and South Florida grow February through May and August through October.

WHERE TO PLANT–Needs at least 8 hours of full sun. Beans grow in poor soil, because they fix nitrogen, which enriches the soil. With adequate light and ample water, beans can grow in containers.

HOW TO PLANT–Direct sow in garden. Provide pole beans with support.

WATER NEEDS–Needs lots of water

CARE–Soil that's too rich produces more leaves and fewer beans.

PROBLEMS–None.

HARVEST–Harvest bush, green, and wax beans while pods are still tender. Pole beans produce multiple crops, provided you pick every pod.

SELECTIONS–Some of many good varieties for Florida are 'Contender', 'Greencrop', and 'Tendergreen Improved' (Bush); 'Cherokee Wax' and 'Improved Golden Wax' (Wax); and 'Blue Lake', 'Kentucky Wonder', and 'White Half Runner' (Pole).

BROCCOLI

Brassica oleracea
Cabbage family: Brassicaceae

WHEN TO PLANT–Plant at the onset of cooler weather. A second planting can grow until warm weather returns. Broccoli bolts with too much heat.

WHERE TO PLANT–In full sun, with well-drained, moist soil with added organic matter

HOW TO PLANT–Place one or two seeds per pot containing ¼ inch (6 mm) soil. Cover with fine soil. Place pot in shallow water until soil is saturated. Thin to one seedling per pot. Keep moist in full sun. Plant into garden after three sets of mature leaves develop. Or plant directly in the garden with 2 or 3 seeds per hole and cut off the smaller ones once there are several true leaves. (You can eat these seedlings.) Allow plenty of room, with plants 14 inches (36 cm) apart.

WATER NEEDS–Give plenty of water.

CARE–Keep after the weeds and apply compost top dressing a few times during the growing season.

PROBLEMS–Keep armyworms from young transplants with a 3-inch (7.5-cm) heavy paper collar pushed partially into the ground.

HARVEST–After head or curd forms, but before individual flowers expand, cut the center head about 6 inches (15 cm) below the flower head. Continue to care for the plants and harvest the small flower heads that will sprout for a month or more as the plants try to bloom and set seed.

SELECTIONS–'Green Comet', 'High Dividend', 'Packman' (early season)

CABBAGE
Brassica oleracea
Cabbage family: Brassicaceae

WHEN TO PLANT–This is a cool-season crop. Plant one crop in late fall and another 30 to 45 days later to stagger availability. Stop planting in February or March.

WHERE TO PLANT–In full sun, in average, well-drained soil

HOW TO PLANT–If sown directly into the ground, thin to proper spacing of about 10 inches (25 cm) apart for good growth–too close will yield small, weak plants.

WATER NEEDS–Lots of water.

CARE–Provide rich soil and add compost and/or fish emulsion as plants mature.

PROBLEMS–Occasionally, armyworms cut tender stems of new sprouts or transplants at night. Make barriers of heavy paper and push them halfway into the ground. Once seedlings get a little older (and tougher), remove the collars.

HARVEST–Harvest at any stage.

SELECTIONS–Easy-to-grow cabbage is great for beginners, but there are numerous unique varieties for advanced gardeners. Check with neighborhood gardeners for their best selections. Try 'Bonnie's Hybrid', 'Copenhagen Market', 'Mammoth Red Rock' (red cabbage), 'New Jersey Wakefield', or 'Savoy Chieftain' (densely curled). Chinese cabbages may even be used in ornamental plantings.

CANTALOUPE
Cucumis melo
Squash family: Cucurbitaceae.

WHEN TO PLANT–Plant after frost danger has passed, the earlier the better. Start seeds indoors 2 weeks before planting to get a head start on the season.

WHERE TO PLANT–In full sun in well-drained, organically enriched soil. Good air circulation is necessary to discourage diseases.

HOW TO PLANT–Plant seeds or seedlings either in rows 48 inches (122 cm) apart with individual plants 24 inches (61 cm) apart, or in hills 48 to 60 inches (122 to 152 cm) apart with four to five seeds per hill.

WATER NEEDS– If planting in hills, leave a swale in the center to hold water. Provide ample water until fruit begins to ripen. Then hold off a little for better-tasting melons.

CARE–Use a thick layer of straw or pine needle mulch over entire vine area.

PROBLEMS–Place half-grown fruit on boards or cans to reduce slug or insect damage. Or grow on vertical supports with fruits held by a sling to prevent slugs and keep fruit easy to monitor.

HARVEST–Pick immediately when ripe, when fruit is fragrant and melons release from vine.

SELECTIONS–Cantaloupes are worth the effort and real estate. 'Ambrosia' is still the best hybrid, with intense flavor and disease-resistant vines. 'Minnesota Midget' has 3-foot- (91-cm-) long vines.

CARROT
Daucus carota
Carrot family: Apiaceae

WHEN TO PLANT–Multiple sowings any time between late September and mid-March

WHERE TO PLANT–Plant in well-drained, enriched soil, with all rocks and roots removed. Needs at least 6 hours of full sun.

HOW TO PLANT–Sow very small amount of seed in ¼-inch (6 mm) furrow. DO NOT COVER; just pat into the soil and gently water with a watering can. Even if careful, you probably sowed too many seeds. Seedlings MUST be thinned to one plant every 3 inches (7.5 cm). Gently pull seedlings sideways or cut at ground level to minimize damage to remaining seedlings. Carrots do not tolerate transplanting.

WATER NEEDS–Keep moist

CARE–Carrots past their prime are woody and inedible, so plant crops 4 weeks apart.

PROBLEMS–Rotate crop locations annually. Too long in one spot encourages wire worm infestations. To be safe, when preparing soil, sprinkle in wood ashes, which repel root worms.

HARVEST–Anytime after reaching 3 inches (7.5 cm) long. Leaves are also edible, raw or cooked.

SELECTIONS–Growing 'Chantenay Royal', 'Imperator 58', 'Nantes Half Long', 'Tendersweet'; unusual varieties: 'Cosmic Purple', 'Snow White'. There are also rainbow mixtures with purple, red, orange, and white carrots.

CHIVES
Allium schoenoprasum
Amaryllis family: Amaryllidaceae

WHEN TO PLANT–Chives can tolerate low temperatures down to about 25°F (about-4°C). Plant at any time of the year.

WHERE TO PLANT–Plant chives in full sun, in well-prepared, well-drained soil. With their lovely light-lavender flowers, chives can be planted as a border plant in flower gardens. They are a short-lived perennial that will grow for 3 or 4 years, so keep away from the rotating annual crops.

HOW TO PLANT–Given their reluctance to grow quickly, it's recommended that many chive seeds be planted in small containers with good potting soil, then later planted into the garden after they have reached sufficient size.

WATER NEEDS–Chives prefer moist soil but can also survive drought conditions and be revived with regular applications of water.

CARE–Chives are easy to grow.

PROBLEMS–None.

HARVEST–Chives can be harvested by pulling individual stems or by cutting what's needed with scissors or clippers. Flowers are edible too.

SELECTIONS–There are no known specific varieties of regular chives. However, garlic chives (*A. tuberosum*), also a perennial, performs well in Florida too.

CORN
Zea mays
Grass family: Poaceae

WHEN TO PLANT–In North Florida plant February through April. In Central Florida plant January through April. In South Florida plant October through March.

WHERE TO PLANT–Full sun, in well-drained soil

HOW TO PLANT–Start with fresh seed. Plant in blocks, not long rows, to increase pollination.

WATER NEEDS–Keep moist.

CARE–Add compost regularly during the growing season. To increase chances pollen will reach the ear, shake entire plant several times a day when pollen first appears.

PROBLEMS–Given the number and variety of bugs that attack corn, after one season most gardeners decide it's easier to buy a few ears. Bottom line–growing corn is not easy in most areas of Florida. Pests include birds eating seedlings, fall armyworms, and corn earworms.

HARVEST–Check for ripeness when silks turn brown all the way to the husk or if top kernels squirt "milk" when pushed with a thumbnail.

SELECTIONS–'Early Sunglow' and 'Golden Cross Bantam' (yellow); 'Silver Queen' and 'Sweet Ice' (white)

CUCUMBER
Cucumis sativus
Squash family: Cucurbitaceae

WHEN TO PLANT–In North Florida plant seeds August through September and February through April. In Central Florida plant seeds September and January through March. In South Florida plant seeds September through October, November through December, and January.

WHERE TO PLANT–Full sun in well-drained, enriched soil

HOW TO PLANT–Sow seeds ½ inch (1 cm) deep in rows or grow on strings like pole beans. The upright method requires less space, provides better air circulation, keeps fruits cleaner, and allows easier harvesting.

WATER NEEDS–Maintain a regular watering regimen to prevent misshapen fruit.

CARE–Female flowers need to be pollinated several times before a fruit will develop, so installing a pollinator garden near squash-family crops is a good idea.

PROBLEMS–Lessen powdery mildew infestations by watering in early morning and by not touching wet plants. Oils can protect plants and eradicate powdery mildew but cannot be used when temperatures reach 90°F (32°C). Most cucumbers are susceptible to fungal diseases once the wet season begins.

HARVEST–They can be harvested at any time depending upon your needs, but pick well before ripening to minimize the seediness.

SELECTIONS–MR 17', 'Pixie', 'Straight Eight'; or 'Burpee's Bushmaster' (smaller)

DILL
Anethum graveolens
Carrot family: Apiaceae

WHEN TO PLANT—Dill can be planted for fall or spring gardens and tolerates both extreme heat and freezing temperatures.

WHERE TO PLANT—Plant dill in full sun, in well-prepared, well-drained soil. It can also be planted in butterfly gardens as a caterpillar host plant.

HOW TO PLANT—Dill seed can be direct sown into the garden at 6-inch (15-cm) intervals in rows that are 8 to 16 inches (20 to 41 cm) apart. Seedlings produce very fine foliage, so care must be taken when weeding for the first 4 to 5 weeks.

WATER NEEDS—Dill prefers moist soil but can also survive drought conditions once established.

CARE—Dill is an easy herb to grow. Provide plenty of water and rich soil. Once flowers begin to bloom, foliage production stops.

PROBLEMS—Black swallowtail butterfly caterpillars like dill. Plant an extra row for the butterflies.

HARVEST—Dill foliage can be harvested by cutting individual lacy leaves. The dill seeds can also be harvested.

SELECTIONS—For Florida gardens try 'Fernleaf', 'Hercules', and 'Super Dukat'.

EGGPLANT
Solanum melongena
Nightshade family: Solanaceae

WHEN TO PLANT—Plant seeds of this warm-season vegetable 6 weeks before outdoor planting date. Eggplants love heat.

WHERE TO PLANT—Full sun in average, well-drained soil

HOW TO PLANT—Uncommon varieties are usually only available from seed. Sow seeds ¼ inch (6 mm) deep and provide bottom heat when possible. Plant individual plants 20 inches (51 cm) apart, in 20- to 36-inch- (51- to 91-cm-) wide rows. Space smaller types closer.

WATER NEEDS—Although eggplants can withstand drought, production is severely curtailed when plants go dry. Keep soil moist. Add mulch to conserve moisture.

CARE—Apply compost when planting, then again halfway through the season.

PROBLEMS—Eggplants are virtually pest free. Keep heavy fruits off the ground by gently tying individual branches to a pole or slipping cardboard under the fruits.

HARVEST—Harvest while still glossy and cut the stem above the calyx (the green star at the top) on fruit to prolong shelf life.

SELECTIONS—'Black Beauty', 'Calliope', 'Casper', 'Cloud Nine', 'Florida High Bush', 'Green Goddess'

LETTUCE
Lactuca sativa
Daisy family: Asteraceae

WHEN TO PLANT—Plant directly in the garden or extend the season by planting seeds indoors 4 to 5 weeks before planting outdoors. Plant every 2 or 3 weeks for a season-long supply. In North Florida plant September through October and February through March. In Central Florida plant September through March. In South Florida plant September through January.

WHERE TO PLANT—Needs at least 6 to 8 hours of full sun, in enriched, well-drained soil.

HOW TO PLANT—Sow seeds directly by sprinkling a seed every 2 to 3 inches (5 to 7.5 cm) apart into a ¼-inch (6 mm) furrow; barely cover with fine soil. Or transplant started seedlings. *Gently* water with a watering can. Carefully thin seedlings to distance specified on packet.

WATER NEEDS—Keep moist but not wet. Mulch retains moisture and keeps leaves cleaner.

CARE—Use fresh seed and refrigerate opened seed packets for later sowings. Water with a little organic fertilizer when transplanting.

PROBLEMS—If plants are kept too wet, slugs or snails can be a problem. Hand pick in early evening or early morning.

HARVEST—Pick outer leaves or entire head.

SELECTIONS—'Black-Seeded Simpson', 'Buttercrunch', 'Oak Leaf', 'White Boston'. There are hundreds of varieties. Some seed packs include several varieties and may be called chefs' mix.

MINT

*Mentha spp. Peppermint: (M. × piperita);
Spearmint: (M. spicata); Apple mint: (M. suaveolens)*
Mint family: Lamiaceae

WHEN TO PLANT–Able to withstand extremes in temperatures and can be planted at any time of the year.

WHERE TO PLANT–Mint is a vigorous grower. It's recommended that it only be planted in containers or in a perennial bed where it can fill in between other tough plants. Plant mint in full sun to part shade, in well-prepared, well-drained soil.

HOW TO PLANT–Mint can be direct sown into containers with a good-quality, well-drained potting soil. Mint can also be planted with annuals and perennials for an attractive mixed ornamental planter.

WATER NEEDS–Mint prefers moist soil but can also survive drought conditions.

CARE–Mint is an easy herb to grow. Give it plenty of water and a dash of organic fertilizer after established and mint will grow very well.

PROBLEMS–Spreads aggressively via rhizomes. Plant in pots or install above- and below-ground barriers around mint plantings.

HARVEST–Mint foliage can be harvested at any time.

SELECTIONS–For Florida gardens try peppermint, spearmint, apple mint, pineapple mint, and chocolate mint.

OKRA

Abelmoschus esculentus
Mallow family: Malvaceae

WHEN TO PLANT–Will grow in Florida's summer heat and humidity. In North and Central Florida plant seed March through August. In South Florida plant in August and September.

WHERE TO PLANT–Plant in full, hot, blazing sun in deeply tilled, well-drained soil.

HOW TO PLANT–Direct sow seed 1 inch (2.5 cm) deep after frost danger has passed and soil has warmed. Or start early by sowing seeds in coir cups indoors. Give okra plenty of room–plant seed 18 to 24 inches (46 to 61 cm) apart in rows 36 inches (91 cm) apart.

WATER NEEDS–In well-drained soil you can't water okra too much. It's a good idea to plant them in a grid with swales between the plants so water can soak into the root zone between the plants.

CARE–Unpicked pods remaining on the plant cause it to stop making new pods.

PROBLEMS–Harvest pods with clippers. Don't twist them off or leave unpicked.

HARVEST–Pods longer than 4 or 5 inches may be tough, so pick okra every day or two.

SELECTIONS–Varieties include 'Alabama Red', 'Baby Bubba' (for small gardens and containers), 'Clemson Spineless', 'Cow Horn', 'Evertender', 'Little Lucy' (burgundy dwarf), 'Red Burgundy', and 'White Velvet'.

ONION

Allium cepa
Amaryllis family: Amaryllidaceae

WHEN TO PLANT–Onions prefer cool weather. Plant October through January throughout Florida.

WHERE TO PLANT–Plant in full sun in enriched, well-prepared soil.

HOW TO PLANT–Onions can be planted three ways. Seeds, sets, and pre-started plants. Space at 4 inches (10 cm) for the best bulbs. Mulch with 3 or 4 inches (7.5 or 10 cm) of pine needles or straw.Mulch with 3 or 4 inches (7.5 to 10 cm) of pine needles or straw.

WATER NEEDS–Average water needs

CARE–Onions are heavy nitrogen feeders. Enrich the soil and apply organic fertilizer such as fish emulsion as they start to send up leaves and again in midwinter.

PROBLEMS–Weeds are the biggest problem. Cultivating is difficult around the plants, so extreme care is needed.

HARVEST–Onions can be harvested any time, but the main harvest should be after the leaves turn yellow and fall over. When this happens, stop all irrigation and let soil dry out before the harvest. Hang by the leaves in a dry warm spot for 2 or 3 weeks to cure the onions so they can be stored longer.

SELECTIONS–Only buy "short-day" onions for Florida.

OREGANO
Origanum vulgare
Mint family: Lamiaceae

WHEN TO PLANT—Oregano seeds are usually planted spring through fall; cuttings or plants can be planted at any time.

WHERE TO PLANT—Oregano is a low-growing herb with ¼-inch- (6 mm-) long leaves. Plant oregano in full sun to part shade, in rich, well-prepared, well-drained soil. Oregano is somewhat tolerant of frost, so it's a perennial herb throughout Florida.

HOW TO PLANT—Oregano seeds can be direct sown into containers with a good quality, well-drained potting soil. Oregano can also be planted with annuals and perennials for an attractive mixed ornamental planter.

WATER NEEDS—Oregano prefers somewhat moist soil. Not drought tolerant.

CARE—Oregano is an easy herb to grow.

PROBLEMS—None.

HARVEST—Oregano foliage can be harvested by cutting stems or individual leaves at any time.

SELECTIONS—For Florida gardens try 'Greek' oregano, 'Hot and Spicy' oregano, 'Harrenhausen', and 'Kent Beauty'.

PEPPERS, BELL
Capsicum annuum
Nightshade family: Solanaceae

WHEN TO PLANT—Peppers enjoy warm temperatures. In North and Central Florida plant February through March and again July through September. In South Florida, plant August through September.

WHERE TO PLANT—Needs at least 8 hours of full sun in compost-amended, well-drained soil.

HOW TO PLANT—Growing from seed is easier indoors than outdoors. Follow spacing specified on packet when planting in the garden.

WATER NEEDS—Peppers like moist but not wet soil. Mulch helps moderate soil temperatures and retains moisture.

CARE—Peppers are major feeders. A fish emulsion fertilizer a couple of times during the season is ideal.

PROBLEMS—Prevent brittle stems with fruit from breaking by staking plants. Occasionally, aphids appear on emerging growth.

HARVEST—Can be picked before mature color develops, but they won't be as sweet or as hot.

SELECTIONS—Sweet: 'Big Bertha', 'Gypsy', 'Pimento', 'Purple Beauty', 'Sweet Banana', 'Yolo Wonder'; hot: 'Caribbean Red', 'Habañero', 'Scotch Bonnet', 'Super Chili'. Peppers can also grow in containers.

POTATO, SWEET
Ipomoea batatas
Morning glory family: Convolvulaceae

WHEN TO PLANT—Plant March through June. It's a hot-weather plant.

WHERE TO PLANT—Plant in full sun, in compost-enriched soil. Avoid areas that have been fallow or where sweet potatoes have grown in the last 3 years.

HOW TO PLANT—Prepare soil properly before planting. Create 10-inch- (25-cm-) tall, 12-inch- (30-cm-) wide linear mounds. Enrich soil with compost. Place rooted slips into the top of mounds 12 to 14 inches (30 to 36 cm) apart, in rows 48 to 60 inches (122 to 152 cm) apart.

WATER NEEDS—Provide adequate water. In final 2 weeks, reduce irrigation amount.

CARE—Requires very little care

PROBLEMS—Sweet potatoes perform best where soil was turned over 1 or 2 months before planting to reduce nematodes. Even better, use a cover crop of marigolds in beds before planting sweet potatoes. Deer may occasionally eat leaves, which won't have a significant effect on tubers' size or quality.

HARVEST—Tubers can be harvested at any time. Cut vines away, gently remove soil, and cure in sun for 2 or 3 days. They will continue growing as long as tops are green.

SELECTIONS—'Beauregard', 'Hernandez', 'Picodito' (boniato)

ROSEMARY
Salvia rosmarinus
Mint family: Lamiaceae

WHEN TO PLANT–Rosemary can withstand the extremes in Florida temperatures and can be planted into the garden at any time.

WHERE TO PLANT–Depending on the selection, rosemary can grow either as a ground cover or as a low-growing shrub to 48 inches (122 cm) tall. Plant rosemary in full sun to part shade, in well-prepared, well-drained soil.

HOW TO PLANT–Rosemary is most often planted into the garden as a transplant or cutting.

WATER NEEDS–Rosemary prefers soil that is allowed to dry out between waterings.

CARE–Rosemary is an easy herb to grow. More rosemary plants are killed from too much water than anything else. Just pretend it doesn't exist and it will perform well in the garden.

PROBLEMS–Do not overwater!

HARVEST–Rosemary can be harvested by removing individual leaves and/or stems at any time.

SELECTIONS–For Florida gardens try upright rosemary, creeping rosemary, white rosemary, 'Blueboy', 'Dancing Waters', and 'Spice Island'.

SPINACH
Spinacia oleracea
Spinach family: Amaranthaceae

WHEN TO PLANT–This cool-weather vegetable "bolts" in heat. In North and Central Florida plant in October and November. In South Florida plant October through January. Plant successive crops every 3 weeks for continuous yield.

WHERE TO PLANT–Needs enriched, well-drained, deep loamy soil. Requires full sun and good air circulation. If necessary, plant in aboveground containers or raised beds.

HOW TO PLANT–Start seeds indoors or direct sow into the garden.

WATER NEEDS–Keep moist but not wet.

CARE–Feed lightly with fish emulsion once a month.

PROBLEMS–Weed often. Apply straw to reduce weeds, conserve water, and keep leaves cleaner.

HARVEST–Harvest single outside leaves or entire plant. Watch for flower stalks, then harvest immediately before it becomes bitter.

SELECTIONS–Good plain-leaf spinach varieties for Florida include 'Giant Nobel', 'Olympia', and 'Space'. Of the crinkled (savoyed) leaf varieties, 'Bloomsdale Longstanding' performs well. Other savoyed varieties include 'Melody', 'Tyee', and 'Vienna'. There are also spinach substitutes–Malabar spinach (*Basella alba*) and New Zealand spinach (*Tetragonia tetragonoides*)–that can be grown through the summer.

SQUASH
Cucurbita spp.
Squash family: Cucurbitaceae

WHEN TO PLANT–In North Florida plant in March and again in September; in Central Florida plant in February and again in September; in South Florida plant in January and again in October. Summer squashes are used right after harvest, while winter squashes can be stored for months or into winter.

WHERE TO PLANT–In full sun with compost-enriched, deeply tilled, well-drained soil

HOW TO PLANT–Build mounds with swales in the center and plant seeds on the edges of the mounds 24 inches (61 cm) apart.

WATER NEEDS–Water in the morning by filling up the swales in the mounds. Provide good circulation to reduce mildew and fungal infestations.

CARE–There are male and female flowers, and the female flower, which sits atop a tiny fruit, must be pollinated several times for the fruit to grow.

PROBLEMS–For stem borers and pickle worms, which bore into the fruit, apply Bt to deter them. Most squashes are susceptible to fungal infestations during our hot, wet summers.

HARVEST–About 45 days from seed

SELECTIONS–'Caserta', 'Cocozelle', 'Eightball', 'Early Butternut', 'Peter Pan', 'Prolific Straightneck', 'Summer Crookneck', 'Spaghetti', 'Table King'. Seminole pumpkin (*C. moschata*) does well in our hot, wet summers and has a tough skin that repels most borers.

THYME
Thymus vulgaris
Mint family: Lamiaceae

WHEN TO PLANT—Thyme is native to the Mediterranean and is adapted to hot, dry summers. Here in Florida, our summers are wet, so if you're planting seed, do so in the spring, but transplant at any time.

WHERE TO PLANT—Plant thyme in full sun to part shade, in well-prepared, well-drained soil.

HOW TO PLANT—Thyme can be planted by transplant, cutting, or seed. The seeds are so tiny they should be sown indoors to start.

WATER NEEDS—Well-drained soil

CARE—Thyme is an easy herb to grow. More thyme plants are killed from too much water than anything else.

PROBLEMS—No known problems

HARVEST—Thyme can be harvested by removing individual leaves or stems at any time after establishment.

SELECTIONS—There are more than a hundred varieties of thyme, with the most common being garden thyme and lemon thyme (*T. citriodorus*).

TOMATO
Solanum lycopersicum
Nightshade family: Solanaceae

WHEN TO PLANT—Plant early in the spring to get a full harvest before summer, because most tomatoes do not set fruit when the low nighttime temperatures are higher than 70°F (21°C) and because the wet summers bring in the fungal wilts. You can plant again in the fall.

WHERE TO PLANT—Plant in the ground or large containers, in 8 or more hours of full sun. Use enriched, well-drained soil.

HOW TO PLANT—Sow seeds indoors 6 to 8 weeks before last frost. Plant transplants (taller ones are better) with only top 4 inches (10 cm) above soil.

WATER NEEDS—Prefers constantly moist soil, but cannot tolerate soggy roots.

CARE—Tomatoes are commonly staked, grown in cages, or supported like pole beans.

PROBLEMS—Tomatoes are highly susceptible to several diseases. Do not pick fruit or groom plants when leaves are wet. In names, the letters "VFN" indicate built-in resistance: "V" for Verticillium wilt, "F" for Fusarium wilt, and "N" for nematodes.

HARVEST—60 to 90 days, depending on variety

SELECTIONS— 'Better Boy' (VFN), 'Sun Coast' (VF), 'Walter' (F), 'Floramerica' (F), 'Red Cherry', 'Sweet 100', 'Floragold', 'Florida Petite'. The Everglades tomato (*S. pimpinellifolium*), which produces tiny cherry tomatoes, does okay in the summer.

WATERMELON
Citrullus lanatus
Squash family: Cucurbitaceae

WHEN TO PLANT—North Florida: plant seeds March and August. Central Florida: plant seeds February and August. South Florida: January through March and August through September.

WHERE TO PLANT—Most soils except muck, in full sun.

HOW TO PLANT—Plant seeds 1½ inches (4 cm) deep, 36 inches (91 cm) apart, in rows 7 to 8 feet (2 to 2.5 m) apart.

WATER NEEDS—Needs lots of water

CARE—To retain moisture, keep out competing weeds, and keep fruit clean, plant seeds through a tillable newspaper/hay layer.

PROBLEMS—Worms can be controlled with DiPel (*Bacillus thuringiensis*).

HARVEST—Matures in 80 to 100 days from seed, depending on variety. Although difficult to determine ripeness, check when the melon bottom turns bright golden yellow or the closest tendril turns from green to brown.

SELECTIONS—Florida is the nation's leading watermelon producer. Large watermelons: 'Charleston Grey 133', 'Crimson Sweet', 'Jubilee' (Florida Giant). Smaller melons: 'Mickeylee', 'Sugar Baby'.

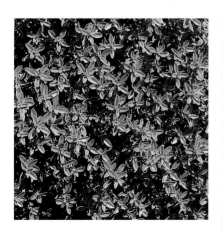

HERBS

NAME	SPACING (INCHES)	HOW TO START	PART USED	WHEN TO PLANT	HEIGHT (INCHES)	GROWTH HABIT
Anise	Oct.–May	18–24	Spreading	18	Seed	Seeds when ripe
Basil	Oct.–May	18–24	Rounded	12	Seed	Leaves any stage
Bay Laurel	Year-round	60–72+	Upright	48	Cuttings	Leaves any stage
Borage	Oct.–May	18–24	Sprawling	24	Seed	Leaves and flowers
Caraway	Oct.–May	18–24	Upright	12	Seed	Seeds
Cardamom	Oct.–May	36–48	Clumping	24	Divisions	Seeds
Chervil	Oct.–May	18–24	Spreading	12	Seed	Leaves any stage
Chives	Oct.–May	12–18	Clumping	10	Seed, division	Leaves any stage
Coriander	Oct.–May	12–36	Spreading	12	Seed	Leaves and seed
Cumin	Mar.–April	8–12	Spreading	4	Seed	Seeds
Dill	Oct.–May	48–60	Upright	12	Seed	Leaves and seed
Fennel	Oct.–Mar.	24–36	Upright	12	Seed	Leaves and seed
Garlic	Oct.–Dec.	24–30	Upright	6	Cloves	Bulbs and leaves
Ginger	Year-round	24–36	Clumping	12	Rhizomes	Rhizomes
Horehound	Year-round	12–24	Spreading	12	Seed, cuttings	Leaves before flowers
Lemon Balm	Oct.–May	18–24	Clumping	12	Seed, cuttings	Leaves any stage
Lovage	Oct.–Mar.	24–36	Upright	12	Seed	Leaves any stage
Marjoram	Oct.–May	6–8	Spreading	12	Seed	Leaves any stage
Mint	Year-round	12–24	Spreading	18	Seed, cuttings	Leaves any stage
Nasturtium	Nov.–Feb.	12–18	Spreading	6	Seed	Leaves and flowers
Oregano	Year-round	6–8	Spreading	12	Seed, cuttings	Leaves any stage
Rosemary	Year-round	24–36	Upright	24	Seed, cuttings	Leaves any stage
Sage	Oct.–April	18–24	Spreading	18	Seed, cuttings	Leaves any stage
Savory	Oct.–Mar.	10–12	Upright	12	Seed	Leaves any stage
Tarragon	Year-round	24–36	Upright	18	Seed, cuttings	Leaves young
Thyme	Year-round	4–12	Spreading	12	Seed, cuttings	Leaves any stage
Watercress	Oct.–Mar.	6–8	Spreading	6	Seed, cuttings	Leaves young

COOL-SEASON VEGETABLES

| NAME | WHEN TO PLANT | | | PLANTING METHOD | SPACING (INCHES) | DAYS TO HARVEST |
	NORTH	CENTRAL	SOUTH			
Asparagus	Year-round	Year-round	Will not grow here	Crowns	12–18	2 years
Beets	Sept.–Mar.	Oct.–Mar.	Oct.–Feb.	Seed	3–5	50–65
Broccoli	Aug.–Feb.	Aug.–Jan.	Sept.–Jan.	Seed, plants	12–18	55–90
Brussels Sprouts	Sept.–Dec.	Oct.–Dec.	Nov.–Dec.	Seed, plants	18–24	75–90
Cabbage	Sept.–Feb.	Sept.–Jan.	Sept.–Jan.	Seed, plants	12–24	70–100
Carrot	Sept.–Mar.	Oct.–Mar.	Oct.–Feb.	Seed	1–3	65–80
Cauliflower	Jan.–Feb. Aug.–Oct.	Oct.–Jan.	Oct.–Jan.	Seed, plants	8–24	55–90
Celery	Jan.–Mar.	Sept.–Feb.	Oct.–Jan.	Seed, plants	6–10	80–125
Chinese Cabbage	Oct.–Jan.	Oct.–Jan.	Nov.–Jan.	Seed, plants	8–12	60–90
Collards	Feb.–Mar.	Aug.–Dec.	Sept.–April, Sept.–Feb.	Seed, plants	10–18	40–80
Endive/ Escarole	Feb.–Mar., Sept.	Jan.–Feb., Sept	Sept.–Jan.	Seed	8–12	80–95
Kale	Oct.–Feb.	Oct.–Feb.	Nov.–Jan.	Seed	8–16	50–60
Kohlrabi	Mar.–April, Oct.–Nov	Feb.–Mar., Oct.–Nov	Nov.–Feb.	Seed	3–5	70–80
Lettuce	Feb.–Mar., Sept	Sept.–Mar.	Sept.–Jan.	Seed, plants	8–12	40–90
Mustard Greens	Sept.–Mar.	Sept.–Mar.	Sept.–Mar.	Seed	1–6	40–60
Onion	Sept.–Dec.	Sept.–Dec.	Sept.–Nov.	Seed, plants	4–6	110–160
Parsley	Feb.–Mar.	Oct.–Jan.	Sept.–Jan.	Seed	8–12	70–90
Peas, English	Jan.–Mar.	Oct.–Feb.	Oct.–Feb.	Seed	2–3	50–70
Potato	Jan.–Mar, Sept.–Oct..	Feb.	Sept.–Jan.	Seed pieces	8–12	85–110
Radishes	Sept.–Mar.	Oct.–Mar.	Nov.–Mar.	Seed	1–2	25–30
Radishes, Winter	Sept.–Oct.	Sept.–Nov.	Sept.–Dec.	Seed	4–6	60–70
Rhubarb	Year-round	Aug.–Oct.	Aug.–Oct.	Seed, divisions	24–30	100–150
Spinach	Oct.–Nov.	Oct.–Dec.	Oct.–Jan.	Seed	3–5	45–60
Strawberry	Sept.–Oct.	Sept.–Oct.	Oct.–Nov.	Plants	10–14	90–110
Swiss Chard	Sept.–Mar.	Sept.–Mar.	Sept.–Mar.	Seed, plants	8–10	40–60
Turnip	Jan.–April, Aug - Oct	Jan.–Mar.	Oct.–Feb.	Seed	4–6	40--60

WARM-SEASON VEGETABLES

| NAME | WHEN TO PLANT | | | PLANTING METHOD | SPACING (INCHES) | DAYS TO HARVEST |
	NORTH	CENTRAL	SOUTH			
Bean, Lima	Mar.--Aug.	Mar.--June; Sept.	Aug.--April	Seed	3--4	65--75
Bean, Snap	Mar.--April, Aug.--Sept	Mar.--May, Sept.--Oct.	Sept.--April	Seed	3--4	55--70
Cantaloupe	Mar.--April,	Mar--April	Feb.--Mar., Aug.--Sept.	Seed, plants	24--36	65--90
Corn, Sweet	Mar.--April; Aug.	Feb.--Mar., Aug.--Sept.	Aug.--Mar.	Seed	12--18	60--95
Cucumber	Feb.--April, Aug.--Sept.	Feb.--Mar., Aug.--Sept.	Sept.--Mar.	Seed, plants	12--24	40--70
Eggplant	Feb.--July, Aug.--Sept.	Feb.--Mar., Aug.--Oct.	Dec.--Feb.	Seed, plants	24--36	75--100
Okra	Mar.--July	Mar.--Aug., Aug.--Sept.	Feb.--Mar.	Seed	6--12	50--75
Peanut	Mar.--May	Mar.--April	Feb.--Mar.	Seed	24--48	75--150
Peas, Southern	Mar.--Aug.	Mar.--Sept.	Aug.--April	Seed	2--3	60--90
Pepper	Mar.--April, July--Aug.	Mar.--April, Aug.--Sept.	Aug.--April	Seed, plants	12--24	60--100
Potato, Sweet	Mar.--June	Mar.--July	Feb.--July	Plants	12--14	120--140
Pumpkin	Mar.--April, July--Aug.	Mar.--April, July--Aug.	Jan.--Feb., July--Sept.	Seed, plants	36--60	80--120
Squash, Summer	Mar.--April, Aug.--Sept.	Mar.--April, Aug.--Sept.	Jan.--Mar., Aug.--Oct.	Seed, plants	24--36	35--55
Squash, Winter	Mar.	Mar. & Aug.	Jan.--Feb.	Seed, plants	36--48	70--110
Tomato	Mar.--April; Aug.	Mar.; Aug.--Sept.	Aug.--Mar.	Seed, plants	18--24	75--110
Watermelon	Mar.--April, July--Aug	Feb.--Mar.; Aug.	Jan.--Mar., Aug.--Sept.	Seed, plants	15--60	75--95

JANUARY

❏ This is the middle of Florida's cool-season gardening. South Florida gardeners can plant mixes of cool- or warm-season crops.
❏ Weeding and almost-daily harvesting will be your major chore.
❏ During this cool but drier time, crops will use less water. Keep up your regular checks for moisture needs. Do not overwater or root rot may result.
❏ Start seeds of peppers, tomatoes, or eggplant in flats inside, so they'll be ready to plant in the garden beds in early March. Make it a first-of-the-month priority.
❏ Insects and diseases are not a major winter problem. However, caterpillars stay active. Hand pick or apply natural control. Aphids or whiteflies may also appear.

FEBRUARY

❏ Prepare soil for warm-season crops. Dig out deep-rooted perennial weeds, apply mulch, and remove weeds from rest of garden.
❏ Tend to your started seedlings. Mist to keep them moist. Begin weekly feeding of half-strength liquid fertilizer when seedlings sprout. Provide plenty of air movement. Increase fertilizer to full strength when seedlings reach garden size with 4 to 6 true leaves.
❏ Since it is still cool, plants don't require as much moisture. However, regularly check the garden to see if surface soil is dry.
❏ Whiteflies can be a problem during winter. Control with water spray, especially on undersides of leaves, when first noted. You may also see aphids, caterpillars, and mites.

MARCH

❏ Although it's time for warm-season crops, central and northern growers can plant one last crop of quick cool-season plants, such as lettuce.
❏ Plant seedlings of warm-weather crops into the beds. Be sure to water them well as they adapt to the garden.
❏ Follow instructions on seed packets for most plants.
❏ Keep up harvests and remove plants when production drops.
❏ Make sure soaker hoses and micro sprinklers are working. These are the two best systems to use in the garden. They conserve water and put it only where needed.
❏ Corn may need extra feedings. However, beans may need fewer to keep from producing lots of foliage but not as many flowers or fruit.
❏ Pests become more active this month. The leafminer may be found on tomatoes, basil, melons, beans, and cucumbers. You may also notice aphids, caterpillars, mites, slugs, and snails–hand pick or rinse with water. Look for root knot nematode damage on roots of crops at the end of their cycle.

APRIL

❏ Plant the last corn, melons, and other spring crops that need only around 50 days. Reliable hot-weather herbs include dill, oregano, chives, and thyme.
❏ As cool-season crops finish up, add new plantings. You can start sweet potatoes at home from sprouting potatoes.
❏ When adding herbs, plant some in containers. Some that have trouble surviving the hot rainy season survive in pots that can be moved. Control spreading herbs by harvesting, sharing with friends, or feeding the compost pile.
❏ It's hot and dry. Make sure plants get moisture needed for production.
❏ Tomatoes are most affected by insects and diseases. The worst are wilts and leaf spots (blight). The only controls for wilts are planting early in the season, using resistant varieties, crop rotation, or planting the next crop in hay bales or containers. You may also see aphids, caterpillars, mites, slugs, snails, and whiteflies. Hand pick or rinse with water.

MAY

❏ Crops that take heat are peppers, okra, sweet potatoes, and Seminole pumpkins. Many herbs are in full growth, but as hot rainy weather arrives, they often decline. Gather and preserve them now.

❏ When crops finish, many gardeners give up for the summer and plant a cover crop of French marigolds to reduce nematodes or legumes to enrich the soil.

❏ Harvest crops as needed. Crops left in the garden attract critters, so clean them out.

❏ After corn and melons form, no more fertilizer is needed. Most remaining warm-season crops should be fed regularly.

❏ Stay alert to numerous pests and control as needed. Look for aphids, caterpillars, leaf spots, mites, slugs, snails, and whiteflies until crop production is finished.

JUNE

❏ Try some real tropical crops like boniato, calabaza, chayote, dasheen, Jerusalem artichoke, or malanga. Start them from produce found at your local food store.

❏ Keep up harvests of warm-season crops. Preserve or share excess with friends or a local soup kitchen. Do not allow them to decline in the garden.

❏ Less watering will be required during the rainy season. Check garden whenever a few days pass between rains.

❏ Feed crops that are still actively growing with a side dressing of composted manure. Do not feed crops that are about finished with production.

❏ A few of the more common pests at this time of year are caterpillars, garden flea hoppers, leaf spots, slugs, snails, and whiteflies.

JULY

❏ Prepare beds for new plantings. Remove unproductive herbs or vegetable plants, enrich the soil with organic matter, use weed prevention measures, and solarize soil against nematodes.

❏ In mid-month, start seeds of tomatoes, eggplants, and peppers for an August planting. Feed seedlings weekly with half-strength balanced fertilizer.

❏ Don't let summer crops get out of control. Prune to keep in-bounds and they will still produce a good crop.

❏ Summer rains may provide necessary watering, but also areas that are too wet. Consider raised beds for the next crop.

❏ Container plantings may need additional feedings if growth slows or foliage yellows.

❏ Pests are still active, but summer crops are durable. They won't mind a few chewed leaves or some missing sap. Control grasshoppers, caterpillars, garden flea hoppers, leaf spots, slugs, snails, and whiteflies with hand picking and water spray.

AUGUST

❏ Get ready for 9 months of great gardening. The first crops are warm-season types, followed by cool-season crops (planted in fall), then another round of warm-season crops (planted when spring arrives). This is very different for gardeners used to planting first crops in early spring.

❏ Start easy-to-grow crops from seeds. Add a little fertilizer to water used to start new seeds. Apply first feedings 2 to 3 weeks after planting. Keep granular fertilizer or composted manure away from stems.

❏ If growing transplants, look for varieties with strong stems and bright-green leaves. Avoid spindly or damaged plants.

❏ Explore the garden daily for water needs and potential pest problems.

❏ Do not allow newly seeded areas or transplants to get dry. Water when surface soil feels dry, and mulch.

❏ Beware of cutworms. Place paper collars around the base of transplants to protect them. Other pests to watch for are aphids, caterpillars, mites, slugs, snails, and whiteflies.

SEPTEMBER

❏ Warm-season gardens begun last month in Central and North Florida should be completed as soon as possible. These regions will soon become too chilly for good production.

❏ Although it is traditional to plant in rows, it's not necessary. Some prefer using small paths between the crops, square-foot gardening, or wide-row planting arrangements.

❏ Remove weeds. Be careful not to remove sprouting seedlings.

❏ The rainy season may end shortly. Make sure irrigation system and sprinklers are working. Consider using soaker hoses and micro irrigation. Apply irrigation during early morning hours to conserve water.

❏ Caterpillars may be your major pest this time of year. Hand pick. More pests found in the fall warm-season garden are aphids, grasshoppers, mites, slugs, snails, and whiteflies.

OCTOBER

❏ The chill in the air signals the end of warm-season and the beginning of cool-season crops everywhere but South Florida. Fall also means herb-growing season.

❏ Lots of cool-season crops can be planted from seeds. It takes about 4 to 8 weeks for transplant size. Cover the seeds to keep them moist and speed germination. When first sprouts are noticed, remove covering and check for pests. Transplants are easier and quicker than seeds.

❏ Thick mulch of pine needles or straw reduces the need for cultivation, keeps out weeds, and retains moisture.

❏ Growth during cooler weather is slower, so less water is needed. Allowing several days between waterings helps plants develop deeper, pest-resistant root systems. Check to see if plants need moisture, especially container plantings.

❏ Stay alert to mite problems; rinse away with water. Other pests to watch for are aphids, caterpillars, grasshoppers, slugs, snails, and whiteflies.

NOVEMBER

❏ Don't let one garden area sit without a growing crop. If you want to take a break, consider sowing a cover crop of rye grass or maybe some pollinator plants such as tropical sage. Scatter seed over any tilled soil and water it in. It can be mowed down and tilled in at planting time.

❏ As the warm-season crops finish, have seeds or transplants of the cool-weather vegetables ready. Continue planting herbs in the garden and containers. This is the time of most rapid growth.

❏ November can produce bountiful harvests for Thanksgiving. Keep crops picked to encourage new production.

❏ Check plants and containers frequently during this cool but dry time of year.

❏ Insects are less active during cooler days. A few to still watch for are aphids, caterpillars, slugs, snails, and whiteflies.

DECEMBER

❏ Happy holidays! Your harvest can add to the big family feasts.

❏ Use seeds and transplants in small pots or cell-packs to keep the garden growing when a spot becomes available. Start tomatoes inside and plant in the garden as soon as possible to produce a good crop before summer.

❏ Keep protective covers handy, as many North and Central Florida areas may get a frost or freeze this month. A blanket or some hay may be enough to hold in some heat. Young plants can be protected with an overturned pot, box, or garbage can.

❏ Continue checking for water needs of the plants. Both in-ground and container plants can go a bit longer between waterings.

❏ The plants are still active. Maintain feeding schedules with minor variations. Increase the time between feedings.

❏ Most pests don't like the really cold weather. Most active will be caterpillars in big-leafed crops. Control by hand picking.

LAWNS
for Florida

The all-American lawn is a centuries-old leftover from European nobility, when a large lawn indicated how wealthy the residents were, because they had to pay people to hand-cut it with scythes. America's love affair with lawns began after World War II when developments were built to house families and where each household had a lawn small enough to be mowed with a hand-pushed lawnmower. Upon invention of gas-powered mowers, lawns grew larger. And in this century, the lawn acreage around the country is so vast that it is the largest irrigated crop in the country, with five times the acreage of corn, the second-largest crop. In Florida alone, there are more than 4 million acres of lawn.

Home turf can serve as a play area, supporting family football games, inviting croquet, or being the spot to tumble with a family pet. Many people prefer a simple open space created by a lawn in the landscape and as a result, lawns have become the default landscape for Florida and elsewhere. The majority of Florida's homeowners' associations (HOAs) have regulations that promote lawns to unify the look of the neighborhood.

Because it's not easy keeping a monoculture of turf grass in Florida where insects can attack and weeds can intrude in the blink of an eye, most Florida homeowners hire lawn-care companies to do the work. They routinely apply landscape-wide insecticides, fungicides, and herbicides, and since those products are not good for the soil ecosystem, they then apply synthetic fertilizers to keep the grass alive. Also, in the winter, when lawns would normally go dormant, they over-seed the whole lawn with rye grass seed, so the lawn stays unnaturally green.

There have been significant destructive environmental consequences as a result of our love of high-maintenance lawns in Florida. Some of the synthetic fertilizers, pesticides, and herbicides wash from our landscapes into the storm drain systems and have polluted our waterways, turning them green with slime or causing toxic red tides as algae reacts to all those nutrients. The products that are not absorbed right away soak into the soil and pollute our aquifers—the source of 90 percent of our drinking water. In several areas in the state, there are now fertilizer bans throughout the wet season and year-round regulations disallowing synthetic fertilizers with phosphorous, so the NPK numbers on a bag of fertilizer may now look like this: 16-0-8 or 15-0-15.

Landscape-wide insecticide applications harm our native bees and other beneficial insects and destroy their nesting habitat, which is often in the ground. In addition, there is mounting evidence that these products are not good for us or our pets either. Thankfully, for the many Floridians who would like to have a lawn at their home, there are measures gardeners can take to reduce the negative consequences of lawns.

Smaller and more sustainable lawns are growing in popularity, as they require fewer resources and lower maintenance. These lawns are less expensive to care for and less harmful to the environment.

LIVING WITH A LAWN

The best lawns grow in full-sun locations. So when planning a new lawn or reducing an existing one, many cultural problems can be eliminated by planting turf grass only where it gets a full day of sun. Keep lawns away from trees because not only are light levels too low under most of the canopy, the turf also has to compete with tree roots for water and nutrients. It is better to plant more shade-tolerant and vigorous ground covers under trees. Also, avoid putting lawns in low areas that may accumulate water and hold it for more than a few hours. Such wet locations encourage shallow root systems and disease problems. Plant rain garden plants there instead.

Keep the mower in mind when defining or redefining the edges of the lawn. There should be no vertical edges and no sharp corners. The mowing should be accomplished in one clean sweep.

Because of prolific weeds in Florida, most lawns are started with sod, but seeds or plugs are alternatives. In general, seeds and plugs are better suited to filling bare spots in older turf. Most Florida soils are suitable for growing turf. Soils rich in organic matter or clay hold more moisture than sandy soils, but both are capable of supporting a good lawn. Adding compost or other organic matter is beneficial; it helps hold moisture and provides some nutrients for turf growth, but more importantly, it adds life to the soil.

All turf types can be established by sod, which gives an instant lawn and helps shut out weeds that may grow among seeded and plugged turf. Choose the species of grass that best suits your location. Most sod is sold in rectangular portions. It can be purchased by the piece or on a pallet. A pallet of sod may contain 400 to 500 square feet (122 to 152 square m), so ask about the quantity before you buy.

Have the soil prepared and damp when the sod arrives. If for some reason the sod cannot be immediately installed, keep it in a shady location. Sod that sits on the pallet for longer than 48 hours quickly declines. Install the sod by laying pieces next to each other, abutting the edges. Cut sections to fill in any small spaces. After the sod is laid, water the turf thoroughly. A good rule to keep the sod moist is to water every day for the first week. The second week, water every other day, and the third week every third day. After 3 weeks, water only as needed to keep the turf from wilting.

MAINTAINING LAWNS

After establishment, caring for home lawns is a combination of adding nutrients, irrigating, and mowing. From March through October, most lawns need regular mowing. During the cooler months, cutting may not be necessary at all in North Florida, and just every third week or so in Central and South Florida. The general rule is to remove no more than one-third of the grass blade at any one time, but allowing more time between mowings is a more sustainable approach. Another good mowing tip is to keep a sharp blade and mow in different directions across the lawn at each cutting.

BAHIA GRASS

Paspalum notatum

HARDINESS–Zones 8–11

MOWING HEIGHT–3 to 4 inches (7.5 to 10 cm)

WATER NEEDS–Drought tolerant once established. With drought will turn brown but revives once seasonal rains return.

CARE–Provide first feeding in 3 to 4 months. Apply 16-0-8 fertilizer around March with iron feeding. Prefers acidic soil with pH between 5.5 and 6.5. Tolerates filtered open shade.

PROBLEMS–Readily forms seed heads in the summer.

USES AND SELECTIONS–Bahia grass is a good-looking lawn requiring minimal care. It's one of Florida's most drought-tolerant turf types, tough enough for backyard football games. Bahia is a multipurpose turf, growing well from seed and establishing easily from sod. Different varieties are available.

BERMUDAGRASS

Cynodon spp.

HARDINESS–Zones 8–11. Turns brown with frost but recovers with warm weather.

MOWING HEIGHT–To 2 inches (5 cm)

WATER NEEDS–Drought tolerant once established

CARE–Provide first feeding in 3 to 4 months. Apply 16-0-8 fertilizer in March to this high-maintenance lawn. Tolerates pH extremes if supplied with trace elements. Remove thatch layer once a year.

PROBLEMS–Diseases include dollar spot, brown patch, and leaf spots. An established Bermuda lawn is weed resistant.

USES AND SELECTIONS–This finely textured turf is popular on golf courses and athletic fields. It is also drought and salt tolerant. 'FloraTeX' needs fewer feedings, has some nematode tolerance, and has good potential as a care-free home lawn.

CARPETGRASS

Axonopus fissifolius

HARDINESS– Zones 8–11. Tolerates heat but turns brown with frost and slowly re-greens in warmer weather.

MOWING HEIGHT–2 to 3 inches (5 to 7.5 cm)

WATER NEEDS–Poor drought tolerance. Needs abundant water. Tolerates wet soil.

CARE–This wide-bladed turf grows in acidic soil (pH 5.0 to 5.5). It is low-maintenance, but with a little care produces good green color and dense growth. Needs less fertilizer than other lawn turf.

PROBLEMS–Produces numerous seed heads. Has poor nematode and cold resistance. Also susceptible to armyworm, cutworm, grubs, mole crickets, brown spot, and dollar spot.

USES AND SELECTIONS–Carpetgrass is also called flatgrass and Louisiana grass. This is the grass for wet, poorly drained soil. It has a shallow root system, so it needs abundant water. It does have some shade tolerance but is not as good as St. Augustine grass in lower light locations. Grows from sprigs, seeds, or sod.

CENTIPEDE GRASS

Eremochloa ophiuroides

HARDINESS– Zones 8-11

MOWING HEIGHT–2 to 3 inches (5 to 7.5 cm)

WATER NEEDS–Keep new plantings moist to encourage growth. Some drought tolerance once established, for deep-rooted lawns. Shallow-rooted lawns may need frequent waterings.

CARE–Feed at half recommended rate 4 to 6 months after new growth begins. Fertilize in March. Prefers slightly acidic soil (pH of 6.0). If pH cannot be altered, add minor nutrients. Tolerates light shade.

PROBLEMS–Gardeners in North Florida grow best-looking centipede grass, with fewest pests. In sandy, warm soils nematodes are a problem, and high pH requires periodic iron applications.

USES AND SELECTIONS–Centipede grass is sometimes called poor man's turf due to its ability to grow in infertile soils with minimal feedings. It has good green color, grows in light shade, and can tolerate drought. It can be quite vigorous with the right care and can grow from seed, plugs, or sod. Different varieties are available.

CLOVER

Trifolium spp.
Legume family: Fabaceae

HARDINESS– Zones 8-11. Tolerates heat and cold.

MOWING HEIGHT–4 inches (10 cm)

WATER NEEDS–Good drought tolerance. Also tolerates wet soil.

CARE–Because it's a legume, it fixes its own nitrogen and enriches the soil. It only grows to 5 or 6 inches (12.5 to 15 cm) tall, so frequent mowing is not necessary.

PROBLEMS–Tolerates moderate foot traffic, but not heavy use. It's a short-term perennial, so reseeding may be necessary every 3 or 4 years.

USES AND SELECTIONS–Clover used to be part of every seed mix for lawns until the 1960s, but then was considered a weed. Dutch clover (*T. repens*) seed is widely available and can be sown onto an existing, but thoroughly dethatched, lawn. There are several native clovers as well.

FREEDOM LAWN

Hundreds of species

HARDINESS– Zones 8-11. Plant mix varies depending on location and conditions.

MOWING HEIGHT–Highest setting on the lawn mower.

WATER NEEDS–Exists on natural rainfall but may look better with some irrigation when droughts occur during the growing season.

CARE–No special care except occasional mowing. In North Florida, freedom lawns go dormant in the winter and may not need mowing from November through March.

PROBLEMS–None. If one plant has problems, another one will soon fill in. It's 100 percent safe for the kids and pets all the time.

USES AND SELECTIONS–A freedom lawn is free of insecticides, fungicides, herbicides, synthetic fertilizer, over-seeding, and over-irrigation. The mixture of grass species included depends on the region and the lawn's starting point prior to conversion to a freedom lawn. If it was a St. Augustine lawn, there will probably still be this grass in many places. But if it was a meadow, the only grass may be bunching grasses. It also depends on the length of time that it's been under natural care.

RYEGRASS

Lolium spp.

HARDINESS– Zones 8-11

MOWING HEIGHT–2 to 3 inches (5 to 7.5 cm)

WATER NEEDS–Keep moist during growing season, fall through early spring.

CARE–Sow seed soon after cooler weather arrives for best growth and longest time to enjoy the bright-green lawn. Use about 8 to 10 pounds (3.5 to 4.5 kg) for every 1,000 square feet (305 square m). Germinates in 10 to 14 days. It is best sown on prepared planting soil. Till the soil, rake it smooth, and then scatter the seeds. After sowing, rake the seeds into soil lightly and then moisten. Fertilize during growing season.

PROBLEMS–Ryegrass is a cool-season grass and cannot take heat. No matter which species you choose, it will decline during spring as the weather warms.

USES AND SELECTIONS–Both the annual (*L. multiflorum*) and perennial (*L. perenne*) species are fast-growing lawns that survive during winter months. Ryegrass is often used for over-seeding and for establishing a temporary lawn and can be used to quickly fill bare spots.

SEASHORE PASPALUM

Paspalum dissectum

HARDINESS–Zones 8-11

MOWING HEIGHT–2 to 2½ inches (5 to 7 cm)

WATER NEEDS–Drought tolerant. Can be irrigated with lower-quality recycled water or salty water found in many coastal wells. Periodically flush with less saline water–such as from rainfall–to prevent salt toxicity.

CARE–This turf has a fine leaf blade and is dark green. It is tolerant of wear, cold, heat, varying soil acidity, and high salt levels. Seashore paspalum spreads rapidly. It prefers frequent and light feedings. The turf also benefits from extra potassium, but never apply it in the wet season.

PROBLEMS–Needs frequent mowing. Susceptible to armyworm, billbug, cutworm, mole crickets, sod webworm, spittlebug, and white grubs. Nematodes may also be a problem.

USES AND SELECTIONS–Ideal for use in seaside plantings or other areas where water may be salty. It can be mowed close to give a well-manicured turf look. Grows from sprigs and sod.

ST. AUGUSTINE GRASS

Stenotaphrum secundatum

HARDINESS–Zones 8-11

MOWING HEIGHT–To 4 inches (10 cm)

WATER NEEDS–Keep new plantings moist to encourage growth. Requires irrigation during drier weather.

CARE–Provide first feeding in 3 to 4 weeks. Apply complete fertilizer once in spring and fall. If turf become slightly yellow in summer, apply iron.

PROBLEMS–Check for chinch bugs, caterpillars, and brown patch during warmer months.

USES AND SELECTIONS–This is native to Florida and is probably the best all-around Florida turf. Although coarser-bladed than northern turfs, it has good shade tolerance (up to 25 percent filtered sun) and pest resistance. Gardeners like the blue-green color and vigor. Grow with mixture of shade-loving and full-sun-loving plants. St. Augustine grass has several selections suited to differing conditions, including shade, pests, and cold. Color and mowing height also vary depending on the selection. May be grown from plugs or sod.

ZOYSIA GRASS

Zoysia spp.

HARDINESS–Zones 8-11. In northern sections of Florida, Zoysia will turn totally brown with cold, and to many people it looks dead.

MOWING HEIGHT–1 to 2 inches (2.5 to 5 cm)

WATER NEEDS–Very drought tolerant, but during dry weather will turn brown without adequate water.

CARE–Sunny sites are best, but can tolerate light shade. It grows in all soil types and tolerates alkaline soils. Apply 16-0-8 once during spring and once during fall. Mechanically remove thatch as needed from this slower-growing turf.

PROBLEMS–Billbugs can cause decline in patches. They may need a chemical control.

USES AND SELECTIONS–This is a fine-bladed grass for a well-maintained look. Once established, it can beat out weeds and withstand wear. It's also drought tolerant, cold hardy, and resistant to salt levels. Many varieties are available as plugs or sod, and one type as seed. The selection 'Empire' has a wider blade and more compact growth habit.

JANUARY

❑ Gardeners usually delay adding new turf until it's a little warmer, when seeds will germinate and freezes aren't a problem for young grass. But working outdoors now is comfortable, so get areas ready.

❑ In warmer areas of the state, begin sodding and plugging.

❑ No mowing is necessary unless rye grass has been over-seeded.

❑ If grass is dormant, little water is needed. Turn off automatic system.

❑ Don't expect many pest problems during winter. If weather is warm, areas affected by brown spot disease can be controlled with fungicide. Control cool-weather weeds manually or with herbicide that permits replanting.

FEBRUARY

❑ Now is the time to establish new lawns. Prepare the site for planting. If using sod, order it to arrive the day it's needed so it isn't left on pallets. If picking it up, find out when new shipments arrive so you can get fresh sod. Soak the prepared soil before planting. Fit the pieces closely together. Water it as it is laid out so it never dries out. Start a watering program.

❑ Mow all lawns as needed, but it probably will not be necessary in North Florida.

❑ Established turf won't need a lot of water at this time of year. Help extend the time between waterings by mowing at the highest recommended height.

❑ First-of-the-year feedings start in South Florida and work their way northward this month. Apply fertilizer when the blades are dry, then water.

❑ Crabgrass is a problem this month. The trick to eliminate it is to prevent seed germination. Watch for brown spot in lawns and chinch bugs in St. Augustine grass lawns.

MARCH

❑ Lawns grow rapidly this month. Begin mowing at desired height.

❑ Now that weather is warmer, check irrigation system to make sure it hits all areas of the lawn. Adjust and replace heads as needed.

❑ Complete all feedings. This is the one time all lawn types could get a complete fertilizer with all three major nutrients. It is best to select a fertilizer with the minor nutrients also, including iron and magnesium. If lawn turns yellow immediately after feeding, it could have iron deficiency.

❑ Chinch bugs may become very active in St. Augustine grass lawns.

APRIL

❑ Watering requirements vary for different lawn types. Some can survive on only rain, but don't look lush. Stretch time between waterings by waiting until spots turn gray-green and leaves curl. Give a thorough soaking. Keep mower at highest setting. Do not apply weed killers to drought-stressed lawns.

❑ Complete spring feedings by early in the month.

❑ This is the last chance to do selective weed control without affecting your turf. Lawn caterpillars may be starting to appear. The most common are sod webworm, armyworm, and grass looper.

MAY

❑ All grass types can now be added. Whether you choose seed, sod, or plugs, prepare the soil properly.

❑ Sharpen the lawn mower blades. Mow when the lawn is dry to prevent slipping and clogging. Cut at the same recommended height year-round. Mow in different directions each time to prevent ruts. Leave clippings on the lawn.

❑ The rainy season may begin late in this month. Until it does, water as usual. Recheck your irrigation system and look for dry spots.

❑ It's the beginning of the mole cricket season for Bermuda, bahia, and zoysia lawns. Other pests may be very active too. Check for chinch bugs, dollar spot, lawn caterpillars, mushrooms, and slime mold.

JUNE

❑ During heavy rains, suppliers may not harvest sod, so you may have to wait. Be selective and make sure you get high-quality sod.

❑ This is the beginning of the wet season, and many areas do not allow any fertilization from now until November. It's a great time to fill in with plugs and seed because Mother Nature often does the watering.

❑ Keep the mower blades sharp, especially for bahia lawns.

❑ Mole crickets are becoming more obvious. Check to see if chinch bugs or lawn caterpillars are present. Using weed killers during hot weather can damage turf. Dig out, mow, or spot-kill weeds with herbicides.

JULY

❏ Give your lawn mower a midsummer checkup.

❏ It's normal for turf to turn a lighter green in July. Some gardeners don't mind, and it may be more pest-resistant turf.

❏ One disease that runs rampant during summer is "take-all root rot." It affects lawns that receive too much water, are competing with other plants, have nematodes, and are under general stress. Many other problems may affect summer lawns. Check for chinch bugs, lawn caterpillars, and mole crickets. Mow, dig out, or spot-kill weeds.

AUGUST

❏ All lawn grasses can be established during summer by seeding, plugging, or sodding. Grasses commonly grown from seed include Bermudagrass, carpetgrass, bahiagrass, and centipedegrass.

❏ Water newly seeded lawns whenever the surface feels dry. Gradually reduce watering to an as-needed basis after 6 to 8 weeks. Mow as needed.

❏ Summer rains can be counted on for most of the water. Turn the sprinkler on periodically to make sure it is operating properly.

❏ Most lawn grasses will not receive a major feeding at this time.

❏ A healthy lawn is more resistant to pest problems, but somehow sod webworms, root rots, and others still cause some damage. Check the lawn weekly for signs of decline. Look for chinch bugs, lawn caterpillars, mole crickets, and the fungus called take-all root rot. When early damage is noted take the appropriate control. Delay use of selective weed-control products another month or two.

SEPTEMBER

❏ By the end of October, bahia stops producing new shoots, but most grasses grow very well during fall. To fill bare spots, try adding plugs or sections of sod.

❏ Don't let up on your mowing. If you go on vacation, have someone do the job. Cutting it when overgrown is a real shock to the grass. Leave clippings on the lawn, unless they form piles due to infrequent mowing.

❏ Summer pests will affect your lawn for at least another month. Look for declining turf weekly. Take steps to control chinch bugs, lawn caterpillars, mole crickets, and take-all root rot. Wait until the later part of the month to begin selective weed control.

OCTOBER

❏ It's too late to start a new permanent lawn from seed, but you can continue with sodding and plugging.

❏ Keep up the mowing. The grass will not stop producing new growth until the weather really gets cool. Check your lawnmower. The blade should be sharpened monthly.

❏ It is getting drier. However, downpours or storms may dump many inches of water, which may cause some root damage. Water as needed, letting the lawn tell you when it is dry.

❏ Some pests may be slowing down. There are still a few pests that linger on: chinch bugs, lawn caterpillars, and mole crickets.

❏ Mowing, digging out, or spot-killing weeds with non-selective herbicides can continue.

NOVEMBER

❏ Gardeners often want to improve sandy soils for turf by adding organic matter, such as compost or topsoil. Another way to increase water-holding ability is by adding colloidal phosphate at the rate of 1 to 2 cubic yards (1 to 2 cubic m) for 1,000 square feet (305 square m) of lawn surface.

❏ Slow down the mowing frequency, and in North Florida, stop mowing until March.

❏ Suddenly it's the dry time, with only a few rainy days each month. Grass grows slower during cooler, shorter days. Water when the lawn tells you it is dry with folded blades and gray-green color.

❏ Looks for grubs, chinch bugs, lawn caterpillars, and mole crickets.

DECEMBER

❏ Most temporary winter lawns in Central and North Florida are planted with ryegrass, but other grasses can be utilized. They are normally not planted until cool weather is here.

❏ Mowing is continued only for temporary winter grass.

❏ It's a dry but cool time. Most lawns only need one watering a week. If cold weather is expected, it's best to water the lawn to prevent drying from associated winds. Only Bermudagrass normally needs feeding at this time of year. Use a nitrogen-only fertilizer.

❏ Only brown patch is active now. Gardeners are more likely to experience frost or freeze damage in cooler areas of the state. After the grass is damaged, maintain a moist but not abnormally wet soil. Do not apply special feeding to encourage growth. Mow as needed at normal height. Refrain from making pesticide applications. Do not panic, most will recover with warm weather. Some gardeners over-seed with ryegrass.

ORNAMENTAL GRASSES
& GROUND COVERS
for Florida

G round covers and bunching grasses offer interesting solutions to problem areas in modern landscaping.

PLANNING
GROUND COVERS: Some grow upright and others spread out across the soil surface. Ground covers often are transition plantings forming a bridge between the trees, shrubs, and lawn areas.

- Many grow in shady spots under trees where lawns and other plants can't compete with the roots.
- Fill in the hard-to-mow spots or areas where it is difficult to maintain plantings.
- Use ground covers in dry spots, areas of poor soil, and on banks.
- Some make excellent seaside plantings in areas where salt levels prevent other plants.
- Add them to containers for spots of greenery or combine with flowers.
- Use ground covers as a sustainable lawn substitute, especially where there is minimal foot traffic.

ORNAMENTAL GRASSES: You are familiar with turfgrasses—now meet their relatives. These are grasses with a bunching growth habit that grow tall and often have attractive inflorescences. They add a prairie and meadow look to the landscape and are often used in natural settings. Ornamental grasses are usually low maintenance and provide wildlife food and shelter.

- Create a view barrier, hedge, or foundation planting.
- Use as an edging, or plant in a mass to fill an area in the landscape.
- Create accent features that have showy inflorescence or colorful foliage.
- Mix together wildflowers and grasses to build a meadow.

PLANTING
Ground covers and ornamental grasses aren't very particular about planting sites. Most do best in a well-drained soil, but it can be sandy, clayey, or peaty. Care is made a lot easier if the soil is enriched with organic matter. Once established, most are drought tolerant. Here are a few tips for the best preparation:

Remove unwanted plants from the area and apply a 2-inch (5-cm) layer of mulch to conserve water and reduce weeds. Follow general planting directions on page 118. The plants should be fairly close together so the overall view is of plants, not great expanses of mulch.

CARE
Primary care involves guiding the growth of the new plants and keeping older plants in-bounds.

Ground covers may need their runners directed across the soil. If needed, creeping ground covers can have their ends pinched back to cause branching and new growth. They may also need coaxing to stay in-bounds, so bend the runners back into the ground cover area. You may need to check these plantings monthly for errant growth during warm weather. Bunching grasses don't need much attention, but in highly visible locations, you may trim them back at the beginning of February before spring growth.

WATERING

After planting ground covers and ornamental grasses, you should give each enough water to establish a root system and begin growth out into the surrounding soil. Hand water individual plants to maintain a moist root ball and surrounding soil.

Water daily for the first week or two. Then reduce the waterings to every other day for a few more weeks. When the plants begin growth and roots can be found in the surrounding soil, reduce to an as-needed schedule. Too much water can cause many ground covers and grasses to develop root rot problems. After establishment, they can mostly exist with seasonal rains.

FERTILIZING

Feeding is needed only to encourage growth during the establishment period. After ground covers grow together and grasses produce spring growth, little fertilizer is needed. Just apply a topdressing of compost once in March, if needed to encourage growth, and add mulch in the planted area. Most ground cover and ornamental grass plantings are never fertilized after establishment. They obtain nutrients from decomposing mulches.

PEST CONTROL

Most ground covers and ornamental grasses can tolerate the few leaf spots and holes made by occasional pests. See the appendix page 224 for more on pests and what actions to take.

AFRICAN DAISY

Gazania spp.
Daisy family: Asteraceae

HARDINESS–Grows best fall through spring. Tolerates light frosts. Summer rains cause rot problems.

NATIVE RANGE–Southern Africa

COLOR(S)–Yellow, orange, red flowers; blue-green foliage

PEAK SEASON–Year-round flowering

MATURE SIZE–6 to 12 inches x 12 to 24 inches (15 to 30 cm x 30 to 61 cm)

WATER NEEDS–Very drought tolerant. Does not tolerate soggy roots.

CARE–Requires well-drained soil. Does best in enriched soil. Thrives in hot, dry areas and needs full sun for blooming. On cloudy days flowers might not open all the way. When used as a ground cover, plant 12 to 18 inches (30 to 46 cm) apart. Also grown as a perennial.

PROBLEMS–May get root rot if kept too wet.

USES AND SELECTIONS–The low-growing gazania provides mounds of blue-green foliage with cheery daisylike flowers. It is invaluable in sunny, dry areas where other things won't grow. Use as a ground cover, edging, and to control erosion. It is also suitable for xeriscaping, rock gardens, and containers.

ARTILLERY PLANT

Pilea microphylla
Nettle family: Urticaceae

HARDINESS–Zones 10-11, with winter protection in colder areas

NATIVE RANGE–Florida, Mexico, Central & South America

COLOR(S)–Finely textured foliage is lime green. Flowers are inconspicuous.

PEAK SEASON–Evergreen

MATURE SIZE–6 to 10 inches x 18 inches (15 to 25 cm x 46 cm)

WATER NEEDS–Requires well-drained soil. Water well for first few weeks if it doesn't rain. Established plants will tolerate some drought.

CARE–For ground covers, space about 18 inches (46 cm) apart. Periodically remove older woody stems or renew plantings. Easily propagates from cuttings.

PROBLEMS–This durable plant holds up well in heat or cold, as well as dry and wet weather. Snails may appear but are not usually a problem. Can become weedy since seeds are easily spread.

USES AND SELECTIONS–Artillery plant fills in quickly and can be planted in beds or containers. Use under palms or other trees.

BLUE DAZE

Evolvulus glomeratus
Morning glory family: Convolvulaceae

HARDINESS–Zones 9b-11; may not survive hard freeze

NATIVE RANGE–South America

COLOR(S)–Abundant flowers are blue; foliage is silvery blue-green

PEAK SEASON–Flowering and foliage year-round

MATURE SIZE–12 inches x 24 inches (30 x 61 cm)

WATER NEEDS–Once established, it is moderately drought resistant.

CARE–Space about 12 to 18 inches (30 to 46 cm) apart. Fairly fast growing in almost any soil, requiring almost no maintenance. Fertilize lightly. In partial shade it flowers a little less.

PROBLEMS–Requires good drainage. If kept too wet, fungus may set in.

USES AND SELECTIONS–This multipurpose plant blooms in the morning. It can be used in containers (draping over the sides), hanging baskets, or in the ground. It looks good cascading down a wall, in mass plantings, in borders, and as a ground cover. Since it is salt tolerant, it also serves well in seaside gardens or oceanfront balconies. There are four species of *Evolvulus* native to Florida that may be good alternatives.

BUGLE WEED

Ajuga reptans
Mint family: Lamiaceae

HARDINESS–Zones 8-10; southern plantings prefer more shade.

NATIVE RANGE–Europe and western Asia

COLOR(S)–White, pink, purple flowers; dark-green, bronze, or purple foliage

PEAK SEASON–Spring through summer

MATURE SIZE–10 inches (25 cm) x spreading runners

WATER NEEDS–Drought tolerant but makes best growth in enriched moist soil. Water during severe droughts. Does not tolerate soggy soil.

CARE–Plant in well-drained soil, spaced 10 to 12 inches (25 to 30 cm) apart. Mulch to retain moisture and control weeds. Feed in spring, summer, and early fall.

PROBLEMS–This slow grower needs good drainage and air movement to prevent root rot, especially in summer. Hand pick any caterpillars and slugs or use recommended pest control. May grow into nearby plantings.

USES AND SELECTIONS–Useful for edging, ground covers, and mass plantings. Best suited for smaller spaces or gardens where the dense, tight foliage covers the ground in front of or around shrubs. Use around patio stones or plant in containers.

CAST IRON PLANT

Aspidistra elatior
Asparagus Family: Asparagaceae

HARDINESS–Zones 8-11; leaves are cold sensitive. Prune off any freeze-damaged leaves before spring growth begins.

NATIVE RANGE–Japan

COLOR(S)–Large dark-green leaves

PEAK SEASON–Foliage year-round

MATURE SIZE–2 to 3 feet x 2 feet (61 to 91 cm x 61 cm)

WATER NEEDS–Drought tolerant but makes best growth in moist soils. During severe drought, water weekly.

CARE–Space about 10 to 18 inches (25 to 46 cm) apart. Apply a top dressing of compost 4 to 6 weeks after planting. Cast iron plant is slow growing, requiring almost no maintenance.

PROBLEMS–Prefers well-drained soil.

USES AND SELECTIONS–It is durable, takes most soil conditions, and even tolerates deep shade. Dense tropical leaves make good backdrop for smaller plants or can be used as a ground cover. Use near patios, along walkways, in containers, or wherever greenery is desired. There are varieties with variegated, striped, and spotted leaves.

CREEPING FIG

Ficus pumila
Mulberry family: Moraceae

HARDINESS–Zones 8-11

NATIVE RANGE–Southeast Asia, Korea, Japan

COLOR(S)–Bright-green leaves; inconspicuous flower

PEAK SEASON–Year-round foliage. Juvenile plants have small oval leaves 1 inch (2.5 cm) long. On older plants the leaves are oblong, 2 to 4 inches (5 to 10 cm) long.

MATURE SIZE–6 to 8 inches x 3 feet or more (15 to 20 cm x 91 cm). It also climbs structures or trees.

WATER NEEDS–Drought tolerant but makes best growth in moist soils. During severe drought, water weekly.

CARE–Prefers well-drained soil. Space about 12 inches (30 cm) apart in compost enriched soil. Fertilize with fish emulsion in the spring after planting, but not after that.

PROBLEMS–Is an aggressive plant that can climb trees, shrubs, and nearby buildings. Periodic trimming is needed to control. Pests are usually few.

USES AND SELECTIONS–Use as a ground cover leading up to turf and walkways, as a wall covering, in hanging baskets, to cover water-garden rocks, or to cover topiaries. It forms an excellent backdrop for sunny annuals or shade-loving perennials. Some varieties have variegated or lobed leaves.

FAKAHATCHEE GRASS

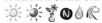

Tripsacum dactyloides and dwarf Fakahatchee grass: T. floridanum
Grass family: Poaceae

HARDINESS–Zones 8–11; dwarf Fakahatchee is cold sensitive and occurs only in South Florida.

NATIVE RANGE–Florida, Eastern North America, Central America, and northern South America

COLOR(S)–Golden-brown flowering stems; green foliage

PEAK SEASON–Summer and fall flowering; year-round foliage in most of Florida

MATURE SIZE–3 to 4 feet x 3 feet (91 to 122 cm x 91 cm). The dwarf Fakahatchee: 1 to 2 feet x 2 feet (30 to 61 cm x 61 cm)

WATER NEEDS–Once established, is drought tolerant. Tolerant of a wide range of conditions, from dry to wet.

CARE–Plant in enriched soil 24 to 36 inches (61 to 91 cm) apart. It's optional to cut back in late winter to within 6 inches (15 cm) of the ground. If they get too large for a space, they can be divided and replanted: you'll need to cut through the crown with a sharp shovel.

PROBLEMS–Pests are seldom a problem.

USES AND SELECTIONS–Also called eastern gama grass. Use as a border for native plant settings or in a meadow with asters, blanket flower, coreopsis, and other grasses. It also grows in wetlands and salt marshes.

FOGFRUIT

Phyla nodiflora
Verbena family: Verbenaceae

HARDINESS–Zones 8–11

NATIVE RANGE–Southern North America, including all of Florida, cosmopolitan in the southern hemisphere around the world.

COLOR(S)–Tiny white flowers; foliage green

PEAK SEASON–Summer and fall flowering; year-round foliage in most of Florida

MATURE SIZE–6 inches (15 cm) x trailing

WATER NEEDS–Once established, is drought tolerant. Tolerant of a wide range of conditions, from dry to wet.

CARE–Plant in any soil 10 to 24 inches (25 to 61 cm) apart. If it trails out onto sidewalks, bend it back to form a thicker covering. Some people trim it back with a string trimmer once or twice a year for a neater or denser texture.

PROBLEMS–Pests are seldom a problem.

USES AND SELECTIONS–Also called capeweed or turkeytangle. Use as an edging for native plant settings or as a turfgrass substitute. Tolerates some foot traffic. Highly salt tolerant.

LILYTURF

Liriope muscari
Asparagus family: Asparagaceae

HARDINESS–Zones 8–10

NATIVE RANGE–Southeast Asia, Korea, and Japan

COLOR(S)–Lavender, white, pink, blue flowers; green leaves

PEAK SEASON–Summer blooms; evergreen foliage

MATURE SIZE–1 foot x 1 foot (30 cm x 30 cm)

WATER NEEDS–Drought tolerant when established.

CARE–Space 8 to 10 inches (20 to 25 cm) apart in well-drained soil. Plant dwarf types closer. Some shade is preferred for most varieties. Fertilize in spring. Divide full container-bought plants before planting.

PROBLEMS–Grasshoppers. Hand pick.

USES AND SELECTIONS–This slow-growing plant is a good, all-purpose ground cover. It is also useful as a border plant and when planted with shrubs such as croton or brugmansia. Also works well planted with garden structures such as decks, steps, or boulders. Several cultivars are sold, varying in size, leaf coloration, and sun tolerance.

LOPSIDED INDIAN GRASS

Sorghastrum secundum
Grass family: Poaceae

HARDINESS–Zones 8-11; throughout the state, this native Florida grass turns golden brown in the fall and declines after flowering.

NATIVE RANGE–Florida and other southeastern states

COLOR(S)–Golden-brown flowering stems; green foliage

PEAK SEASON–Fall flowering

MATURE SIZE–2 feet (61 cm) (foliage), 6 feet (183 cm) (flowers) x 2 feet (61 cm)

WATER NEEDS–Once established, is drought tolerant. Add mulch to retain moisture. Does best if watered during drier times. Is tolerant of a range of conditions, including damp soils and light shade.

CARE–Plant in enriched soil 18 to 24 inches (46 to 61 cm) apart. Optional pruning in late winter.

PROBLEMS–Caterpillars may appear but are seldom a serious problem.

USES AND SELECTIONS–Plant clusters to create a ground cover for a golden fall accent, or mix with perennials including gaillardia, black-eyed Susans, goldenrod, and asters for a native Florida look. The large seed stalks of this native may be used in flower arrangements.

MEXICAN HEATHER

Cuphea hyssopifolia
Loosestrife family: Lythraceae

HARDINESS–Zones 8b-11; in spring, cut back freeze-damaged branchlets and they will resprout.

NATIVE RANGE–Mexico and Central America

COLOR(S)–Purple, pink, white flowers; small green leaves

PEAK SEASON–Spring and summer blooms; evergreen foliage

MATURE SIZE–12 inches x 30 inches (30 cm x 76 cm)

WATER NEEDS–Somewhat drought tolerant when established. However, it does best in enriched, well-irrigated soil. Apply mulch and do not allow to dry out completely.

CARE–Space about 18 inches (46 cm) apart in well-drained enriched soil. Add compost topdressing once a year in the spring.

PROBLEMS–Vigorously growing plants are less susceptible to pests.

USES AND SELECTIONS–Also called false heather, use this dwarf shrub massed as a ground cover, as edging, or toward the front of a planting bed, where readily visible. Also looks good in a container when used alone or as edging for a larger plant. Several cultivars are available.

MONDO GRASS

Ophiopogon japonicas
Asparagus family: Asparagaceae

HARDINESS–Zones 8-10

NATIVE RANGE–Southeast Asia, Korea, and Japan

COLOR(S)–Dark-green leaves

PEAK SEASON–Year-round foliage

MATURE SIZE–3 to 4 inches (7.5 to 10 cm)

WATER NEEDS–Drought tolerant when established. Grows in any well-drained soil. However, it does best when it is enriched. Apply mulch to retain moisture and keep down weeds. Water during severe drought.

CARE–Space about 8 to 10 inches (20 to 25 cm) apart. Although slow growing, may invade nearby areas.

PROBLEMS–Does not take heavy foot traffic. May be infected by scale.

USES AND SELECTIONS–Mondo grass can substitute for grass among steppingstones, in shady areas under trees, or on hard-to-mow slopes. The ¼-inch- (6 mm-) wide leaves have a turf-like look. Plant as filler along walkways, in large beds, or in Oriental gardens. It is an excellent ground cover for shady areas where other plants cannot take the drier or shadier conditions. Several selections are available, including a dwarf form.

MUHLY GRASS

Muhlenbergia capillaris
Grass family: Poaceae

HARDINESS–Zones 8-11

NATIVE RANGE–Florida, Eastern North America, Central America, Cuba

COLOR(S)–Pink to purple flowering stems; green foliage

PEAK SEASON–Fall flowering

MATURE SIZE–3 feet x 3 feet (91 x 91 cm)

WATER NEEDS–Once established, is drought tolerant. Add mulch to retain moisture. Does best if watered during drier times of the year.

CARE–Plant in enriched soil 12 to 18 inches (30 to 46 cm) apart. Optional pruning in late winter.

PROBLEMS–None.

USES AND SELECTIONS–Also called pink muhly or sweet grass, it provides mounds of fine, delicate foliage with flowering stalks high above them. Good as an accent, as a border planting, in perennial gardens and natural settings, or as ground cover, even in dry areas. Enjoy the fall color when mixed with other grasses, asters, goldenrod, and daisies.

ORNAMENTAL SWEET POTATO

Ipomoea batatas
Morning Glory family: Convolvulaceae

HARDINESS–Zones 9-11; often declines in winter and tends to die back in colder areas of North and Central Florida.

NATIVE RANGE–Mexico

COLOR(S)–Foliage chartreuse, dark purple, multi-hued

PEAK SEASON–Warm-season foliage; summer blossoms

MATURE SIZE–1 to 2 feet (30 to 61 cm) x trailing

WATER NEEDS–Once established, underground tubers retain some moisture.

CARE–Plant in well-drained soil. Keep pruned to control the vigorous vines and to encourage branching. Grows well in full sun, but does better with some shade.

PROBLEMS–Holes caused by beetles may be ignored in this fast-growing plant. Keep the plant within bounds.

USES AND SELECTIONS–Varieties come in several colors and are often planted together for maximum visual impact. It makes a colorful ground cover in both sun and partial shade. It also does well around the rocks and sides of water gardens. Use it to make a bold statement in container plantings, especially when cascading over the edges.

PAMPAS GRASS

Cortaderia selloana
Grass family: Poaceae

HARDINESS–Zones 8-11; in warmer areas may remain evergreen. In cooler regions turns brown after first cold.

NATIVE RANGE–Southern South America

COLOR(S)–White to pink flowering stems; green foliage

PEAK SEASON–Blooms late summer and fall

MATURE SIZE–8 feet x 8 feet (2.5 x 2.5 m)

WATER NEEDS–Drought tolerant once established. Add mulch to retain moisture. Does best if watered during drier times.

CARE–Plant in enriched soil 36 to 48 inches (91 to 122 cm) apart. Optional pruning before spring growth begins.

PROBLEMS–Keep sharp foliage away from pedestrian traffic.

USES AND SELECTIONS–Forms an eye-catching accent, view barrier, or garden backdrop. Add other grasses or contrasting native shrubs, perennials, and annual flowers for accents. Good to grow in coastal areas and for dried flower arrangements. Several varieties are available, including dwarf and variegated forms as well as pink foliage. The dwarf may be used in containers and perennial beds.

PURPLE LOVEGRASS

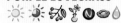

Eragrostis spectabilis
Grass family: Poaceae

HARDINESS–Zones 8-10; foliage turns reddish in fall and declines after flowering, later in South Florida than North and Central areas.

NATIVE RANGE–Eastern North America, including Florida

COLOR(S)–Reddish-purple flowering stems; green foliage

PEAK SEASON–Flowers in fall

MATURE SIZE–2 feet x 2 feet (61 x 61 cm)

WATER NEEDS–Drought tolerant once established. Add mulch to retain moisture. Does best if watered during drier times.

CARE–Plant in enriched soil 12 to 18 inches (30 to 46 cm) apart. Optional pruning in late winter.

PROBLEMS–None.

USES AND SELECTIONS–May be Florida's most attractive grass, forming compact mounds with flowers a foot above foliage, which turns reddish each fall. Use in clusters as a ground cover, add it to natural landscape areas for a Florida look, or plant for a late summer accent of color. Mix with native shrubs or wildflowers of gaillardia, asters, goldenrod, and black-eyed Susans. There are several other native lovegrasses–all are recommended.

SAND CORDGRASS

Spartina bakeri
Grass family: Poaceae

HARDINESS–Zones 8-11

NATIVE RANGE–Florida and a few other southeastern states

COLOR(S)–Brown flowering stems; green foliage

PEAK SEASON–Flowers in May through June

MATURE SIZE–4 feet x 5 feet (122 x 152 cm)

WATER NEEDS–Tolerates both wetland conditions and, once established, drought.

CARE–Plant in enriched soil 30 to 60 inches (76 to 152 cm) apart. Optional pruning in late winter.

PROBLEMS–Once established, this thin-leafed grass forms bunches. It needs room to spread and may not be suitable for small gardens.

USES AND SELECTIONS–Ideal for wetlands, marshlands, lakes, detention ponds, and canal-side plantings. It even tolerates brackish water. This versatile plant can be used to create a view barrier, accent planting, space divider, or backdrop with seasonal flowers as accents. Also use as a ground cover grouped with dwarf yaupon holly, Indian hawthorn, and juniper. There are several other Florida native cordgrasses–all are recommended.

SHORE JUNIPER

Juniperus conferta
Cypress family: Cupressaceae

HARDINESS–Zones 8-10a

NATIVE RANGE–Japan

COLOR(S)–Finely textured blue-green leaves

PEAK SEASON–Year-round foliage

MATURE SIZE–2 feet x 6 to 8 feet (61 cm x 183 to 244 cm)

WATER NEEDS–Drought tolerant when established. Grows in sandy or well-drained soil.

CARE–Space about 18 inches (46 cm) apart. Carefree and tolerant of infertile soils. Can also be trained as a bonsai.

PROBLEMS–Do not overwater or prune.

USES AND SELECTIONS–Plant to cascade over sides of low containers, drape over edges of terraces, as a low-lying ground cover, or in rock gardens. The fresh juniper smell, plus its wind, salt, and drought tolerance make this an excellent seaside planting. Mix with other salt-tolerant plants, such as agave, necklace pod, and shore natives. Several cultivars are available, including trailing and compact forms.

SUNSHINE MIMOSA

Mimosa strigillosa
Legume family: Fabaceae

HARDINESS–Zones 8-10

NATIVE RANGE–Southern North America–including most of Florida–and South America

COLOR(S)–Flowers pink; dark-green leaves

PEAK SEASON–Year-round foliage, pink flowers from spring through fall

MATURE SIZE–6 inches (15 cm) x trailing

WATER NEEDS–Drought tolerant once established.

CARE–Space about 24 inches (61 cm) apart in well-drained soil. It's a legume, so it fixes nitrogen and can grow in lousy soil. It tolerates mowing, which might be necessary a couple of times a year to cut back weeds until it fills in. Eventually it will crowd out weeds. Bend vines back from sidewalks to keep in-bounds. Trimming will stimulate new growth.

PROBLEMS–No serious pests.

USES AND SELECTIONS–Ideal for difficult conditions and areas, such as a lawn substitute, ground cover under high shade of trees, or on slopes. Only a few plants are needed to densely fill large areas. It grows low and can tolerate light foot traffic.

WIREGRASS

Aristida stricta
Grass family: Poaceae

HARDINESS–Zones 8-11; during fall, wiregrass declines after producing flowers and seed heads.

NATIVE RANGE–Southeastern states, including most of Florida

COLOR(S)–Yellow flowering stems; green foliage

PEAK SEASON–Flowers in summer

MATURE SIZE–30 inches x 30 inches (76 x 76 cm)

WATER NEEDS–Although drought tolerant, prefers water during droughts

CARE–Plant in sandy soil 10 to 18 inches (25 to 46 cm) apart. Does best with some weeding. Fertilizer is not needed, but a compost topdressing can enhance initial growth.

PROBLEMS–None.

USES AND SELECTIONS–This bunching grass is best for coverage of wide-open spaces with wildflowers. It could also be used alone as ground cover. Since it grows in poorer soils, it's ideal for site restoration. Create a Florida look with clusters of wiregrass beds among other native plantings of wax myrtles, hollies, asters, goldenrods, pines, and palmettos. Leaves are thin and wiry, with plants eventually growing to a mounded shape.

GROUND COVERS

NAME	AREA OF FLORIDA	HEIGHT (INCHES)	LIGHT NEEDED	FLOWER COLOR/ SEASON	BEST USES
Asiatic Jasmine	NCS	8–12	Sun, shade	Seldom flowers	Under trees, open areas
Beach Morning Glory	CS	4–60	Sun	Purple/Summer–fall	Banks, seashores
Beach Sunflower	NCS	12–24	Sun	Yellow/Year-round	Open areas, seashores
Bromeliads	CS	6–36	Light shade	Variable/Year-round	Under trees
Bugleweed	NC	6–10	Sun, light shade	Purple/Summer	Under trees, edging
Cast Iron Plant	CS	18–30	Shade	Purple/Spring	Under trees
Confederate Jasmine	NCS	10–18	Sun, shade	White/Spring	Under trees, open areas
Coontie	NCS	12–24	Sun, light shade	Inconspicuous	Under trees, open areas
Creeping Fig	NCS	8–12	Sun, light shade	Inconspicuous	Banks, open areas
Daylily	NCS	12–24	Sun, light shade	Numerous/ Spring-summer	Open areas
Dichondra	NCS	1–20	Sun, light shade	Inconspicuous	Under trees, open areas
Dwarf Gardenia	CS	6–12	Sun, light shade	White/Spring	Under trees, open areas
Fogfruit	NCS	4–10	Sun, light shade	White/Spring	Under trees, open areas
Holly Fern	CS	12–18	Shade	None	Under trees
Ivy, Algerian	NCS	6–10	Light shade, shade	Inconspicuous	Under trees, banks
Juniper, Chinese	NC	12–24	Sun	Inconspicuous	Banks, open areas
Juniper, Shore	NCS	12–24	Sun	Inconspicuous	Banks, open areas
Lantana, Trailing	CS	18–24	Sun	Lavender	Banks, open areas
Leatherleaf Fern	CS	18–24	Light shade, shade	None	Under trees
Lilyturf	NCS	12–24	Sun, light shade	Purple-white/ Summer	Under trees, edging
Mondo Grass	NCS	6–18	Sun, light shade	Purple-white/ Summer	Under trees, edging
Sunshine Mimosa	NCS	4–6	Sun, light shade	Pink/Spring- summer-fall	Open areas under trees, edging

N = North Florida   C = Central Florida   S = South Florida

ORNAMENTAL GRASSES

NAME	GROWTH HABIT	HEIGHT (INCHES)	INFLORESCENCE COLOR/MONTHS	BEST USES
Chalky Bluestem	Upright	12–18	White/Sept.–Oct.	Ground cover
Elliott Lovegrass	Mounded	12–24	Silver/Aug.–Sept.	Ground cover
Fakahatchee Grass	Arching	24–36	Gold/June–Sept.	Ground cover
Florida Gammagrass	Arching	12–24	Gold/Sept.–Oct.	Ground cover, accent
Fountain Grass	Arching	36–48	Purple/Aug.–Oct.	Ground cover, view barrier
Giant Plumegrass	Upright	24–30	Pink, purple/Sept.–Oct.	Ground cover, accent
Great Dame	Upright/creeping	6–12	Green/Year-round	Ground cover
Lopsided Indiangrass	Upright	12–24	Gold/Sept.–Oct.	Ground cover
Muhly Grass	Mounded	24–30	Pink/Sept.–Oct.	Ground cover, accent
Pampas Grass	Upright	72–96	White, pink/Aug.–Oct.	Accent, view barrier
Pineland Dropseed	Mounded	18–24	Maroon/June–July	Ground cover
Purple Lovegrass	Mounded	12–24	Pink/Aug.–Sept.	Ground cover, accent
Sand Cordgrass	Upright	48–60	Brownish/May–June	Ground cover, view barrier
Short-spike Bluestem	Arching	12–24	Golden/Sept.–Oct.	Ground cover
Wiregrass	Upright	12–18	Bronze/June–Oct.	Ground cover

N = North Florida   C = Central Florida   S = South Florida

JANUARY

❏ Ground covers and ornamental grasses may need some grooming. It's optional to trim top of brown grasses to the basal clumps, within 6 to 12 inches (15 to 30 cm) of the ground. Edge ground covers creeping over walkways.

❏ Water new plantings daily for first few weeks. Ground covers and ornamental grasses usually become established very quickly. Established plants only need to be watered during drought.

❏ In South Florida, many plants may begin growth; add compost only if you want to encourage growth. In Central and North Florida, wait until February or March.

❏ Most insects do not become active until growth begins. However, scale can appear at any time. Winter is a good time to control with oil spray, if applied when temperatures are above 40°F (4°C). Insects and sooty mold slowly flake off after a month or more.

FEBRUARY

❏ Most ground covers and ornamental grasses are tough, needing little site preparation.

❏ It's optional, but prune ornamental grasses just before their spring growth. You don't have to prune every year, but if there is a lot of brown among plants, do a major pruning job. Mulch after pruning.

❏ Water new plantings every day for the first week or two. For the next few weeks, water every day or two. Hand water to make sure moisture runs through the root system. Use soaker hoses or micro sprinklers where possible. Established plants usually need waterings only during drought.

❏ Most ground covers and ornamental grasses get nutrients from decomposing mulches.

❏ Aphid presence can be ignored unless populations are high. Skip the sprays if beneficial insects are present. Other pests this month are mites, mealybugs, scale, and powdery mildew.

MARCH

❏ If you have bare spots where turf won't grow, consider adding a ground cover.

❏ Very few grasses like shade. Once you have the right spot, planting is easy. With only a plant or two, just open the hole, loosen the surrounding soil, and then add the plant. When planting a large area, loosen the entire area and add lots of organic matter.

❏ Some ground covers grow out onto walkways and other plants. Trimming them back will cause more growth, so turn the stems back into the growth area instead.

❏ This is the dry season. Make sure new plantings have adequate moisture. The first month or two is usually the critical period. Older, established plants only need water during drought or when plants wilt.

❏ Mites are a common pest during drier months. Other problems include aphids, caterpillars, powdery mildew, and scales. Hand pick or rinse away with water.

APRIL

❏ Adding ground covers and ornamental grasses can continue throughout the year, though it's best to buy creeping ground covers early in the season.

❏ Now is a good time to divide ground covers. Dig the entire plant or just a portion to divide. Set the portions in the new site at the same depth they were in the garden. Add mulch and water thoroughly. Full pots from the nursery can also be divided.

❏ Established plantings can often go a week or two without irrigation. Make sure new plantings have adequate moisture.

❏ No fertilizer is needed for ground covers and grasses at this time. Add compost to containers to rejuvenate the soil.

❏ Some insects are becoming active. Check for grasshoppers, mealybugs, mites, powdery mildew, and scale.

MAY

❏ Continue planting any ground covers and ornamental grasses you might like. You don't have to give special soil preparation, but in large beds the addition of organic matter helps stretch the time between waterings.

❏ Your plants and the weeds will grow well. Once your new plants are in the ground, weed control is up to you. Add a layer of mulch, apply pre-emergence weed control product, and remember that hoeing and pulling are still good ways to control weeds.

❏ This is our last month of dry weather. Keep up regular watering of newly planted ground covers and ornamental grasses. Once established, make periodic checks.

❏ Caterpillars may be present at this time of year, so anticipate all the butterflies that you'll have.

JUNE

❏ Check ground covers that may be growing out of control. The start of the rainy season is when you can expect a flush of new shoots. Keep plants off walkways. Some ground covers can climb trunks and should be trimmed back from the base a foot or more. Continue to control weeds.

❏ Most plantings make good growth as the rainy season returns. You may not have to do any watering. However, continue to check the soil of recently added plants.

❏ With the summer rains comes the chance of rot problems. Leaf spots may also be a problem but are often minor and can be ignored. Summer pests include aphids, caterpillars, grasshoppers, and scales.

JULY

❏ If you don't have a lot of room but still want to enjoy ground covers and grasses, use a small area or plant in containers.

❏ Keep up with the growth of your ground covers. Bend them back to growing areas to keep them in-bounds. Many ornamental grasses begin flowering during early summer months. The inflorescence is the attractive portion and should be left on plants until it turns brown to feed the birds. Many gardeners like to cut and dry the flowering portions for arrangements.

❏ Mother Nature is probably helping with waterings. Continue to check the more recent plantings for water needs.

❏ For container gardens, apply compost to renew soil.

❏ Most plantings can tolerate some defoliation from the caterpillars and grasshoppers. Scale may also be active.

AUGUST

❏ Now is the perfect time to pick ground covers to fill small spaces between a building and sidewalk, or between the pavers of a walkway.

❏ Don't let the hot summer keep you from adding plants. Just be sure you have a well-prepared site before planting. Add organic material to help hold moisture. After planting, thoroughly moisten and add a mulch layer.

❏ Ground covers that bloom during spring should get their last trimming of the year.

❏ Regular rains should provide lots of water, but continue to check new plantings to make sure they are moist.

❏ Mealybugs may be found on tropical plants. Other pests and problems include caterpillars, grasshoppers, leaf spots, scale, and root rot.

SEPTEMBER

❏ The weather is becoming a little cooler, and it's easier to spend time outdoors. Garden centers are restocking plants for fall. Ground covers and ornamental grasses can be planted now. Use good planting techniques.

❏ As the rainy season comes to an end, you may have to take over the waterings. The only plants that usually need special watering are new plantings and container plants.

❏ Caterpillars are often heavy in fall. Hand pick where needed or wait for butterflies. Other active pests include grasshoppers, mites, leaf spots, and scales.

OCTOBER

❏ This is the perfect time to get outdoors and enjoy the landscape, and it's ideal for making new plantings.

❏ Many ornamental grasses will be making their fall display. If you wish, cut some of the long inflorescences to dry or use in fall displays. When the flower stalks fade, many turn brown and will support the fall birds. Also, some native bees use hollow stems for sheltering over the winter, so leave the stalks through the winter.

❏ Gardeners may begin noticing many leaf spots on deciduous ground covers during fall. Some are getting ready for winter, and leaf spotting as the leaves begin to drop is normal. Even some evergreen types are not as vigorous during fall and may develop brown to yellow patches. This is normal. Pests you might be concerned about are caterpillars, grasshoppers, mites, and scale insects.

NOVEMBER

❏ It continues to be a good time for planting. However, if only adding one or two plants, soil preparation is not needed.

❏ Most plant growth is slowing because of cool weather and shorter days. Your job is to remove ground cover growths that may be overgrown or affecting other plantings. Continue to control weeds.

❏ Cool weather means slower growth and fewer waterings. As always, continue to check new plantings to make sure soil is moist. Well-established plants seldom need watering, except in containers.

❏ Mites can remain a pest during fall. Luckily, ground covers are fairly resistant. Mealybugs may develop, especially in shady spots. Spray with water. Caterpillars and grasshoppers may still be around.

DECEMBER

❏ Shop your garden center early, because they often reduce stock in December for holiday plants. You can keep plants in containers for a while if the time is not right for planting.

❏ Little care is needed. Enjoy the meadow look of browning flower stems on grasses over the winter.

PERENNIALS
for Florida

There is a lot of variety among Florida perennials. Some are quite traditional and grow for years with normal care. Others are treated as long-lived annuals, since they may need more cold temperatures than Florida can provide. Many tropical plants produce almost continuous bloom for years in South Florida.

PLANNING

Use perennials to help make your gardening easier, because perennials may last for years instead of having to be replanted each season. They come in all heights and widths, so they can squeeze into small spaces or be clustered together to fill an entire bed, which could be dedicated to perennials or mixed with annuals in a garden. Perennials can also fill planters and hanging baskets either alone or with annuals.

Perennials provide the best displays when clustered together. Try planting groups of three, five, seven, or more of the same type in any one flower bed. Plan for their size, because they may be in a location for years.

PLANTING

Before planting, check the perennial list on pages 138 and 139. Find a site with the proper light level for the plants you would like to grow. It's important to put the right plant in the right place.

Select a site without a lot of competition to provide years of good growing conditions. Follow general planting guidelines on page 15.

Florida perennials can be planted year-round. It's best to purchase them in a dormant state at garden centers or native plant sales. Or you can grow them from seed. If growing from seed, it may work better to start seeds in containers and move them to the garden when they are an appropriate size.

After planting, add compost and then mulch to control weeds and maintain moist soil at a uniform temperature. Keep the mulch back from the base of the plants.

WATERING

Keeping soil moist is especially important during the establishment period. New garden perennials may have a limited root system that needs time to grow out into the surrounding soil. It's best to water daily for the first week or two. After that, the perennial garden can be placed on an as-needed watering schedule.

- Use the plants as a guide. If they wilt, a good watering is probably needed.
- Get to know the type of plants you are growing. Some, like blanket flower and butterfly weed, are drought tolerant. Others, including hosta and violet, like moist soil.
- Using temporary soaker hoses and/or micro sprinklers often increases the success rate of these plantings.

FERTILIZING

Most perennials are not heavy feeders. You can use a general organic fertilizer such as fish emulsion 4 to 6 weeks after planting and again the following March. Compost is still the best bet, because when you take care of the soil, it feeds your plants.

PEST CONTROL

Perennials are usually tough and durable. You may rinse away aphids, leafminers, and whiteflies, and hand pick grasshoppers. And as noted in other sections, learn to tolerate a few insects. Get to know your plants, then treat major pest problems as noted. See the appendix on page 224 for more on pests and what actions to take.

BEEBALM

Monarda spp.
Mint family: Lamiaceae

HARDINESS–Zones 8–10

NATIVE RANGE–North America, including Florida

COLOR(S)–Red, white, pink, pastel flowers

PEAK SEASON–Blooms mid- to late-summer

MATURE SIZE–2 to 3 feet x 1 to 2 feet (61 to 91 cm x 30 to 61 cm)

WATER NEEDS–Prefers moist soil, but do not overwater.

CARE–Easy to grow when provided with rich, well-drained soil.

PROBLEMS–Leaves often affected by mildew. Provide adequate air circulation and distance between plants to avoid it. Newer cultivars may be resistant.

USES AND SELECTIONS–Beebalm's big showy flower heads are irresistible to hummingbirds, and bees and butterflies also visit. Plant in wildflower and butterfly gardens. The leaves are aromatic. Common names include Oswego tea and bergamot. Many cultivars are available, including: 'Aquarius', 'Cambridge Scarlet', 'Petite Wonder', and 'Snow Queen'. Dotted horse mint (*M. punctata*) is a good native for most of Florida.

BLACK-EYED SUSAN

Rudbeckia spp.
Daisy family: Asteraceae

HARDINESS–Zones 8–9

NATIVE RANGE–Baltic region and North America, including Florida

COLOR(S)–Yellow, orange, and black flowers

PEAK SEASON–Blooms summer and fall

MATURE SIZE–2 to 3 feet x 2 feet (61 to 91 cm x 61 cm)

WATER NEEDS–Drought tolerant but also tolerates higher moisture levels

CARE–Needs well-drained soil. Salt tolerant. Requires little care. Blooms on many varieties don't require staking. Tends to be a short-lived perennial that needs replanting.

PROBLEMS–Pests and diseases aren't usually a problem on most varieties, especially natives.

USES AND SELECTIONS–Rudbeckias are good bloomers. There are nine species native to Florida with *R. hirta* being the one with the largest native range in Florida. Plant as a border, for cut flowers, or as a mixer in perennial displays with plants like beebalm, daylilies, and bunching grasses. Also good for wildflower and native plant gardens. There are numerous variations, including the PPA Plant of the Year for 1999, *R. fulgida* var. *sullivantii* 'Goldsturm', which has larger flowers.

BLANKET FLOWER

Gaillardia spp.
Daisy family: Asteraceae

HARDINESS–Zones 8–9

NATIVE RANGE–North America, including Florida; also South America

COLOR(S)–Yellow, red, and combination flowers

PEAK SEASON–Blooms summer and fall

MATURE SIZE–2 to 3 feet x 1 to 2 feet (61 to 91 cm x 30 to 61 cm)

WATER NEEDS–Drought tolerant

CARE–Plant forms tidy clumps of somewhat fuzzy foliage. Once established, it is carefree. This rugged plant is tolerant of poor soil, drought, and heat.

PROBLEMS–Trouble-free foliage

USES AND SELECTIONS–A short-lived perennial. Two species are native to Florida–lanceleaf blanketflower (*G. aestivalis*) and firewheel (*G. pulchella*). Use in xeriscape plantings, wildflower beds, and butterfly gardens. Use cheerful blanket flower for low-maintenance borders with other bright colors, including yellow daisies or coreopsis, or red salvia. Some of the best cultivars are wine-red 'Burgundy', which combines beautifully with blue perennials, and the new 'Mesa Yellow', a prolific, shorter cultivar that is a 2010 All-America Selection. 'Goblin' is a dwarf cultivar.

BLUE PHLOX

Phlox divaricate
Phlox family: Polemoniaceae

HARDINESS–Zones 8-9

NATIVE RANGE–North America, including only a few counties in North Florida

COLOR(S)–Light blue, lavender, pink flowers

PEAK SEASON–Blooms late spring through summer

MATURE SIZE–1 to 1½ feet x 1 foot (30 to 45 cm x 30 cm)

WATER NEEDS–Prefers moist conditions.

CARE–Needs humus-rich, well-drained soil and mulch to protect shallow root system. Too much sun may cause the plant to slow its growth. Feed in spring with compost.

PROBLEMS–With too much moisture and humidity, it may develop mildew. Provide plenty of air circulation, good drainage, and space between plants to help prevent it.

USES AND SELECTIONS–Blue phlox is perfect for the front of a shade border, wildflower garden, or as a woodland ground cover. The flowers are scented, explaining one of its common names, wild sweet William. Cultivars include 'Chattahoochee', which has lavender-blue flowers with dark-purple centers, and the prolific white-flowered 'Fuller's White'.

BUSH DAISY

Euryops chrysanthemoides
Daisy family: Asteraceae

HARDINESS–Zones 9-11. If frozen, regrows from base each spring.

NATIVE RANGE–South Africa

COLOR(S)–Yellow flowers

PEAK SEASON–Blooms year-round in South and much of Central Florida

MATURE SIZE–2 to 4 feet x 3 to 4 feet (61 to 122 cm x 91 to 122 cm)

WATER NEEDS–Somewhat drought tolerant. However, it flowers best with regular waterings.

CARE–Plant in any soil. Requires little care. Growth habit is loose, so trim occasionally to encourage dense growth.

PROBLEMS–Only nematodes are a serious concern.

USES AND SELECTIONS–Use this rounded plant as a tall colorful ground cover, small shrub, or perennial border. The delicate leaves are fernlike. Bush daisy also makes a nice specimen or foundation planting. It can be used in xeriscape and butterfly gardens, or in front of a fence where its loose growth is not important. *E. pectinatus* has a more compact growth habit and blooms better.

CENTURY PLANT

Agave spp.
Asparagus family: Asparagaceae

HARDINESS–Zones 8-11

NATIVE RANGE–Southern states (but not Florida), Mexico, Central America, and northern South America

COLOR(S)–White or yellow flowers; foliage light bluish-green

PEAK SEASON–Year-round foliage, but each plant only blooms once.

MATURE SIZE–2 to 5 feet x 3 feet (61 to 152 cm x 91 cm), but flower spikes can be 15 feet (4.5 m) depending upon species.

WATER NEEDS–Water when young. Very drought tolerant when established.

CARE–Requires good drainage. To improve drainage, create a mound with sandy, rocky soil. Plant at any time except while flowering. Little care is needed. It tolerates heat, drought, and some salt exposure.

PROBLEMS–Most century plants have sharp spines.

USES AND SELECTIONS–Use as specimen or grouped together. Plant in sandy beds, rock gardens, or areas without irrigation. Agaves are excellent choices for the rocky Florida Keys. A plant flowers after about 10 years, not 100, but then it dies. Normally, small offshoots will have formed by then, and these can be left in place or replanted. There are several different species, including the dwarf, spineless foxtail century plant (*A. attenuata*).

CONEFLOWER

Echinacea purpurea
Daisy family: Asteraceae

HARDINESS–Zones 8-9

NATIVE RANGE–Eastern states, including only one county in North Florida

COLOR(S)–Lavender flowers

PEAK SEASON–Blooms spring to fall

MATURE SIZE–2 to 4 feet x 1 to 2 feet (61 to 122 cm x 30 to 61 cm)

WATER NEEDS–Somewhat drought tolerant in partial shade

CARE–Plant in well-drained soil. This low-care Florida native has excellent heat tolerance. Cut back in early summer to encourage bushier growth and more flowers. Tends to be an annual in most of Florida because it requires cold winters.

PROBLEMS–None.

USES AND SELECTIONS–Use coneflowers along walkways, in borders, in mixed beds, in wildflower gardens, for naturalizing, containers, butterfly gardens, and xeriscapes. They make excellent cut flowers. New varieties 'Sunrise', 'Sunset', and 'Sundown' are orange, gold, and red.

COREOPSIS

Coreopsis spp.
Daisy family: Asteraceae

HARDINESS–Zones 8-10

NATIVE RANGE–North America, including all of Florida; also South America and the Balkans

COLOR(S)–Yellow flowers

PEAK SEASON–Blooms summer

MATURE SIZE–1 to 3 feet x 2 to 3 feet (30 to 91 cm x 61 to 91 cm)

WATER NEEDS–Drought tolerant

CARE–This carefree plant withstands intense heat and low soil fertility. It doesn't even mind salt and wind. It keeps providing masses of flowers for months on end.

PROBLEMS–Problem free

USES AND SELECTIONS– Coreopsis is the Florida state wildflower, with thirteen native species. Interest in coreopsis (also called tickseed) has increased as interest in native and drought-tolerant plants has grown. They fit in and among all sorts of other perennials, creating an appealing look that is lush and casual. Use them along walkways as well as in borders, mixed beds, wildflower gardens, containers, butterfly gardens, and xeriscapes. Cultivars provide varying petal shapes, different growth habits, and more intense colors, but the native species are best for the pollinators.

FERNS

Ferns are perennial, non-flowering plants that are grown in landscapes for their interesting foliage. There are many genera, species, and varieties of ferns, which are grouped here because most require similar care. There are a few ferns listed separately under the Tropical Plants section. Many ferns are native to Florida, but there are some non-native ferns that have become invasive. Ferns can be epiphytic or terrestrial.

HARDINESS–Zones 8–11

COLOR(S)–Green foliage

MATURE SIZE–6 inches to 6 feet (15 to 183 cm) x various

WATER NEEDS–A few ferns can tolerate some drought, but most require moist soil. Some, like the native leather fern, need constant moisture.

CARE–Terrestrial types need good drainage and enriched soil. Planting in mulch is ideal. Epiphytic ferns are usually attached to trees and live with just the moisture and dust in the air.

PROBLEMS–If you use ferns native to your area, there are no problems.

USES AND SELECTIONS–In subtropical and tropical gardens, ferns are all-purpose plants. They can hover by walkways, serve as ground covers, fill hanging baskets, creep on trees, encircle palms, and act as accents. They bring grace to everything they do.

CINNAMON FERN
(Osmundastrum cinnamomeum) Zones 9–10:

USES AND SELECTIONS–This large, bunching fern can grow to 5 feet (152 cm) under ideal conditions. Its fertile fronds are the color of cinnamon and are produced in the spring and again in the fall as the sterile fronds are fading for the winter. It likes wet feet, but can tolerate drier conditions, if there is more shade.

LEATHER FERN

(Acrostichum danaeifolium) Zones 9–11:

USES AND SELECTIONS–This is the beefiest and largest native fern in Florida, growing to 6 feet (183 cm) tall. The fronds are wide and stiff, not delicate. These large ferns look good at a natural pool's edge, a canal bank, a lakefront, or other low-lying area where its feet stay wet. For streamside, they are made to order. A single clump at a pond's edge makes a bold statement.

NETTED CHAIN FERN

Woodwardia areolata Zones 9–10:

USES AND SELECTIONS–This Florida native running fern makes a good foot- (30-cm-) high ground cover at edges of wooded areas or under single trees in a lawn. It dies back in winter, leaving only its stiff fertile fronds standing.

ROYAL FERN

(Osmunda regalis var. spectabilis) Zones 9–11:

USES AND SELECTIONS–This 4-foot- (122-cm-) tall bunching fern has deeply divided fronds for a lacy look. The spores are produced at the tops of the fronds in the spring, and once the spores are released the remainder of the fronds stay in place for the season. It prefers wet or continuously moist locations.

SWAMP FERN

(Telmatoblechnum serrulatum) Zones 9b–11:

USES AND SELECTIONS–This Florida native (also called toothed fern) is an excellent ground cover for large, moist areas, like the edge of ponds, swamps, or marshes.

SWORD FERNS:

Giant sword fern (*Nephrolepis biserrata*) and sword or Boston fern *(N. exaltata)* Zones 8–11:

USES AND SELECTIONS–Plant as ground cover beneath tree canopies and palms, since they prefer some shade. The giant grows much larger and is best suited for spacious naturalistic gardens. Two non-natives (*N. brownii* and *N. cordifolia* (both have little tubers)) are invasive in Florida. Pull out the invasives whenever possible.

FIRECRACKER PLANT

Crossandra infundibuliformis
Acanthus family: Acanthaceae

HARDINESS–Zones 9-11

NATIVE RANGE–India, Sri Lanka, and Bangladesh

COLOR(S)–White, orange, red, salmon, yellow flowers

PEAK SEASON–Blooms summer through fall

MATURE SIZE–To 3 feet x to 3 feet (to 91 cm x to 91 cm)

WATER NEEDS–Somewhat drought tolerant, but blooms best with regular moisture

CARE–Plant in well-drained, enriched soil. It loves rain, heat, and humidity. Apply compost in March. Grow as a small shrub or trim regularly to be bushy and compact.

PROBLEMS–It readily reseeds and can become weedy. Pull up all the seedlings or use a sterile cultivar like 'Orange Marmalade'.

USES AND SELECTIONS–The brilliant firecracker plant flowers stand out against their glossy, dark-green foliage. They also attract butterflies. Use this showy plant in borders, as a ground cover, or in containers and planters. Cultivars include 'Orange Marmalade', 'Tropic Flame', and 'Florida Sunset'.

FIRESPIKE

Odontonema cuspidatum
Acanthus family: Acanthaceae

HARDINESS–Zones 8-11. In colder regions, dies back in winter and resprouts in spring.

NATIVE RANGE–Central America

COLOR(S)–Crimson flowers on spikes

PEAK SEASON–Blooms midsummer through winter

MATURE SIZE–To 6 feet x 6 feet or more (to 183 cm x 183 cm or more)

WATER NEEDS–Tolerates short periods of drought. Grows best with weekly watering during dry times. Blooms best with more regular moisture.

CARE–Plant in well-drained, enriched soil. This prolific bloomer does well even in partial shade. It spreads by underground root suckers, forming clumps. Stems also root when they fall to the ground. Pruning may be necessary to control growth and also to encourage denser growth.

PROBLEMS–Usually trouble free

USES AND SELECTIONS–Use firespike as an accent, in mixed borders, and as background planting. Ideal for butterfly gardens and locations to enjoy hummingbirds attracted by the red tubular flowers.

FOUR O'CLOCK

Mirabilis jalapa
Four o'clock family: Nyctaginaceae

HARDINESS–Zones 8-11. Mulch in colder areas for winter frost protection.

NATIVE RANGE–Mexico and Central America

COLOR(S)–Red, magenta, pink, yellow, white, and bicolor flowers

PEAK SEASON–Blooms summer

MATURE SIZE–2 to 3 feet x 2 to 3 feet (61 to 91 cm x 61 to 91 cm)

WATER NEEDS–Regular moisture during growing season. Reduce watering in winter.

CARE–Plant in any soil. Does best in full sun. Because these fast-growing, tough perennials develop deep tubers, they may outlast most other perennials.

PROBLEMS–Essentially trouble free. It readily self-seeds and if not controlled when seedlings are young, tubers are difficult to remove. Plants are poisonous if ingested.

USES AND SELECTIONS–The easy-to-grow four o'clock has a long southern gardening tradition. Use in beds and borders. The sweetly scented flowers last from evening (not four o'clock) until the next morning. They are still colorful when not open. Use in gardens around patios or entryways, where the fragrance and flowers can be appreciated after hours.

GERBERA DAISY

Gerbera jamesonii
Daisy family: Asteraceae

HARDINESS–Zones 9-11

NATIVE RANGE–Southern Africa

COLOR(S)–White, cream, pink, red flowers

PEAK SEASON–Blooms summer through fall

MATURE SIZE–To 18 inches x 12 inches (to 46 cm x 30 cm)

WATER NEEDS–Allow to dry out between waterings. Avoid soggy soils.

CARE–Plant in deep, well-drained, enriched soil. Prefers full sun. Feed monthly throughout summer or use time-release fertilizer. Use fertilizer containing iron and magnesium.

PROBLEMS–Treat as an annual in areas with prolonged freezes or plant in containers and provide winter protection. The plant can rot (newer varieties have most problems) when watered too much or planted too deep. Hand pick caterpillars and cutworms.

USES AND SELECTIONS–Use as a border plant, in containers, or anywhere bright color is needed. Plant a bed with a single color or mix-n-match. Also called Transvaal daisy, gerberas make long-lasting cut flowers. There are single and double flower forms, with blooms reaching 7 inches (18 cm) across. Select old garden varieties for best growth and in-ground planting.

GOLDENROD

Solidago spp.
Daisy family: Asteraceae

HARDINESS–Zones 8-11

NATIVE RANGE–Cosmopolitan across much of the world, including Florida

COLOR(S)–Yellow flowers

PEAK SEASON–Blooms late summer to fall

MATURE SIZE–1 to 6 feet (30 to 183 cm), depending on species.

WATER NEEDS–Tolerates moist to dry conditions

CARE–Plant in any well-drained soil; even poor soils produce bountiful spires of golden flowers. These perennials are easy to care for and tough enough for roadside plantings.

PROBLEMS–Erroneously blamed for causing hay fever. Pollen grains are heavy and sticky because they are insect pollinated. Wind-pollinated ragweed, with its insignificant flowers, blooms at the same time.

USES AND SELECTIONS–Goldenrod's sunny color complements other mid- and late-season bloomers. Besides nineteen native Florida species, there are some terrific cultivars. Plant goldenrod in mixed or single species wildflower gardens and in native plant gardens. Choose natives to better support pollinators. 'Fireworks' is a compact, clump-forming plant, 3 to 4 feet (91 to 122 cm) tall. 'Golden Fleece' is a dwarf selection, less than 2 feet (61 cm) tall, that's ideal for smaller garden spaces.

HOSTA

Hosta cultivars
Asparagus family: Asparagaceae

HARDINESS–Zones 8-9a

NATIVE RANGE–Eastern Asia, Korea, and Japan

COLOR(S)–Green, blue-green, chartreuse, variegated foliage; lavender, white flowers

PEAK SEASON–Bloom period varies by species and cultivar

MATURE SIZE–1 to 2 feet x 1 to 5 feet (30 to 61 cm x 30 to 152 cm)

WATER NEEDS–Requires constant moisture, especially during summer.

CARE–Plant in enriched soil. Hosta only grows in northernmost Florida since it doesn't tolerate extended heat and humidity and requires cold winters. Check for the cultivars that grow well in your area.

PROBLEMS–Slugs and snails are common pests. Hand pick.

USES AND SELECTIONS–Plant hosta in shady borders, mass plantings, containers, and along walkways. Sometimes the flowers, which appear on an upright spike, are fragrant. Don't expect hosta plantings in Florida to look as lush as those in more temperate zones.

MILKWEEDS

Asclepias spp.
Dogbane family: Apocynaceae

HARDINESS–Zones 8–11. If it freezes back, it usually returns in spring.

NATIVE RANGE–North America, including all of Florida; Central & South America and sub-Saharan Africa

COLOR(S)–Pink, white, red, orange, and yellow flowers

PEAK SEASON–Blooms spring to fall

MATURE SIZE–10 inches to 4 feet x 6 inches to 3 feet (25 to 122 cm x 15 to 91 cm) depending upon species

WATER NEEDS–Some species are drought tolerant once established, while others like pink swamp milkweed (*A. incarnata*) require more moisture.

CARE–Some of the milkweeds are easy to grow, while others require specific conditions.

PROBLEMS–Aphids may infest the leaves. Milkweeds are poisonous if ingested.

USES AND SELECTIONS–Plant in perennial borders, wildflower gardens, and for naturalizing. This exceptional butterfly plant is important as a nectar source and larval food for Monarchs and other butterflies. The unusual pods are used in dried arrangements. There are more than a dozen milkweeds native to Florida, but scarlet milkweed (*A. curassavica*) is a non-native species often sold in the trade that causes problems for Monarch butterflies. If you have this species, cut to the ground from late Nov. through Feb.

PENTAS

Pentas lanceolata
Madder family: Rubiaceae

HARDINESS–Zones 9–11. Use as annual in colder locations.

NATIVE RANGE–Arabian Peninsula and eastern Africa

COLOR(S)–Pink, white, lilac, red blooms

PEAK SEASON–Spring through summer

MATURE SIZE–To 30 inches x 18 inches (to 76 cm x 46 cm)

WATER NEEDS–Water new plantings daily for a week or two. Taper off to water once or twice weekly.

CARE–These rapid, easy-care growers need good drainage. Use compost at planting time, and again each March. Cut back in early spring to rejuvenate. They get woody and leggy after 3 or 4 years. Take cuttings to replace old plants with new. Cover during freezes for protection in Central Florida.

PROBLEMS–Control spider mites with water spray or horticultural oil.

USES AND SELECTIONS–Mix with other butterfly plants. Use a wave of single color for best effect and to attract butterflies. Plant in a meadow with other wildflowers. Both regular and dwarf sizes are available, so use as background shrubs or foreground flowers.

PERIWINKLE

Catharanthus roseus
Dogbane family: Apocynaceae

HARDINESS–Zones 8–11

NATIVE RANGE–Madagascar

COLOR(S)–Pink, white, rose, purple flowers

PEAK SEASON–Year-round blooms

MATURE SIZE–To 24 inches x 12 inches or more (to 61 x 30 cm or more)

WATER NEEDS–Keep new plantings moist for first month or so, then gradually taper off watering. Don't water too much.

CARE–Prefers dry, sandy soil. Don't pamper. Relatively drought resistant when established; heat tolerant. An application of compost at planting is sufficient. They look best when trimmed.

PROBLEMS–Poisonous if ingested. Newer selections less susceptible to rot problems.

USES AND SELECTIONS–Plant in beds, containers, and window boxes. Use as edging, ground cover, or camouflage for leggy shrubs. White periwinkles are also visible at night. There are many beautiful selections with different colors and growth habits. These beautiful, rugged plants were among the first flowering plants traded by South Florida pioneers.

PLUMBAGO

Plumbago auriculata
Plumbago family: Plumbaginaceae

HARDINESS–Zones 9-11. Prune freeze damage after spring growth begins.

NATIVE RANGE–Southeastern Africa

COLOR(S)–Cobalt-blue flowers

PEAK SEASON–Blooms spring through summer

MATURE SIZE–3 to 4 feet x 8 feet (91 to 122 cm x 2.5 m)

WATER NEEDS–Moderately drought tolerant when established. Water during dry season.

CARE–Plumbago blooms best with enriched soil. Apply compost in March each year. The plant falls over and roots, so prune to keep in-bounds. Or, tie to supports such as arbors or gates for a dramatic effect. Prune back hard at the end of winter.

PROBLEMS–Provide good air movement to avoid summer leaf and stem diseases.

USES AND SELECTIONS–Use as a short shrub or giant ground cover. The color complements magenta bougainvillea or yellow flowers. Because plumbago sprawls, it can serve as an underplanting around taller shrubs. The mounding shape also works well at an entry gate or in containers and planters. Red and white varieties are available.

POINSETTIA

Euphorbia pulcherrima
Spurge family: Euphorbiaceae

HARDINESS–Zones 9b-11. Frosts and freezes damage stems and foliage.

NATIVE RANGE–Mexico

COLOR(S)–Red, white, pink bracts that look like flowers

PEAK SEASON–Winter

MATURE SIZE–Varies

WATER NEEDS–Keep moderately moist, but never wet

CARE–Move holiday poinsettias outdoors when the weather warms. Before planting in full sun, gradually accustom it to increasing light levels. Plant in enriched, well-drained soil. Prune to within 12 to 18 inches (30 to 46 cm) of the ground in early spring after blooming is over and frost danger has passed. Prune until early September to get a compact plant.

PROBLEMS–Do not plant near night lights, because poinsettias need long nights for flowering. One flash of light after mid-September will stop the flowering. Normally, it flowers at Winter Solstice. Some people are sensitive to the sap of poinsettias, but they are not poisonous to people or pets.

USES AND SELECTIONS–The species grows to 10 feet (3 m) and has less showy bracts (often thought to be the flowers). A native poinsettia, painted leaf (*E. cyathophora*), occurs throughout Florida and has similar but smaller set of bracts that turn red with the long nights.

SHASTA DAISY

Leucanthemum x superbum
Daisy family: Asteraceae

HARDINESS–Zones 8-9a

NATIVE RANGE–Eurasia

COLOR(S)–White flowers with orange centers

PEAK SEASON–Blooms spring and summer

MATURE SIZE–1 to 3½ feet x 2 to 3 feet (30 to 107 cm x 61 to 91 cm)

WATER NEEDS–Drought tolerant

CARE–Plant in enriched, well-drained soil. Easy to grow well.

PROBLEMS–Performs better in cooler summers, so provide afternoon shade and water during summer. Grow as an annual in Southern Florida.

USES AND SELECTIONS–Use for long-lasting cut flowers, mass plantings, and in meadows and butterfly gardens. Shasta daisy's white blooms also make beautiful additions to night gardens. Find a locally adapted selection for best growth in your area of Florida. There are many cultivars. 'Becky' is long blooming and stands up to heat and humidity. It won the 2003 PPA Award. Shorter varieties, like 'Esther Read', are also available. The long-blooming 'Aglaia' is fringed, for a totally different look.

SPANISH BAYONET

Yucca aloifolia
Asparagus family: Asparagaceae

HARDINESS–Zones 8-11

NATIVE RANGE–Southeastern states, including all of Florida; Central America

COLOR(S)–White flowers

PEAK SEASON–Evergreen foliage; spring blooms

MATURE SIZE–8 to 12 feet x 4 feet (2.5 to 3.5 m x 122 cm)

WATER NEEDS–Drought tolerant

CARE–Requires excellent drainage

PROBLEMS–The sharp leaf tips make an effective home-protection system when planted along property lines. Avoid planting in areas where children play or visitors may walk.

USES AND SELECTIONS–Salt and drought tolerant; group Spanish bayonet with other plants that don't need much water, in seaside gardens, or in beds with plenty of sand. They are interesting for vertical elements, as background plants, or at fence corners. Low-growing shore juniper can be used to accent a clump of these growing on sand dunes. There are two other natives that are somewhat shorter: Adam's needle (*Y. filamentosa*) and moundlily yucca (*Y. gloriosa*).

STOKES' ASTER

Stokesia laevis
Daisy family: Asteraceae

HARDINESS–Zones 8-9

NATIVE RANGE–Southeastern states, including North Florida

COLOR(S)–Blue, lavender, yellow, white flowers

PEAK SEASON–Blooms late spring and summer

MATURE SIZE–1 to 2 feet x 1 to 2 feet (30 to 61 cm x 30 to 61 cm)

WATER NEEDS–Prefers moist soil.

CARE–Does best in enriched soil. Requires little care.

PROBLEMS–Untroubled by pests

USES AND SELECTIONS–The large flowers are up to 4 inches (10 cm) across. Plant at the front edges of mixed wildflower and butterfly gardens as well as containers and cutting gardens. Besides the Florida native species, there are several cultivars. Two of the best cultivars are lavender-blue 'Blue Danube' and powder-blue 'Klaus Jelitto'. 'Alba' is white and 'Mary Gregory' is yellow. There are also dwarf varieties with compact growth.

VARIEGATED FLAX LILY

Dianella tasmanica
Asphodel family: Asphodelaceae

HARDINESS–Zones 8-11

NATIVE RANGE–Southeastern Australia, including Tasmania

COLOR(S)–White and green foliage

PEAK SEASON–Evergreen

MATURE SIZE–To 3 feet x to 3 feet (to 91 cm x to 91 cm)

WATER NEEDS–Very drought tolerant

CARE–Plant in any well-drained soil. Dianella is somewhat salt tolerant and tough enough for street plantings. It will grow in most light levels.

PROBLEMS–Parts may be poisonous if eaten.

USES AND SELECTIONS–This plant is grown for its foliage; the small blue flowers are insignificant. The brightly colored leaves complement both flowering and foliage plantings. It can also lighten a dark tropical shade garden. Use it as ground cover, edging, or background planting for shorter annuals or perennials. It is suitable for containers as well as xeriscape gardens. Some cultivars are available.

VERONICA

Veronica spicata
Plantain family: Plantaginaceae

HARDINESS–Zones 8-9a

NATIVE RANGE–Eurasia

COLOR(S)–Blue-purple, red flowers

PEAK SEASON–Blooms summer

MATURE SIZE–1 to 2 feet x 1 to 2 feet (30 to 61 cm x 30 to 61 cm)

WATER NEEDS–Prefers average moisture levels, neither too wet nor too dry.

CARE–Plant in average soil. This carefree perennial does well when growing in the northern parts of the state.

PROBLEMS–Doesn't do well in the extended heat and humidity of some central areas and Southern Florida. Pests and diseases are not a problem.

USES AND SELECTIONS–With its full, showy flower spike, veronica is a good choice for sunny or partially sunny perennial displays. Its long, dense flower spikes appear throughout the summer. Use with other mid-border perennials. One of its most sensational editions is the 18- to 20-inch- (46- to 51-cm-) high 'Sunny Border Blue', which won top PPA honors in 1993 and continues to be popular. Other attractive species form 8-inch (20-cm) compact dwarf mounds or have silvery-gray leaves.

WILD PETUNIA

Ruellia caroliniensis
Acathus family: Acanthaceae

HARDINESS–Zones 8–11. May freeze to ground but will regrow from roots.

NATIVE RANGE–Mid-Atlantic and southeastern states, including all of Florida

COLOR(S)–Blue-lavender flowers

PEAK SEASON–Summer blooms

MATURE SIZE–20 inches (51 cm) x various

WATER NEEDS–Water daily for a week, then gradually taper off. Drought tolerant once established. Do not keep too wet.

CARE–Little care is required after it is established. Not fussy about soil. Can reseed themselves, given right conditions.

PROBLEMS–This is a Florida native. It is less compact and bushy than numerous invasive non-native ruellias sold at nurseries, including Mexican petunias, which are a Category I invasive plant. Consider this when selecting plants for your garden.

USES AND SELECTIONS–Ruellia works well in butterfly gardens and water-conserving native areas.

YARROW

Achillea millefolium
Daisy family: Asteraceae

HARDINESS–Zones 8–9

NATIVE RANGE–Cosmopolitan in the northern hemisphere, including North Florida

COLOR(S)–Yellow, white, red, rose, pink, salmon, or mixed flowers

PEAK SEASON–Summer blooms

MATURE SIZE–2 to 3 feet x 2 to 3 feet (61 to 91 cm x 61 to 91 cm)

WATER NEEDS–Drought tolerant once established

CARE–Once established, the plants are self-sufficient. The flat-topped blossoms, usually up to 5 inches (12.5 cm) across, are actually tight clusters of tiny flowers.

PROBLEMS–In the warmer parts of the state, yarrow may not be as reliable as a flower. However, it can be used for its bright green, delicate foliage.

USES AND SELECTIONS–Ideal in locations with plenty of sun and average soil. Yarrow provides good color all summer long. It looks great in sweeps or clumps, or interspersed throughout a perennials bed–anywhere you want dependable color. They make good cut flowers, fresh or dried. The ferny foliage at the base of the plants makes an attractive, gray-green, off-season ground cover.

PERENNIALS

NAME	AREA OF FLORIDA	HEIGHT (INCHES)	WIDTH (INCHES)	FLOWER COLOR/ SEASON	LIGHT NEEDED
African Iris	Throughout	24	24	White, blue, yellow/ Year-round	Sun–light shade
Angelonia	Throughout	18	12	White, purple/ Year-round	Sun
Beebalm	NC	36	30	Reddish/April–June	Sun
Bird of Paradise	CS	36	36	Orange, blue/ Year-round	Sun–light shade
Blanket Flower	Throughout	18	18	Yellow, orange, red/ Mar.–Nov.	Sun
Blue Daze	Throughout	12	18	Blue/Year-round	Sun
Blue Ginger	CS	36	24	Blue/May–Oct.	Light shade
Blue Phlox	N	12	12	Blue/Mar.–April	Light shade
Blue Sage	CS	60	30	Blue/Dec.–Mar.	Light shade
Bush Daisy	Throughout	24	24	Yellow/Year-round	Sun–light shade
Milkweed	Throughout	36	36	Yellow, orange/ Year-round	Sun–light shade
Cardinal's Guard	CS	72	48	Scarlet/ May–Oct.	Light shade
Cat's Whiskers	CS	36	30	White, lavender/ Mar.–Nov.	Sun–light shade
Coneflower	NC	30	12	White, purple/ April–Aug.	Sun
Coreopsis	Throughout	18	18	Yellow/April–Oct.	Sun
Crossandra	Throughout	12	12	Orange/May–Oct.	Sun–shade
False Dragon Head	Throughout	24	24	White, pink, lavender/Sept.–Oct.	Sun–shade
Firespike	Throughout	72	36	Red/Year-round	Sun–light shade
Four O'Clock	Throughout	36	36	White, yellow, red/ April–Oct.	Sun–light shade
Gaura	NC	24	18	White, pink/Year-round	Sun
Gerbera Daisy	Throughout	18	18	Varied/Year-round	Sun–light shade
Goldenrod	NC	36	24	Yellow/May–Oct.	Sun

N = North Florida   C = Central Florida   S = South Florida

PERENNIALS

NAME	AREA OF FLORIDA	HEIGHT (INCHES)	WIDTH (INCHES)	FLOWER COLOR/ SEASON	LIGHT NEEDED
Heliconia	CS	60	24	Yellow, orange, red/ Year-round	Sun–light shade
Hosta	NC	18	18	White, lavender/ June–Aug.	Shade
Jacobinia	CS	48	36	White, pink/Year-round	Shade
Lantana	Throughout	24	24	Cream, yellow, red, lavender/Year-round	Sun
Lion's Ear	Throughout	48	18	Orange/Oct.–April	Sun
Mexican Heather	Throughout	18	18	White, purple/Year-round	Sun–light shade
Pentas	Throughout	48	36	White, pink, red, lavender/Year-round	Sun–light shade
Philippine Violet	Throughout	48	36	White, lavender/ Sept.–April	Sun–light shade
Poinsettia	CS	72	72	White, pink, red, bracts/Dec.–Mar.	Sun–light shade
Black-eyed Susan	NC	30	18	Yellow/May–Oct.	Sun
Ruellia	Throughout	36	24	Blue, violet, pink/ April–Nov.	Sun–light shade
Salvia	Throughout	48	48	Blue, red, pink, white, yellow/Year-round	Sun
Shasta Daisy	NC	24	12	White/May–June	Sun
Shrimp Plant	Throughout	60	48	Reddish-brown/ March–Oct.	Sun–light shade
Stokes' Aster	Throughout	12	12	White, blue/May–July	Sun–light shade
Veronica	NC	18	18	Blue, white/May–July	Sun–light shade
Violet	NC	10	12	White, blue/Mar.–June	Light shade
Yarrow	NC	18	18	Yellow, rose, white/ May–June	Sun
Yellow Alder	CS	24	24	Yellow/Year-round	Sun

N = North Florida   C = Central Florida   S = South Florida

JANUARY

❏ Protect cold-sensitive plants. Move containers to warmer area. Cover plantings to the ground with blankets or cloths. (Plastic provides little protection.) Turn trashcans or cardboard boxes over plants. Use outdoor-approved electric lights under covers for a little heat.

❏ Use perennials for bouquet material. Some provide only greenery this month, but many have flowers. A little pruning can also be done now.

❏ Most plantings need minimal amounts of moisture. Give good soakings when watering is required. Keep new plantings extra-moist for first few weeks. Then gradually reduce waterings to an as-needed basis.

❏ Plants are not very active this month. Yellowing plants in southern regions can receive a top dressing of compost to enrich the soil.

❏ Cut away winter damage to prevent rot problems and improve appearance. A few mealybugs, slugs, and snails might still be a problem.

FEBRUARY

❏ February can be quite cold, with frosts and freezes in Central and North Florida. By month's end, most areas enjoy consistently warm weather.

❏ Cold-hardy perennials can be planted now. Keep less hardy plants in their containers until after the average last frost date.

❏ Don't rush to prune out dead or declining portions, as some cold may linger. When winter is over, take out brown plant portions and do any reshaping.

❏ It won't hurt to get a little jump on spring with composting.

❏ Bugs and diseases start to become more active, mostly in South Florida. Look for aphids, mealybugs, slugs, snails, and powdery mildew.

MARCH

❏ There is a diminishing chance of frost in North Florida, and all Florida gardeners can begin perennial plantings. Most grow well during the warmish days and cool nights ahead.

❏ Now is the time to direct plant growth. Prune to correct lopsided growth and nip out tips of developing shoots to encourage fuller plants. Avoid trimming shoots that are starting to flower.

❏ Separate plantings into heavy- and low-water-use areas so irrigation systems can be run only as needed. Keep plants on a low-water usage program. It helps them develop a deeper root system, discourages many pests, and saves watering dollars.

❏ Apply the yearly topdressing of compost this month. Give new plants extra half doses of compost to encourage growth.

❏ Welcome beneficial insects such as lady beetles, lacewings, and praying mantis. Watch for the bad ones: aphids, mealybugs, slugs, and snails. Hand pick or spray with water.

APRIL

❏ If large plants are overgrowing their neighbors, either prune them or divide and transplant them to other areas.

❏ Remove fading flower heads or leave the seed for the birds.

❏ Once perennials establish a good root system, they will draw moisture stored in the ground. Improve sandy soil with compost to hold extra moisture.

❏ Garden fleahoppers are becoming noticeable. Other April garden pests are aphids, mealybugs, slugs, snails, and powdery mildew. Control with a water spray.

MAY

❏ Alkaline soil close to cement walls or foundations may keep acid-loving plants from doing well. Transplant them and replant the area with plants that do well in neutral or alkaline soil.

❏ Make sure each plant has room to grow. Label all perennials so they aren't forgotten during the dormant season.

❏ Leaves damaged by leafminers can be removed or ignored. Control leaf spot with fungicide. Aphids, mealybugs, slugs, and snails could be present.

JUNE

❏ Perennials are not fussy and can be dug and divided almost any time of year. During hot summer months you have choices when dividing: move them to a new bed, grow them in containers, or give them to friends.

❏ The daily rains should do most of the watering this month.

❏ Stop all generalized feedings as the rains return. Too much of it might end up in our waterways and aquifers.

❏ Many perennials have toughened up after spring growth, so bugs don't find them as tasty. New pests may include grasshoppers, katydids, slugs, and snails. Hand pick. Aphids on new growth may be controlled by lady beetles.

JULY

❏ Plan other perennial gardens to replace problem turf areas or old annual beds.

❏ If purchasing perennials now, either add during a cooler time of day or keep them in their pots until fall. Just trim back overgrown portions and keep them well composted.

❏ Cut back stems overhanging walks and pinch out tips of lanky plants to encourage denser growth.

❏ Summer rains still provide most water needs Check container plantings daily. They may dry quickly in the heat.

❏ Some pests are sure to be feeding. Many can be tolerated if only a few plant portions are affected. Hand pick when possible. If pests are more numerous, you may need an insecticide.

AUGUST

❏ If you started rooting cuttings a month or so ago, they may be ready for containers. If you tug a little and they resist, roots are forming. Lift out gently. When the root ball is about the size of a quarter, it's ready for a pot. Most transplants should then grow rapidly and be ready for the garden in 6 to 8 weeks.

❏ Correcting poor drainage can prevent root rot. Aphids, garden fleahoppers, grasshoppers, slugs, and snails are active and may need control.

SEPTEMBER

❏ A long, hot summer is hard on plants, and many spots may need renovation. If you have some replacements from cuttings, divisions, or seeds, you will be ready.

❏ Cut back to a branch angle or bud, or to the ground. If you want a plant to fill in from the base, cut about a foot above where new branches should begin. A good pruning now prepares plantings for growth in milder fall weather.

❏ Be prepared to water more often if the rainy season fades away early.

❏ Poinsettias form their flower buds next month, but only if they have no nighttime light. Move containers to an area with no outdoor lights, or cover plants near streetlights from before sundown until sunrise.

❏ With drier weather, mites increase. Pests that continue their activity through fall are aphids, garden fleahoppers, grasshoppers, slugs, and snails.

OCTOBER

❏ Prepare beds for fall planting. With new plants, be conscious of water needs, because the dry season is coming. Consider using perennials in large pots of varying sizes. Container gardens can last for months, but gradually the plants run out of room. When this happens, remove the perennials and add them to the landscape.

❏ Container plantings should continue with their liquid fertilizer feeding every other month and should receive a compost topdressing.

❏ Some pests will fade. However, stay alert to the presence of aphids, garden fleahoppers, mites, slugs, and snails.

NOVEMBER

❏ This is a pleasurable time to add perennials to the landscape. Consider keeping new cold-sensitive ones in containers in northern areas until spring.

❏ Mulches can be very important during fall and winter. Besides retaining moisture, loose mulch near plants can provide cold protection. Keep a bale or two of weed-free hay or pine needles handy for protection when cold is predicted.

❏ Edging makes perennial beds look more attractive and can be done any time. However, it is a lot easier during these cooler months.

❏ Perennials don't need much water during cooler months and can exist for a week or more without irrigation. Water only when necessary.

DECEMBER

❏ Perennials can be planted at any time. Most garden centers are clearing their shelves, so look for good buys and keep warm until spring. More perennials will become dormant with cooler temperatures.

❏ Beware of freezing temperatures by month's end. Keep cold protection ready for sensitive perennials. Although South Florida gardeners can often ignore this cold talk, they must stay alert to surprise freezes.

❏ Most plants need minimal watering during this dry, cool time of year. Most can last a week or more without a watering if they are mulched. Only plants in pots should be of real concern and checked daily.

❏ Cold weather in Florida slows insect pests down. Plants in protected locations and in warmer areas of the state may find some aphids, mites, slugs, and snails still active.

SHRUBS
for Florida

S hrubs build unity and layers in the landscape design with repeating foliage color and leaf shape. Shrubs may bear attractive flowers, colorful berries, and unique leaf shapes. Some only offer seasonal interest; when the show is over, they fade into the background with other landscape plantings. Others are on display year-round. These are often permanent accents given a prominent spot where they are sure to be noticed by visitors.

Shrubs can be used for hedges, hedgerows, or screening of sights, sounds, and dust. Small shrubs can be used as foundation plantings. Cluster shrubs together with trees to create good habitat. You can probably think of other uses for shrubs in your landscape.

PLANNING

Consider shrubs to be a long-term feature in your landscape. Yes, they could be dug up and moved, but it's not a fun job, and for this reason, it's wise to have a plan.

In our shrub tables (pages 160 to 162), we have tried to make the selection of shrubs easy by noting the best regions for each. Do your research to determine whether or not a shrub is suited to your area. Natives are always a good choice. How many shrubs do you need? Should they be tall or small? Do you want flowers?

It is usually best to plant a cluster, using odd numbers to avoid symmetrical designs. Use the eventual width of the plants as a guide when deciding how many to plant in a space (half to three-quarters the width is the best between-plant spacing). Arrange plants according to light requirements. Don't allow tall plants to hide smaller shrubs.

PLANTING

Most shrubs grow well in sandy or clay soil, but you can make care a lot easier by enriching these sites with organic matter. Work in compost, coconut coir, or composted manure. Use the general planting directions in the introduction. (See page 15.)

Make sure the soil has good drainage. If in doubt, mound up the planting site a bit to help extra moisture move away from the root system. In some wet locations, consider using more formal raised beds, or developing swales to move moisture to other areas of the landscape. To prevent soil from washing away, avoid planting shrubs near the dripline of a roof.

CARE

Don't trim shrubs for a year after planting, but then they may need direction, whether a light pruning to keep limbs from reaching over paths, or a full seasonal pruning to renew vigor. Make sure you prune the plants at the best time so as not to remove flower buds from the more colorful types.

WATERING

Newly planted shrubs need regular attention. How long this period of scrutiny lasts depends on the time it takes the plants to develop roots in the surrounding soil. Some, like azaleas, may take a year or two to establish.

FERTILIZING

One way to promote growth is by using compost to enrich the soil and fish emulsion to augment the nutrients. During good growing weather, shrubs can quickly convert nutrients into new stems and foliage.

- NEW PLANTINGS: Feed lightly 6 to 8 weeks after planting, and again the following March.
- ESTABLISHED PLANTINGS: Apply compost in March if needed to maintain growth and good plant color. Water thoroughly. There is no need to remove mulch—watering moves the nutrients into the ground.

PEST CONTROL

Shrubs generally tolerate pests, some more than others. Some insect damage is very noticeable in the early stages, and this means that the shrubs are playing their role in the local ecosystem. See the appendix on page 224 for more on pests and what actions to take.

AMERICAN BEAUTYBERRY

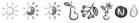

Callicarpa americana
Mint family: Lamiaceae

HARDINESS–Zones 8–11. Grows throughout Florida

NATIVE RANGE–Southeastern states, Cuba, and Bahamas

COLOR(S)–Pink blooms and vibrant purple fruits

PEAK SEASON–Spring blooms, year-round in South Florida, but the peak season is when the fruit ripens.

MATURE SIZE–8 x 10 feet (2.5 x 3 m)

WATER NEEDS–Drought tolerant, but also grows in moist soils

CARE–This Florida native requires minimal care or fertilizer. If additional growth is desired, add compost topdressing in early spring. It has arching branches, which could be pruned in late winter if they grow into pathways. Cut back to a few feet (about 60 cm) above the ground for the best shape.

PROBLEMS–None.

USES AND SELECTIONS–Beautyberry's main beauty is during fall and winter when fruit clusters turn purple on gracefully arching branches. Plant in clusters of three or more for best fall display. Use with other drought-tolerant plants. Berries feed winter birds but are also edible for jellies or breads. Leaves can be used as a mosquito repellant.

AZALEA

Rhododendron spp.
Heath family: Ericaceae

HARDINESS–Zones 8–9. Native azaleas only in colder areas; only a few hybrids of the Asian species will grow in South Florida.

NATIVE RANGE–Florida and most of the Northern Hemisphere.

COLOR(S)–Pink, red, white, purple blooms; green foliage

PEAK SEASON–Spring blooms

MATURE SIZE–2 to 6 feet x 2 to 6 feet (61 to 183 cm x 61 to 183 cm)

WATER NEEDS–Does best with adequate water.

CARE–Prefers acidic soils. Once established, grows well with minimal care. Azaleas may take 2 years to develop. They benefit from added compost in early spring. Water regularly, especially during drought. Every 3 to 5 years give rejuvenation pruning.

PROBLEMS–Too much shade gives poor flowers but good foliage.

USES AND SELECTIONS–Most plantings bloom for 3 to 4 weeks, then fade into the background as a backdrop, space divider, or transition plant. Use lower-growing azaleas as ground covers and small hedges along walkways. Plant in clusters for best color. Florida is home to four native azaleas, but the Asian azaleas are the ones most often offered for sale. It's worth the effort to look for the natives.

CAMELLIA

Camellia japonica
Tea family: Theaceae

HARDINESS–Zones 8–9

NATIVE RANGE–China, Korea, and Japan

COLOR(S)–Flowers in shades of pink, red, white; green foliage

PEAK SEASON–Blooms late November through March

MATURE SIZE–10 to 12 feet x 6 to 8 feet (3 to 3.5 m x 2 to 2.5 m)

WATER NEEDS–Keep moist, especially new plantings. Once established, tolerates short periods of drought if well mulched.

CARE–Prefers lightly shaded locations in acidic, well-drained soil. Apply compost in the fall before blooming cycle. If needed, trim immediately after flowering, before the end of April, when the next year's buds are formed.

PROBLEMS–Dry root balls on new plantings kill many camellias. Tea scale is common. It can be controlled with oil spray, which also treats mites.

USES AND SELECTIONS–Blossoms up to 5 inches (12.5 cm) across put on a major display when few other shrubs are flowering. Use for accent plantings or screening. Plant with shrubs that prefer filtered sun and acidic soil, like azaleas, hydrangeas, and gardenias. Also, use with beds of shade-loving perennials.

CHENILLE PLANT

Acalypha hispida
Spurge family: Euphorbiaceae

HARDINESS–Zones 10b–11; protect from cold in Central and North Florida

NATIVE RANGE–The Philippines and Papua New Guinea

COLOR(S)–Crimson flowers

PEAK SEASON–Blooms spring through fall

MATURE SIZE–8 to 10 feet x 6 feet (244 to 305 cm x 183 cm)

WATER NEEDS–Requires moist soils.

CARE–Does best and becomes readily established in rich, well-drained soil. Add compost after planting. If needed, prune after flowering to keep it in-bounds.

PROBLEMS–Aphids may appear on new growth. Also check for scale and mealybugs. Use insecticidal soap or recommended pesticide.

USES AND SELECTIONS–Plant where the unusual and showy flower is highlighted. Use in a mixed greenery planting of shrubs and lady palms, along a property line, or next to a path. Blend carefully with crotons, hibiscus, and snowbush for a tropical screen. There are several varieties in other colors, including copper or mottled foliage and white flower spikes.

CHINESE FRINGE BUSH

Loropetalum chinense
Witch-hazel family: Hamamelidaceae

HARDINESS–Zones 8–10a

NATIVE RANGE–China and Japan

COLOR(S)–White to deep pink flowers; green foliage, new varieties with reddish leaves

PEAK SEASON–Main blooms February through April

MATURE SIZE–12 feet x 6 feet (3.5 m x 183 cm)

WATER NEEDS–New plants need adequate water. Drought tolerant once established.

CARE–Apply compost 4 to 6 weeks after planting, then in the spring for first 2 years. New plants grow vigorously, forming long shoots. After spring blooming, prune overgrown plants.

PROBLEMS–Decline has been reported with some varieties. Check with your local Extension Agent.

USES AND SELECTIONS–Also called Chinese witch hazel, use for stand-alone accents, hedges, or as view barriers. Take advantage of its drought tolerance by planting with similar shrubs. New varieties have reddish foliage and pink flower forms. There are two fringe trees native to Florida (*Chionanthus virginicus* and *C. pygmaeus*) that can serve the same roles in the landscape.

COCOPLUM

Chrysobalanus icaco
Cocoplum family: Chrysobalanaceae

HARDINESS–Zones 10–11

NATIVE RANGE–Florida, Mexico, Central America, northern South America, and eastern Africa

COLOR(S)–Reddish or purple fruit

PEAK SEASON–Evergreen

MATURE SIZE–3 to 20 feet x 15 feet (91 cm to 6 m x 4.5 m)

WATER NEEDS–Drought tolerant once established

CARE–Has low nutritional requirements, but new plants benefit from a compost topdressing after planting. Tolerates pruning if needed. Once established, grows well with minimal care.

PROBLEMS–Pest free.

USES AND SELECTIONS–This South Florida native is a useful medium-to-large shrub. The coastal salt-tolerant form is low and sprawling. The inland red-tipped variety grows larger but is not as salt tolerant. Cocoplum is ideal for bringing a Florida feel to a landscape that might include cabbage palms, fakahatchee grass, and wax myrtle. Use as a formal or informal hedge, a background planting, or a screen. The fruit is eaten by birds, wildlife, and people, so cocoplum is used when creating a wildlife habitat.

COONTIE

Zamia integrifolia
Zamia family: Zamiaceae

HARDINESS–Zones 8b-11

NATIVE RANGE–Florida, southern Georgia, and Caribbean

COLOR(S)–Green

MATURE SIZE–From 18 to 30 inches x 24 to 30 inches wide (46 to 76 cm x 61 to 76 cm)

WATER NEEDS–Drought tolerant

CARE–Requires well-drained soil. Feed this tough, slow grower with compost or slow-release fertilizer.

PROBLEMS–Fruit is poisonous to pets and people.

USES AND SELECTIONS–Coontie is the only native cycad in Florida. Cycads are primitive non-flowering plants, usually dioecious with male and female plants. It is the only host plant for the Atala butterfly. Coonties are widely used as low hedges because they grow slowly and will never need trimming. Non-native cycads planted in Florida include the cardboard cycad (*Z. furfuracea*) and the sagos (*Cycas* spp.), which may suffer from deadly scale infestations.

FIREBUSH

Amelia patens
Madder family: Rubiaceae

HARDINESS–Zones 10-11. Prune out cold-damaged areas each spring.

NATIVE RANGE–Florida, Mexico, Central America, and South America

COLOR(S)–Scarlet flowers; green foliage with occasional reddish cast

PEAK SEASON–Year-round blooms

MATURE SIZE–15 feet or more x 6 feet (4.5 or more m x 183 cm)

WATER NEEDS–Firebush is a Florida native, very drought resistant once established. Keep moist until established and use mulch to retain moisture.

CARE–This fast-growing shrub is tolerant of Florida heat. It can tolerate light or hard pruning.

PROBLEMS–None.

USES AND SELECTIONS–Incorporate into a butterfly garden or use several near a patio where butterfly and hummingbird activity can easily be seen. Also can be planted in a mixed border with wax myrtle, wild coffee, necklace pod, beautyberry, and cocoplum. Use them along with native trees to create a wildlife habitat, or use where no irrigation is needed. Another firebush that is commonly cultivated and sold as 'African firebush' is *H. patens var. glabra*; it is native to northern South America.

FIRECRACKER PLANT

Russelia equisetiformis
Plantain family: Plantaginaceae

HARDINESS–Zones 9b-11

NATIVE RANGE–Mexico

COLOR(S)–Red, yellow, coral flowers

PEAK SEASON–Evergreen foliage and almost year-round blooms

MATURE SIZE–4 feet x 4 feet (122 x 122 cm)

WATER NEEDS–Somewhat drought tolerant once established, but does best with regular waterings.

CARE–Plant in well-drained, enriched soil. Add compost in the spring after planting. The fast-growing firecracker plant does not require much care and is even tolerant of salt spray.

PROBLEMS–None.

USES AND SELECTIONS–Firecracker plant (also called coral plant) has a unique look, with countless thin, rush-like stems that erupt upward then cascade down to form gentle arches. There are no leaves to speak of, but the stems are filled with clusters of tubular flowers that attract butterflies and hummingbirds. (They can be dried for use in arrangements.) Plant as an accent to fill planter boxes or containers. The weeping habit can also be used to overflow a wall, hide a raised bed, or cover a bank.

FLORIDA PRIVET

Forestiera segregate
Olive family: Oleaceae

HARDINESS–Zones 8b–11

NATIVE RANGE–Florida, Georgia, South Carolina, and the Caribbean

COLOR(S)–Yellow flowers
PEAK SEASON–Blooms winter and spring; leaves usually evergreen

MATURE SIZE–10 to 15 feet x 5 to 10 feet (3 to 4.5 m x 1.5 to 3 m)

WATER NEEDS–Drought tolerant but also does well in moist soils.

CARE–Does well in almost any soil or moisture level. Florida privet is a tough native that even withstands brief flooding and is salt tolerant. It commonly grows in coastal areas. Can tolerate pruning, if using as a hedge.

PROBLEMS–No serious pests or diseases

USES AND SELECTIONS–Also called wild olive, this native has small leaves with dense growth. It makes excellent hedges, screens, and espaliers. Also useful as a specimen plant, in wildlife gardens, for slope erosion, and for seaside landscapes. Hedges can easily be maintained at most heights, or Florida privet can be left completely natural as a small tree. Birds and bees are attracted to the flowers and abundant berries. The Japanese and Chinese privets (*Ligustrum japonicum and L. sinense*) are invasive in Florida, so do not use them and replace what you have with a native.

GARDENIA

Gardenia jasminoides
Madder family: Rubiaceae

HARDINESS–Zones 8b–11

NATIVE RANGE–Eastern Asia and Japan

COLOR(S)–White flowers; dark-green foliage

PEAK SEASON–Blooms spring, sporadic flowers throughout summer; foliage evergreen

MATURE SIZE–12 x 3 or 4 feet (3.5 m x 91 to 122 cm)

WATER NEEDS–Keep moist. Fluctuating soil moisture leads to yellowing leaves.

CARE–Prefers enriched, acidic soils. A lack of micronutrients causes yellow leaves; use a fish emulsion or micronutrient spray. Prune lightly after major flowering to keep shrub compact. Prune any cold damage after new spring growth appears.

PROBLEMS–None.

USES AND SELECTIONS–Use this slow-growing evergreen as a specimen plant, or blend with foliage plants that are colorful in the non-blooming months. 'Miami Supreme' is the biggest-selling cultivar in Florida, with large, fragrant flowers. 'Radicans' is a dwarf. Usually grafted onto nematode-resistant rootstocks.

HIBISCUS

Hibiscus spp. There are native and non-native species, which have differing requirements and uses. They are divided in two groups here.
Mallow family: Malvaceae

NON-NATIVE: *H. rosa-sinensis*

HARDINESS–Zones 9b–11 Not cold tolerant, but can be grown as a container plant in North Florida.

NATIVE RANGE–India

COLOR(S)–All color flowers except blue; green foliage

PEAK SEASON–Blooms spring through summer; evergreen foliage

MATURE SIZE–20 feet or more x 15 feet (6 or more m x 4.5 m)

WATER NEEDS–Fairly drought tolerant once established. May need water in dry season. Don't let roots stand in water.

CARE–Prefers enriched, acidic soils. In cooler regions, grow in protected garden areas, in containers, or as annuals. Prune off cold damage in spring.

PROBLEMS–None.

USES AND SELECTIONS–Although hibiscus blooms last only a day, they flower prolifically. Plant with palms, heliconias, or bananas for a tropical feel.

NATIVE SPECIES: *H. aculeatus: pineland hibiscus; H. coccineus: scarlet hibiscus; H. grandifloras: swamp rosemallow; H. moscheutos: swamp mallow;* and a few others

HARDINESS–Zones 8–11. Not all species occur in all of Florida, but there are some natives in every part of the state.

NATIVE RANGE–Florida and more

COLOR(S)–Red, pink, or white flowers

PEAK SEASON–Blooms spring through summer; plants die back in the winter in North Florida

MATURE SIZE–3 to 10 feet (1 to 3 m) tall depending upon species

WATER NEEDS–Most of these natives like wet feet and will grow well at edges of ponds, but a couple will tolerate drier conditions.

CARE–Prefers enriched, acidic soils.

PROBLEMS–None.

USES AND SELECTIONS–Although hibiscus blooms last only a day, they flower over several weeks. They attract butterflies and other pollinators. The seeds float, so they will spread around the edges of a pond.

HYDRANGEA

Hydrangea macrophylla
Hydrangea family: Hydrangeaceae

HARDINESS–Zones 8-9. Requires some cold weather to do well.

NATIVE RANGE–Japan

COLOR(S)–Pink, blue, white flowers

PEAK SEASON–Blooms spring through summer

MATURE SIZE–May reach 4 feet x 4 feet (122 x 122 cm)

WATER NEEDS–Needs lots of water and will wilt from moisture stress. Check frequently during hot weather and drought.

CARE–Does best with well-drained, enriched soil that retains moisture. Add compost after planting and each spring. Prune any freeze damage in early spring and prune again after flowering in summer. Remove older flower heads and reshape plant.

PROBLEMS–Most of these plants do not survive in Florida for long–it's a short-lived shrub in Florida.

USES AND SELECTIONS–Use in containers for porches, patios, and along walkways. Display in-ground with filtered-sun lovers like allamanda, Indian hawthorn, azaleas, and camellias. For a longer-term hydrangea, try the Florida native oakleaf hydrangea (See page 155).

INDIAN HAWTHORN

Rhaphiolepis indica
Rose family: Rosaceae

HARDINESS–Zones 8-11

NATIVE RANGE–Southeast Asia

COLOR(S)–White, pink flowers; dark-green foliage

PEAK SEASON–Blooms spring; foliage evergreen

MATURE SIZE–3 to 5 feet x 3 feet (91 to 152 cm x 91 cm)

WATER NEEDS–Drought tolerant once established

CARE–Needs well-drained soil. Indian hawthorn is a tough plant that doesn't require much care. It has compact growth, and unlike most other shrubs, doesn't need pruning to be kept as a low hedge or border. It also is somewhat salt tolerant.

PROBLEMS–Indian hawthorn resists most problems, but it's over-planted in Florida.

USES AND SELECTIONS–This compact, slow-growing plant is good for low-maintenance plantings. May be used as foundation plants, low hedges, or borders. The lightly fragrant flowers provide berries for winter birds, making Indian hawthorn useful in wildlife gardens.

IXORA

Ixora coccinea
Madder family: Rubiaceae

HARDINESS–Zones 9b-11

NATIVE RANGE–India and southeast Asia

COLOR(S)–Red, orange, pink, yellow, salmon flowers; green foliage

PEAK SEASON–Blooms spring through summer; evergreen foliage

MATURE SIZE–2½ to 6 feet x 6 feet (76 to 183 cm x 183 cm)

WATER NEEDS–Requires good drainage.

CARE–Ixora likes rich soil to keep producing big balls of flowers called umbels. They prefer acidic soil. They benefit from mulch and fish emulsion for micronutrients. Ixora performs best when not sheared. Wait until spring before pruning freeze damage.

PROBLEMS–May be damaged by nematodes.

USES AND SELECTIONS– Some new cultivars require less shaping, are more tolerant of rocky soils, and are resistant to nematodes. Combine ixora with crotons, palms, or bulbs for easy-care plantings that are colorful but not confusing. New cultivars come in dwarf forms, as well as sizes growing to 12 feet (3.5 m).

JAPANESE ARALIA

Fatsia japonica
Aralia family: Araliaceae

HARDINESS–Zones 8–10

NATIVE RANGE–Korea and Japan

COLOR(S)–White flowers

PEAK SEASON–Blooms in fall

MATURE SIZE–8 feet x 4 feet (244 cm x 122 cm)

WATER NEEDS–Keep moist. Will also tolerate wet soils.

CARE–Prefers slightly acidic, enriched soil. Add compost regularly to maintain lush foliage. The plant may become leggy-looking as older leaves fall off. Either cut back or stake for support. Fatsia is also salt tolerant.

PROBLEMS–Pests or diseases are usually not a problem.

USES AND SELECTIONS–Japanese aralia is grown for its deeply lobed, bold leaves, which are very striking. Use as a patio plant in the ground or in containers. It also works well if carefully mixed with other plants that aren't overwhelmed by the huge leaves. Plant with other low-maintenance, shade-loving plants.

LADY-OF-THE-NIGHT

Brunfelsia americana
Nightshade family: Solanaceae

HARDINESS–9b–11

NATIVE RANGE–Caribbean and Venezuela

COLOR(S)–White flowers

PEAK SEASON–Blooms in summer

MATURE SIZE–10 to 15 feet x 5 to 10 feet (3 to 4.5 m x 1.5 to 3 m)

WATER NEEDS–Water every few days in dry season.

CARE–Add compost after planting. Lady-of-the-night may get cold damage in Central Florida. Prune off damage after new spring growth begins. Prune to shape this naturally sprawling shrub.

PROBLEMS–Plant parts are poisonous if ingested.

USES AND SELECTIONS–Plant where the rich clove-like fragrance in the evening can be appreciated. This shrub blooms profusely all at once. Allow it to sprawl amid groupings of gingers and lady palms. Other species come in different colors and bloom at other times of the year.

LAUREL-LEAF SNAILSEED

Cocculus laurifolius
Moonseed family: Menispermaceae

HARDINESS–Zones 9–11

NATIVE RANGE–India, Southeast Asia, and Japan

COLOR(S)–Insignificant yellow flowers; shiny bright-green foliage

PEAK SEASON–Blooms spring and summer

MATURE SIZE–12 feet x 12 feet (3.5 x 3.5 m)

WATER NEEDS–Relatively drought tolerant once established.

CARE–Grows best in poor but well-drained soils. Once established, grows well with minimal care. If needed, prune to keep compact and full or to trim back any cold-damaged portions in North Florida plantings.

PROBLEMS–May be poisonous.

USES AND SELECTIONS–Called the snailseed because its seeds resemble a snail shell. (Does not fruit in Florida.) Good as an evergreen hedge or border for sun or shade. Can also be used as a contrasting backdrop with perennials of bird-of-paradise, heliconia, ginger, and banana. The foliage is used to make wreaths and is added to arrangements. The Carolina snailseed (*C. carolinus*) is native to North Florida.

NATAL PLUM

Carissa macrocarpa
Dogbane family: Apocynaceae

HARDINESS–Zones 9b-11

NATIVE RANGE–Southeastern Africa

COLOR(S)–White flowers; red fruit; glossy dark-green leaves

PEAK SEASON–Blooms summer; evergreen foliage

MATURE SIZE–Varies

WATER NEEDS–Drought tolerant. Do not overwater.

CARE–Does best in sandy, well-drained soil. Tolerant of salty spray and soil. Grows in partial shade but flowers more in full sun. Only requires light pruning to keep as a hedge.

PROBLEMS–Plant back from walkways so that spines do not interfere with people. All parts of the plant are poisonous, except for ripe fruit.

USES AND SELECTIONS–Natal plums are sweetly fragrant, especially at night, with edible fruit used for preserves. The glossy, dense foliage makes them excellent hedges, ground covers, or screens. They can be used in containers, in planters, and as accent or foundation plants. Carissas are superb plants for seashore landscapes. There are numerous species and cultivars with very diverse growth habits and heights, from dwarf ground covers to small trees.

NECKLACE POD

Sophora tomentosa
Legume family: Fabaceae

HARDINESS–Zones 9b-11

NATIVE RANGE–Florida, Mexico, Central America, South America, Africa, India, Southeast Asia, and Australia

COLOR(S)–Yellow flowers; silvery-green foliage

PEAK SEASON–Blooms winter and spring

MATURE SIZE–6 to 10 feet x 10 feet (183 cm to 3 m x 3 m)

WATER NEEDS–Water well until established, then stand aside. Very drought tolerant.

CARE–Prune in spring to keep long branches in check. In Central Florida, grow in protected area. Prune away cold damage after new spring growth emerges.

PROBLEMS–Hand pick occasional caterpillars or ignore

USES AND SELECTIONS–This durable shrub is salt tolerant and beautiful. Flowering is most plentiful in winter and spring, but may continue throughout the year. Necklace pod produces long, segmented pea pods, like the small pearls of a necklace. Use in borders with other butterfly shrubs. It is perfect for pineland plantings. Use with palmettos, firebush, beautyberry, and other native shrubs.

NIGHT-BLOOMING JESSAMINE

Cestrum nocturnum
Nightshade family: Solanaceae

HARDINESS–Zones 9b-11

NATIVE RANGE–Mexico, Central America, and northern South America

COLOR(S)–White flowers; glossy green leaves

PEAK SEASON–Blooms spring, summer; evergreen foliage

MATURE SIZE–12 feet x 12 feet (3.5 m x 3.5 m)

WATER NEEDS–Can tolerate short periods of drought but makes best growth if watered regularly, especially during drought. Do not let roots get waterlogged.

CARE–Prefers any well-drained soil. Apply compost after planting and again the next spring. This shrub sprawls with long, vine-like stems, and frequent pruning may be needed. Plantings in Central Florida may be affected by freezing weather and need spring pruning to remove damage.

PROBLEMS–Caterpillars and grasshoppers can be hand picked. Plants are poisonous if ingested.

USES AND SELECTIONS–The small flowers pack a powerful, sweet fragrance most noticeable at night. Use as a specimen, in mixed plantings, or as a border. It provides larval food for butterflies.

OAKLEAF HYDRANGEA

Hydrangea quercifolia
Hydrangea family: Hydrangeaceae

HARDINESS–Zones 8-9. Requires some cold weather to do well.

NATIVE RANGE–Southeastern states, including North Florida

COLOR(S)–White flowers that change to pink; reddish fall leaf color

PEAK SEASON–Blooms spring through summer

MATURE SIZE–10 feet tall x 6 feet wide (3 m x 183 cm)

WATER NEEDS–Somewhat drought tolerant after establishment

CARE–Does best with well-drained, enriched soil that retains moisture.

PROBLEMS–None.

USES AND SELECTIONS–Use in informal hedgerows with beautyberry and native azalea, or in groupings as an understory shrub.

OLEANDER

Nerium oleander
Dogbane family: Apocynaceae

HARDINESS–Zones 8-11. In cold areas, it may freeze to the ground, but it grows back from its base.

NATIVE RANGE–Mediterranean and India

COLOR(S)–White, pink, red, salmon flowers

PEAK SEASON–Blooms spring through fall

MATURE SIZE–12 feet x 12 feet (3.5 x 3.5 m)

WATER NEEDS–Very drought tolerant

CARE–Thrives in sand or well-drained soil. For extra growth, add compost to soil after planting. Southern plantings may require regular pruning.

PROBLEMS–All parts are very poisonous. Caterpillars, aphids, and scale may appear. Hand pick or rinse with water.

USES AND SELECTIONS–This showy, sometimes fragrant shrub can be planted as a hedge, space divider, view barrier, or small tree. Plant in clusters for more color. Use large oleanders at the rear of the landscape for distant color. Use dwarf types in foundation plantings and around patios.

PITTOSPORUM

Pittosporum tobira
Pittosporum family: Pittosporaceae

HARDINESS–Zones 8-10

NATIVE RANGE–Korea and Japan

COLOR(S)–White flowers; green, variegated leaves

PEAK SEASON–Blooms spring; evergreen foliage

MATURE SIZE–8 to 12 feet x 8 to 12 feet (2.5 to 3.5 m x 2.5 to 3.5 m)

WATER NEEDS–Drought tolerant once established. Grows best with moderate moisture.

CARE–Not particular about soil. Can be grown as a shrub or small tree, depending upon amount of pruning. It grows faster in enriched soil. In alkaline soils, provide annual micronutrient spray.

PROBLEMS–Undersides of leaves may be affected by aphids and scale. Avoid wet soils, which lead to leaf spot and root rot.

USES AND SELECTIONS–This shrub is used for informal or formal designs. It also can be used in containers or as small patio trees, where the citrusy flower fragrance will be appreciated. Pittosporum is tough enough to be used regularly in commercial plantings and seaside landscapes. A dwarf variety grows only 2 feet (61 cm) high, and another popular cultivar is variegated. Also known as Australian laurel, mock orange, and Japanese cheesewood.

PLUMBAGO

☀ 🦋🌼💧🍃

Plumbago auriculata
Leadwort family: Plumbaginaceae

HARDINESS–Zones 9–11. Prune freeze damage after spring growth begins.

NATIVE RANGE–Southern Africa

COLOR(S)–Cobalt-blue flowers

PEAK SEASON–Blooms spring through summer

MATURE SIZE–3 to 4 feet x 8 feet (91 to 122 cm x 2.5 m). May be trained to climb or crawl.

WATER NEEDS–Moderately drought tolerant when established. Water during dry season.

CARE–Blooms best with enriched soil, so add compost after planting and again the following spring. The plant tends to fall over and root, so prune if it needs control. (Flowers trimmed off will be quickly replaced.) Or, tie to a support such as an arbor or gate for a dramatic effect. Prune back hard at the end of winter.

PROBLEMS–None.

USES AND SELECTIONS–Serves as a short shrub or large ground cover. The color nicely complements magenta bougainvillea or yellow flowers. Because plumbago is low and sprawling, plant it in front of taller shrubs. The mounding shape also works well at an entry gate or in containers and planters. Red and white varieties are available.

PODOCARPUS

☀ ☀ ☀ ☀ 🌼💧🍃

Podocarpus macrophylla
Yellow-wood family: Podocarpaceae

HARDINESS–Zones 8–10

NATIVE RANGE–The Philippines

COLOR(S)–Dark-green leaves

PEAK SEASON–Evergreen

MATURE SIZE–To 30 feet x to 20 feet (to 9 m x to 6 m)

WATER NEEDS–Drought resistant

CARE–Prefers fertile, well-drained soil. Does not tolerate wet roots. This tough plant tolerates heat, drought, sun, shade, and even salt spray.

PROBLEMS–Resistant to most pests and diseases. Seeds and leaves are toxic, but the fruit is not.

USES AND SELECTIONS– Also called yew pine or yew podocarpus. Has narrow needle-like leaves. They have upright dense growth, and there are varieties with different heights and foliage shapes. They are useful where root space is limited. Often planted close to buildings or as foundation plantings. The fleshy fruit attracts birds and branches are useful for arrangements.

ROSES

Rosa spp. and hybrids
Rose family: Rosaceae
Roses are often divided into two groups: modern roses, which were introduced after 1867, and old garden roses (OGRs), aka antique or heritage roses. Roses are further divided into classes. Shrub, hybrid tea, polyantha, grandiflora, and floribunda. Some common classes of OGRs are China, tea, and Bermuda mystery roses, which were grown in Bermuda for more than a century and their origin is unknown.

HARDINESS–Roses grow throughout Florida. Prune winter damage to some roses in North Florida before spring growth begins.

NATIVE RANGE–Florida, North America, and all of Eurasia

COLOR(S)–Flowers in all colors except blue; foliage green

PEAK SEASON–Mostly spring and summer blooms

MATURE SIZE–Depends on the type. Sizes range from small or large shrubs to long vines.

WATER NEEDS–Keep soil moist. Use enriched soil and mulch.

CARE–Once established, add compost in the spring. For modern roses, groom regularly and prune back one third to one half in late winter, keeping to three to seven main stems. In January or February prune back bush types by one third to one half, thinning if needed. Allow climbers to grow, with renewal pruning every 2 or 3 years. For OGRs, prune only lightly where needed. Some very bushy plants may need staking.

PROBLEMS– Black spot can be treated with fungicide sprays in hot, rainy weather. During dry weather, mites can be a major problem. Other pests include thrips, powdery mildew, aphids, and stem cankers. Some of the best selections for Florida are resistant to these problems.

FLORIBUNDA ROSE: USES AND SELECTIONS–Most buds are pointed to slightly rounded and have the hybrid tea rose look. They are considered very hardy and generally pest resistant. Floribundas are suited for smaller gardens or planting in clusters with perennials. The smallest of these multipurpose hybrids are miniatures.

GRANDIFLORA ROSE: USES AND SELECTIONS–Grandiflora have taller bushes than hybrid tea roses, with the full clusters of floribundas. Plant just a bed or create clusters among perennials, annuals, and accent shrubs. Plant with salvias, marigolds, pentas, and heliconia. The first floribunda, 'Queen Elizabeth', is still a favorite.

HYBRID TEA ROSE: USES AND SELECTIONS–Tea roses are bushy and produce stems of single blossoms. Plant in a rose bed or a few clusters. Make sure they have adequate spacing, leaving room for annuals and perennials around the edges including ageratum, alyssum, and periwinkle.

OLD GARDEN ROSE: USES AND SELECTIONS–OGRs include tall shrubs, climbers, and miniature forms. They traveled from Europe to New World settlers' homesteads. They are generally more fragrant than modern hybrids and may be more vigorous. Fill a bed, use as shrubs, or create a backdrop for annual and perennial plants.

'Mrs. B. R. Cant'--this OGR is classified as a tea rose. 'Spice'–a Bermuda mystery rose. 'Louis Philippe'–a China rose also called Florida cracker rose. Knock Out®–a modern rose with resistance to black spot.
The petals and the fruits (known as rose hips) are edible and can be used for jellies and teas, but only from non-poisoned gardens.

SAW PALMETTO

Serenoa repens
Palm family: Arecaceae

HARDINESS–Zones 8–11

NATIVE RANGE–Southeastern states and all of Florida

PEAK SEASON–Spring and summer flowers

MATURE SIZE–6 feet x 6 feet (183 cm x 183 cm)

WATER NEEDS–Keep new plantings moist until roots start growing out. Mulch heavily. Do not let soil dry out for two growing seasons. Once established, is very drought tolerant.

CARE–Plant in any soil. Allow plenty of space for these clump-forming, low-maintenance palms, which grow as wide as tall. Prune away brown fronds as needed. Has high salt tolerance.

PROBLEMS–May be affected by palmetto weevils and palm leaf skeletonizers

USES AND SELECTIONS–Use saw palmettos as space dividers. Most attractive in clusters of three. Add to natural Florida settings with other natives including hollies, pines, ornamental grasses, and coreopsis. Fruit is eaten by wildlife.

SEA GRAPE

Coccoloba uvifera
Smartweed Family: Polygonaceae

HARDINESS–Zones 9–11. Occurs in coastal areas.

NATIVE RANGE–Florida, Mexico, Central America, and northern South America

COLOR(S)–White flowers, purple fruit. New leaves and veins are reddish.

PEAK SEASON–Deciduous in colder winters

MATURE SIZE–20 to 25 feet x 20 feet (6 to 7.5 m x 6 m)

WATER NEEDS–Water daily for first few weeks, then gradually taper off. Drought tolerant once established.

CARE–Plant in full sun with well-drained soil. Apply compost after 4 to 6 weeks and again in the following spring. Can be pruned to single or multiple trunks, as a tree, a large shrub, or a hedge.

PROBLEMS–Virtually pest free

USES AND SELECTIONS–Sea grape lends an exotic look to landscapes and is prized for seaside plantings because of its high salt tolerance. Use in native or wildlife gardens. It can also be used for soil stabilization along the shore. The long fruit clusters are tastier for wildlife than for people, but jellies are good.

THRYALLIS

Galphimia gracilis
Family: Malpighiaceae

HARDINESS–Zones 9–11. Tolerates frost and light freezes. In colder regions, give protected location and prune in late winter.

NATIVE RANGE–Mexico, Central America, and South America

COLOR(S)–Yellow flowers

PEAK SEASON–Blooms spring through fall

MATURE SIZE–8 feet x 6 feet (244 cm x 183 cm)

WATER NEEDS–Tolerates short periods of drought but grows better with regular watering

CARE–Grows in sandy soil, although enriched soil is best. Prune lanky plants in early spring. At lower light levels, it develops more open growth.

PROBLEMS–During transporting and planting, be careful not to break limbs. Hand pick any caterpillars and grasshoppers or use recommended pesticide.

USES AND SELECTIONS–Plant thryallis in clusters to showcase flower spikes above foliage. Plant as backdrops for summer color with cannas, periwinkle, begonias, coleus, and plumbago. Also use as a free-form hedge or barrier. Keep back from walkways because the brittle wood is easily damaged.

VIBURNUM

Viburnum spp. Favorite natives are: maple-leaved viburnum (V. acerifolium); southern arrowwood (V. dentatum); Walter's viburnum (V. obovatum)
Viburnum family: Viburnaceae

HARDINESS–Zones 8-11. Walter's viburnum is the most widespread in Florida. Others occur in north Central and North Florida.

NATIVE RANGE–Florida and more

COLOR(S)–White or pink flowers

PEAK SEASON–Blooms spring; evergreen or deciduous leaves

MATURE SIZE–Varies depending upon species, but most are tall shrubs that can grow to 10 feet (3 m) tall.

WATER NEEDS–Drought tolerant when established. Grows in sandy soils, although well-drained, enriched soil is best. Mulch to retain moisture.

CARE–Apply compost 4 weeks after planting. Can tolerate pruning as needed.

PROBLEMS–None.

USES AND SELECTIONS–Use the taller viburnums as a hedge, screen, or backdrop for lower-growing shrubs and flowers. They do best where they have room to grow and become attractive shrubs with minimal pruning. There are a couple of other natives and also a fragrant Asian species, sweet viburnum (*V. odoratissimum*), that is often sold and used in similar ways.

WAX MYRTLE

Morella cerifera
Myrtle family: Myricaceae

HARDINESS–Zones 8-11

NATIVE RANGE–Mid-Atlantic through southeastern states, including all of Florida; also Mexico, Central America, northern South America, and Caribbean Islands

COLOR(S)–Insignificant greenish flowers and waxy gray berries

PEAK SEASON–Blooms in spring; fall and winter berries; evergreen leaves

MATURE SIZE–15 to 25 feet (4.5 to 7.5 m)

WATER NEEDS–Can flourish under moist or dry conditions. Keep roots moist during first season.

CARE–Once established, requires very little care. It fixes nitrogen, so it can grow in lousy soil. It suckers from the roots, which helps wax myrtle grow into clumps. They may be left alone, shaped, or removed.

PROBLEMS–None.

USES AND SELECTIONS–This supremely versatile native plant grows from the Everglades to the pinelands. Wax myrtle is excellent for xeriscape, low-maintenance, and native landscapes. Use it for a screen or background plant, or with other native shrubs. It can also be shaped into hedges, but grows too large for use close to the home. Male and female flowers are on separate plants. In winter, the female's waxy fruits are appreciated by wildlife and birds.

WILD COFFEE

Psychotria nervosa
Madder family: Rubiaceae

HARDINESS–Zones 9b (if protected)-11

COLOR(S)–Insignificant white flowers; glossy deep-green leaves; red berries

PEAK SEASON–Blooms spring and summer; late summer and fall berries

MATURE SIZE–6 to 15 feet x 5 to 6 feet (183 cm to 4.5 m x 152 to 183 cm)

WATER NEEDS–Keep roots moist until established, then water during drought. Plants wilt when thirsty.

CARE–Add compost a few months after planting and again the following spring. Prune in spring if needed for shaping.

PROBLEMS–None reported.

USES AND SELECTIONS–This native Florida shrub makes a beautiful hedge in semi-shade. Plant beneath palms or gumbo-limbo trees that will provide shade and sun. The leaf texture and shine make wild coffee especially useful in native gardens. Although the flowers are very small, butterflies like them. The shrub stretches out and becomes lanky in shade, but stays compact in partial to full sun. High or partial shade is ideal.

SHRUBS

NAME	AVERAGE SIZE		AREA OF FLORIDA	FLOWER COLOR	SEASON	LIGHT NEEDED
	H. (FT.)	W. (FT.)				
Abelia	4-6	4-6	NC	White	Summer	Sun, light shade
Allamanda, Bush	4-6	4-6	CS	Yellow	Year-round	Sun, light shade
Anise	8-10	6-8	NCS	*		Sun, shade
Aucuba	5-6	2-3	N	*		Shade
Azalea, Indian	6-8	4-6	NC	Varied	Spring	Light shade
Azalea, Kurume	3-4	2-3	NC	Varied	Spring	Light shade
Azalea, Native	5-6	4-6	N	Varied	Spring	Light shade
Banana Shrub	10-12	6-8	NC	Yellow	Spring	Sun, light shade
Beautyberry	5-6	4-5	NC	Lilac	Spring	Sun, light shade
Bottlebrush	8-10	8-10	NCS	Red	Spring	Sun
Brunfelsia	6-8	4-6	CS	Purple	Spring	Sun, light shade
Camellia, Japonica	10-12	6-8	NC	Varied	Winter	Sun, light shade
Camellia, Sasanqua	10-12	6-8	NC	Varied	Winter	Sun
Cape Jasmine	6-8	6-8	CS	White	Spring-summer	Sun, light shade
Cassia	6-8	6-8	CS	Yellow	Fall	Sun
Chaste Tree	10-12	10-12	NC	Blue	Summer	Sun
Cleyera, Japanese	8-10	4-6	NCS	Yellow	Spring	Shade
Cocculus	10-12	6-8	CS	*		Sun, light shade
Cocoplum	10-15	10-15	S	White	Year-round	Sun, light shade
Crape myrtle	6-15	8-10	NC	Varied	Summer	Sun
Crape myrtle, Dwarf	2-4	3-4	NC	Varied	Summer	Sun
Fatsia	5-6	2-3	NCS	*		Light shade
Feijoa	8-10	6-8	NCS	White, red	Spring	Sun, light shade
Firebush	6-8	6-8	CS	Red	Year-round	Sun, light shade
Firecracker Plant	4-5	3-4	CS	Red	Year-round	Sun, light shade
Florida Privet	8-10	6-8	CS	White	Spring	Sun
Florida Yew	8-10	8-10	NC	*		Light shade

* = Inconspicuous Flower Color   N = North Florida   C = Central Florida   S = South Florida

SHRUBS

NAME	AVERAGE SIZE		AREA OF FLORIDA	FLOWER COLOR	SEASON	LIGHT NEEDED
	H. (FT.)	W. (FT.)				
Fortune's Mahonia	3-4	2-3	N	Yellow	Spring	Light shade
Gardenia	6-8	4-6	NCS	White	Spring	Sun, light shade
Hibiscus	8-10	6-8	CS	Varied	Year-round	Sun, light shade
Holly, Chinese	10-12	6-8	NC	White	Spring	Sun, light shade
Holly, Dwarf Burford	5-6	4-5	NC	*		Sun, light shade
Holly, Dwarf Yaupon	3-4	3-4	NCS	*		Sun, shade
Holly, Japanese	2-4	2-3	N	*		Sun, light shade
Holly Malpighia	1-2	1-2	CS	Pink	Spring-summer	Shade
Hydrangea, French	5-6	4-5	NC	Blue-Pink	Spring-summer	Light shade
Hydrangea, Oakleaf	5-6	4-5	NC	White	Summer	Light shade
Indian Hawthorn	3-4	3-4	NCS	White, pink	Spring	Sun, light shade
Ixora	4-6	3-4	CS	Red, yellow	Year-round	Sun, light shade
Japanese Boxwood	3-4	2-3	NC	*		Sun, shade
Jasmine, Arabian	4-5	3-4	S	White	Summer-fall	Sun, light shade
Jasmine, Downy	5-6	4-6	CS	White	Spring-fall	Sun, light shade
Jasmine, Primrose	5-6	5-6	NC	Yellow	Spring-summer	Sun
Jasmine, Shining	4-5	4-5	CS	White	Spring-summer	Sun, light shade
Juniper, Chinese	4-6	4-6	NC	*		Sun
Juniper, Shore	1-2	4-6	NCS	*		Sun
Juniper, Spreading	1	3-4	N	*		Sun
King's Mantle	4-6	4-6	CS	*	Summer	Sun, light shade
Loropetalum	6-8	4-6	NC	White, pink	Spring	Sun, light shade
Natal Plum	6-8	4-6	CS	White	Spring	Sun, shade
Oleander	10-12	6-8	NCS	Varied	Year-round	Sun
Orange Jessamine	10-12	6-8	CS	White	Spring-fall	Sun, light shade
Philodendron, Selloum	6-10	8-10	CS	*		Sun, shade
Pittosporum	8-10	8-10	NCS	White	Spring	Sun, light shade

* = Inconspicuous Flower Color   N = North Florida   C = Central Florida   S = South Florida

SHRUBS

NAME	AVERAGE SIZE		AREA OF FLORIDA	FLOWER COLOR	SEASON	LIGHT NEEDED
	H. (FT.)	W. (FT.)				
Plumbago	4-6	4-6	CS	Blue	Year-round	Sun, light shade
Podocarpus, Yew	20-25	8-10	NCS	Yellow	Spring	Sun, light shade
Powder Puff	8-10	8-10	CS	Red	Winter	Sun, light shade
Pyracantha	8-10	6-8	NC	White	Spring	Sun
Red-tip Photinia	6-8	5-6	NC	White	Spring	Sun
Reeves Spirea	5-6	4-5	NC	White	Spring	Sun
Rose of Sharon	8-10	6-8	NC	Varied	Summer	Sun, light shade
Saw Palmetto	4-6	6-10	NCS	Cream	Spring	Sun, filtered sun
Serissa	1-2	1-2	NCS	White	Spring–summer	Sun, light shade
Silverthorn	10-12	8-10	NC	Tan	Winter	Sun
Simpson Stopper	10-12	6-8	CS	White	Spring	Sun
Snowbush	4-6	4-5	CS	White	Summer	Sun, light shade
Sweet Osmanthus	10-12	6-8	NC	White	Winter	Light shade
Texas Sage	5-6	4-5	NCS	Lavender	Spring–fall	Sun, light shade
Thryallis	5-6	4-6	CS	Yellow	Summer	Sun, light shade
Ti Plant	4-6	3-4	CS	White, pink	Fall	Sun, light shade
Tibouchina	8-10	6-8	CS	Purple	Summer	Sun
Viburnum, Black Haw	6-8	5-6	NCS	White	Spring	Sun
Viburnum, Laurestinis	6-8	4-5	NC	White, pink	Winter	Sun
Viburnum, Sandankwa	5-6	4-5	NCS	White	Spring	Sun, light shade
Viburnum, Sweet	10-12	6-8	NCS	White	Spring	Sun
Wax Myrtle	10-12	6-10	NCS	White	Spring	Sun, light shade

* = Inconspicuous Flower Color   N = North Florida   C = Central Florida   S = South Florida

JANUARY

❑ Winter is great for planting shrubs. If beds are not ready, keep plants in containers and water often. This is also a good time to move plants in your landscape. Roses can be planted year-round when container grown, but bare-root specimens are best planted this month or next.

❑ Prune summer-blooming shrubs if needed. Give roses (except climbing types) their annual pruning. Cut back 1/3 to 1/2, keeping 3 to 7 main stems.

❑ Most shrubs are not heavy water users. All, however, need water in order to become established and produce growth. Even drought-tolerant plants look their best when provided with adequate water. Keep new plantings moist.

❑ In North and Central Florida, feed roses every 6 to 8 weeks until spring. Keep South Florida roses on a monthly fertilizing schedule.

❑ Check plantings for scale and sooty mold. Aphids and mealybugs may appear during warmer winter days. Rinse them with water.

FEBRUARY

❑ Leave cold-damaged plants alone for a few weeks to see what is alive or dead. Water as needed, but do not apply fertilizer until growth begins. If plants are frozen to the ground, wait until late spring before replacing. They might recover.

❑ Container-grown roses can be planted year-round. This is the last month to plant bare-root roses.

❑ If you want plants to have denser growth, pinch out shoot tips.

❑ As plants start growing, cool weather reduces moisture needs. Wait until plants tell you they need water. Keep the root balls of new plantings moist. Use mulch and a soaker hose or micro sprinklers.

❑ In North and Central Florida, feed roses every 6 to 8 weeks until spring. In South Florida maintain the monthly schedule.

❑ Aphids, mealybugs, leaf spot, and scale may start showing up on new shrub growth. Rinse them with water.

MARCH

❑ Spring and fall are the best times to plant roses.

❑ Complete winter pruning of shrubs. Cut out declining portions and reshape winter-damaged shrubs and roses. Winter-flowering shrubs can be trimmed as they finish blooming, but before new growth appears. Prune any winter damage from roses before spring growth begins.

❑ Warmer weather signals increased growth and water needs. Most shrubs are drought tolerant, so check if the upper inch of soil is dry before watering. New shrub and rose plantings should be kept moist, and now is a good time to add a compost topdressing outside the planting holes of shrubs planted in the last year.

❑ Apply monthly feeding to roses. Use 12-4-8 or similar rose fertilizer.

❑ A few pests you may want to control are aphids, mealybugs, leaf spots, and scale. The fungus on azalea flowers is usually ignored. Roses are susceptible to mites and black spot.

APRIL

❑ Plant roses now. Shrubs can be kept in containers until ready for the landscape. Keep the soil moist and apply liquid fertilizer every other week.

❑ Reduce weeds by pulling, applying mulch layers, using a pre-emergence herbicide, and periodically raking or hoeing the soil.

❑ During this hot, dry time of year, frequently check for shrubs that may need water. It does not hurt them to wilt a little. Keep new roses moist. Groom roses throughout the growing season. Continue regular monthly feeding for roses.

❑ Thrips may spoil gardenia flowers. Control with insecticidal spray before the buds open. Look for aphids, caterpillars, mealybugs, leaf spots, and scale. Hand pick or rinse away with water.

MAY

❑ Moving plants at this time of year is difficult. Wait until cooler weather or wetter weather.

❑ After spring growth, some shrubs may need trimming. Up to one-third of the old wood can be removed during spring pruning, but don't do this every year. Roses may be groomed throughout the growing season.

❑ Check plants regularly for water needs during this hot, dry month.

❑ Apply monthly rose feeding.

❑ Plant pests love summerlike weather. Many grasshoppers have recently hatched. Try hand picking these difficult-to-control pests. More summer shrub pests are aphids, caterpillars, mealybugs, and scale. Hand pick or rinse with water.

JUNE

❑ In Florida we add landscape plantings year-round, but it's a lot more stressful for you during summer.

❑ Hurry to complete azalea, camellia, and gardenia pruning as they form buds for next year. Delay pruning plants that flower during summer. Groom roses throughout the growing season.

❑ Summer rains may be doing most of your watering. But check often and when a few days pass without rain, it may be your turn to provide the moisture.

❑ Continue with regular monthly rose fertilizer applications.

❑ Keep your eye out for summer pests. Aphids, caterpillars, grasshoppers, leaf spot, and scale can occur. Black spot may affect roses now.

JULY

❑ It's the wet season, so Nature is providing much of the required irrigation.

❑ Hydrangeas are in bloom and will soon be ready for trimming. Remove old flower heads and trim to reshape the plants. Complete all azalea and gardenia pruning early this month. It's probably too late for additional pruning of camellias without affecting some flowering. Groom roses throughout the growing season.

❑ Keep up with weeding and preventive measures.

❑ You probably won't have to do a lot of watering thanks to frequent summer rains.

❑ Give roses their monthly fertilizer.

❑ The rainy season helps control some pests, like mites, but encourages others. Look for aphids, lace bugs, caterpillars, grasshoppers, and leaf spots. Black spot may affect roses now.

AUGUST

❑ Continue regular hedge pruning, allowing new shoots to grow 6 or more inches (15 or more cm) before shearing. Cut them back to within 1 or 2 inches(2.5 to 5 cm) of previous cuts. Every few years, major prunings to reduce height and width are needed. Groom roses throughout the growing season.

❑ This is still the rainy season, so you probably won't have lots of watering.

❑ Give monthly rose fertilizer application.

❑ Use pesticides only when destructive insects are out of control. Many beneficial insects are in the landscape, including ladybugs, lacewings, and mantids. Pests you may have to control are caterpillars, grasshoppers, lace bugs, and leaf spots. Black spot may affect roses now.

SEPTEMBER

❏ Adding new shrubs and roses should get easier as weather becomes cooler. By late September, the moderating temperatures might coax you outdoors to begin planting. At least you can get the soil ready. Test the pH of the soil so you know what to plant. Enrich sandy soils with organic matter such as coconut coir, compost, or composted manure.

❏ Do some fall shrub pruning. Groom roses throughout the growing season.

❏ Watch the weather to know when to pick up on watering.

❏ Give roses their monthly feeding.

❏ Many bugs develop large populations during summer that keep feeding into fall. You may find aphids, caterpillars, grasshoppers, leaf spots, and mites. Black spot may affect roses now. Develop a pest-control strategy for fall.

OCTOBER

❏ Fall is a great time to add new roses and shrubs. Milder weather allows root systems to grow with little stress on foliage. New plantings need moisture daily for first few weeks. Add layer of mulch. Thereafter, use soil moisture as a guide. Water when top inch of soil starts to dry.

❏ Complete all fall shrub pruning in Central and North Florida. Continue grooming roses as needed.

❏ Wet season is winding down, so water newly planted shrubs until they stop wilting.

❏ Give roses their monthly fertilizer application.

❏ Most gardeners will be fighting some pests for a month or two longer before cooler weather slows their growth. Mites may increase on both shrubs and roses because of the drier weather. Check plantings for caterpillars, grasshoppers, lace bugs, and leaf spots.

NOVEMBER

❏ Adding plants is enjoyable during November. There is less stress on you and the shrubs.

❏ Pruning time is over for all shrubs in Central and North Florida, where trimming done now will encourage growth that might be damaged by cold. South Florida shrubs can be trimmed as needed.

❏ This is a dry but cooler month. Irrigation regulations are limited to once-a-week waterings, but drought-tolerant shrubs won't need it.

❏ In North and Central Florida, reduce rose feedings to every 6 to 8 weeks until spring.

❏ Pest activity starts to slow down in November, but continue regular checks on the landscape. Aphids, caterpillars, grasshoppers, leaf spots, and mites stay active on warm days.

DECEMBER

❏ Winter arrives this month, and it's a great time to add shrubs or relocate them. When moving plants, make sure the soil is moist and try to get a large intact root ball.

❏ Be prepared for cold weather, with protection available for sensitive shrubs when freeze warnings are sounded.

❏ In North and Central Florida, reduce rose feedings to every 6 to 8 weeks until spring.

❏ Only in the warmer locations are pests on shrubs usually active. Look for leaf spots and scale on warm days. During the drier months, mites may attack roses. Spray undersides of leaves with water as first defense.

TREES & PALMS
for Florida

Perhaps there is nothing more useful in the Florida landscape than trees. They provide shade and actually cool the air through transpiration.

Deciding which trees to plant takes careful consideration. Once the tree is in the ground, it's not easily moved. Use our table (page 186) and the palm chart (page 185) to select appropriate trees. It's helpful to see them at plant sales, local garden centers, parks, and botanical gardens.

PLANNING

Take a look at your yard and decide where you want shade. Should it be light shade or filtered? If it is dense, plan on removing lawn from around that tree or group of trees to build a habitat grove. Trees keep the air cooler in your yard. A barrier of trees on the southwest side of the yard can reduce afternoon heat and may significantly reduce your air conditioning use.

Plan ahead for tree size, both above and below ground. As described in the introduction to planning on page 11, call to locate the underground utilities before you plant trees.

PLANTING

Choose small trees with a maximum 1-inch- (2.5-cm-) diameter trunk, because they will become established much more quickly than larger, more expensive container-grown trees, using a lot less water. Use the planting instructions in the introduction on page 15.

Planting palms is a bit different than planting other trees. And the best planting time for dug palms is March through August. Palms make the best root and top growth when the weather is warm. Unlike trees, palms dug from the ground should have about half the older leaves removed at planting time. The remaining leaves are usually drawn up above the bud and tied in place (for about 60 days) to retard water loss. Cabbage palms often have all leaves removed during transplanting. (At no other time should fronds be trimmed like this.) Most field-grown palms require staking for a year or more, because they generate all new roots after transplanting. If container grown, plant palms at any time, and they do not need staking or special pruning.

CARE

New plantings need different care than older, well-established trees. You want new trees to quickly send roots into the surrounding soil to become well anchored.

WATERING

New trees and palms need plenty of water. In addition to the instructions in the introduction, keep in mind that some trees are slow to become established. Dogwoods and magnolias appear to be two of the slowest. Most trees are established after a year. Once trees and palms are established, very few need frequent watering.

FERTILIZING

Most gardeners are surprised to learn that shade and flowering trees need little fertilizer and only during the establishment period. This is when they form new roots and make rapid stem and leaf growth. Three to five years after planting, most special feedings can be discontinued. The first limited feeding is normally applied 4 to 6 weeks after planting. Apply a topdressing of compost outside the planting hole to draw roots into the surrounding soil. For a year or two after planting, apply compost in the spring well before the wet season, and if needed, later in the fall after the wet season. Each time you apply the compost, lay it in a ring a little farther away from the planting hole.

Feed palms on a regular schedule for their lifespan. Current recommendations call for feeding twice a year in the spring before the wet season and again in the fall after the wet season.

PEST CONTROL

Trees and palms do have pests, but most established plantings are resistant and can withstand some holes and defoliation. The real concern is associated with new plantings. Because of their size, very few large established trees or palms are sprayed.

Check your young trees and palms during walks in the yard for pest problems. If noted, many can be hand picked from the plants and destroyed. See pages 224 to 227 for pest descriptions and controls.

ARECA PALM

Dypsis lutescens
Palm family: Arecaceae

HARDINESS–Zones 10-11

NATIVE RANGE–Madagascar

PEAK SEASON–Evergreen; spring flowers

MATURE SIZE–To about 20 feet x 15-plus feet (to about 6 m x 4.5-plus m)

WATER NEEDS–Keep roots moist the first year, then only irrigate during droughts.

CARE–Some nursery arecas are adapted to shade and must gradually be acclimated to sun. Tolerant of many soils. When arecas have potassium deficiency, older leaves get yellow spots. Feed with palm fertilizer with high potassium plus micronutrients.

PROBLEMS–Remove suckers from clump interior to allow circulation, reducing vulnerability to fungus, scale, and mealybugs.

USES AND SELECTIONS–Graceful arching fronds are feather-like with golden bases. Arecas form thick clumps and are widely used for screening, hedging, or background plantings. When kept pruned, they're beautiful specimen plants. Arecas are compatible with many flowering shrubs, serving as a backdrop to display blooms. Use as container plants in cooler locations.

BALD CYPRESS

Taxodium distichum
Cypress family: Cupressaceae

HARDINESS–Zones 8-11

NATIVE RANGE–New York to Texas (including all of Florida) and Mexico

COLOR(S)–Bright-green leaves in summer that turn coppery in fall before dropping

MATURE SIZE–100 feet x 30 feet (30.5 m x 9 m)

WATER NEEDS–Typically grows in water or at water's edge, where it does best. However, this Florida native can grow in dry soils. Keep roots moist, but not waterlogged, until established. Once established, only needs water during severe drought.

CARE–If planted out of water, feed in March and June for first 2 or 3 years. Trees in water need no special feedings. Prune during winter after planting if needed to keep straight trunk and even branching.

PROBLEMS– Cypress roots develop short protrusions above ground called "knees" that help stabilize the tree or perhaps exchange gases, so make sure it's planted where there is plenty of knee room.

USES AND SELECTIONS–One of Florida's few trees that grow in wet or dry soils. Best used lakeside with one or two trees and other wet-root plantings. The needle-like leaves have a feathery appearance and fall in the winter. Another native, pond cypress (*T. ascenders*), also occurs throughout Florida, but it requires moist or wet soil.

BISMARCK PALM

Bismarckia nobilis
Palm family: Arecaceae

HARDINESS–Zones 9b-11. Bismarck palms recover from occasional light freeze damage.

NATIVE RANGE–Madagascar

MATURE SIZE–40 to 70 feet x 15 to 20 feet (12 to 21 m x 4.5 to 6 m)

WATER NEEDS–Water daily for first few weeks, then reduce waterings but keep root zone moist for first growing season. Plant at beginning of rainy season to reduce need for irrigation. Established palms are very drought tolerant.

CARE–Plant in well-drained soil. Prefers full sun. When young, use palm fertilizer in spring. Mature palms usually need no special care. Bismarck palm doesn't exhibit nutritional deficiencies like other palms and is somewhat salt tolerant.

PROBLEMS–None.

USES AND SELECTIONS–Bismarck palms are massive and striking. Their huge trunks and light blue-green fronds (to 4 feet (122 cm) across) are beautiful and command attention, even from a distance. They make excellent specimens in large gardens and can be planted along driveways or paths for a showy entrance. For maximum impact, plant in front of dark-green vegetation.

CABBAGE PALM

Sabal palmetto
Palm family: Arecaceae

HARDINESS–Zones 8-11

NATIVE RANGE–Southeastern states and Cuba

PEAK SEASON–Evergreen; blooms summer

MATURE SIZE–40 feet x 10 feet (12 x 3 m)

WATER NEEDS–Until roots begin growing out from new plantings, thoroughly wet the root ball. Make sure soil does not dry out for several growing seasons. Established cabbage palms only need watering during extreme drought. However, they also tolerate moist soils.

CARE–Transplant in late spring to midsummer, with all fronds removed, and stake firmly for a year or more. Mulch to retain moisture. Fertilize in March with compost and/or palm fertilizer for a couple of years after planting. After establishment, it's recommended that old fronds not be trimmed, but if desired, trim only those that sag below horizontal.

PROBLEMS–Few problems.

USES AND SELECTIONS–The official state tree of Florida. The palm has been used for hats, baskets, roofs, and food. After older fronds drop, the remaining bases, called boots, add interest to the trunk. Can be used as a single specimen, but it looks best in clusters of three or more. The native dwarf palmetto (*S. minor*) is found throughout Florida as an understory plant to 12 feet (3.5 m) tall.

CHINESE FAN PALM

Livistona chinensis
Palm family: Arecaceae

HARDINESS–Zones 9b-11

NATIVE RANGE–China and Japan

PEAK SEASON–Evergreen foliage

MATURE SIZE–20 to 30 feet x 15 feet (6 to 9 m x 4.5 m); fronds 3 to 6 feet (91 to 183 cm) wide

WATER NEEDS–Established trees need little more than occasional irrigation in dry season.

CARE–This tough palm is not fussy. Add compost and fertilizer a couple of months after planting and in March the following year. If removing brown fronds, wait until leaf stems are brown. Palms can use needed potassium from the old leaves as they age.

PROBLEMS–Keep area around base open for air circulation, which helps prevents fungal disease. Susceptible to palm leaf skeletonizer.

USES AND SELECTIONS–Grow in containers in areas where freezing temperatures are likely. Older (taller) palms allow the use of bromeliads planted beneath or around them. Seeds are deep blue-green and pretty, ripening summer through fall. The drooping frond ends are divided, so they seem to be hung with split ribbons.

CRAPE MYRTLE

Lagerstroemia indica
Loosestrife family: Lythraceae

HARDINESS–Zones 8-10

NATIVE RANGE–Southeast Asia

COLOR(S)–Red, pink, lavender, coral, white flowers; green foliage

PEAK SEASON–Blooms summer and fall

MATURE SIZE–20 feet x 20 feet (6 x 6 m)

WATER NEEDS–Drought tolerant and does well in many soils but not standing water. Mulch to retain moisture.

CARE–Often hacked off at 6 feet (183 cm) or so to induce more flowering. Some have called this "crape murder." You can restore to a tree shape by selecting only a few of the shoots to grow and prune away others. It can become a decent tree in your landscape. It is likely to sucker from the base. Select those you want to grow into new trunks and remove the others while they are small.

PROBLEMS–This non-native tree is so over-planted in Florida that you could add diversity to the neighborhood by selecting something else for your landscape.

USES AND SELECTIONS–Use this reliable bloomer in mixed informal planting or as a specimen. The leaves turn yellow then orange-red before falling in midwinter.

DOGWOOD

Cornus florida
Dogwood family: Cornaceae

HARDINESS–Zones 8-9

NATIVE RANGE–Eastern North America, including most of Florida.

COLOR(S)–White flowers; reddish fall color

PEAK SEASON–Blooms early spring; foliage deciduous

MATURE SIZE–20 to 35 feet x 25 to 35 feet (6 to 10.5 m x 7.5 to 10.5 m)

WATER NEEDS–Needs moist soil for best growth, especially in sandy soil. Mulch heavily. Do not let roots get soggy.

CARE–Plant in enriched, well-drained soil. Hard to establish in sandy soils. Prune to either one or several trunks. Leaves turn red and purple in autumn, more vividly in northern areas.

PROBLEMS–Susceptible to several diseases, plus aphids and scale.

USES AND SELECTIONS–Plant as specimen, background, or framing tree. Its size is ideal near patios and in smaller gardens for shade. It also does well beneath large oaks or pines. Numerous selections have different bract (flower) and tree forms–most do not thrive in Florida. Red berries ripen in fall, remain into winter, and are relished by birds and wildlife. Native to Florida.

FLORIDA SILVER PALM

Coccothrinax argentata
Palm family: Arecaceae

HARDINESS–Zones 10b-11

NATIVE RANGE–South Florida, Bahamas, and Colombia

MATURE SIZE–20 feet x 5 feet (6 x 1.5 m)

WATER NEEDS–Water daily for first few weeks, then reduce waterings but keep root zone moist for first growing season. Plant at beginning of rainy season to reduce irrigation. When established, are very drought tolerant.

CARE–For 2 years after planting, use compost and/or palm fertilizer in March. Mature palms get along on their own, unless leaves become off-color. Then apply nutrients. Grow in containers and protect from freezing in Central and North Florida.

PROBLEMS–Overwatering or wet feet can cause disease.

USES AND SELECTIONS–This very slow-growing small native has drooping fronds with silvery undersides. The fragile-looking silver palm is extraordinarily tough, being highly salt and drought tolerant. It is good for seaside homes plus xeriscape and native landscapes. It is suitable for patio and townhouse gardens with limited space. It looks good in groups of three to five or combined with other plants.

GEIGER TREE

Cordia sebestena
Borage family: Boraginaceae

HARDINESS–Zones 10-11

NATIVE RANGE–Caribbean, Central America, and northern South America

COLOR(S)–Orange flowers

PEAK SEASON–Blooms year-round

MATURE SIZE–25 feet x 15 feet (7.5 x 4.5 m)

WATER NEEDS–Established trees need little more than occasional irrigation in dry season.

CARE–Add compost in spring and fall only. This tough little tree is salt and drought tolerant, but not cold tolerant. Leaves will turn brown when temperatures dip below 45°F (7°C). In a freeze, it dies to the ground but resprouts from the roots.

PROBLEMS–Geiger beetle

USES AND SELECTIONS–Plant with sea grape for a natural coastal setting, or give it a place of its own. Hummingbirds are attracted to the bright flowers. Use as a background for a butterfly garden. Plant where irrigation does not reach. The Texas wild olive is a cold-tolerant, white-flowering relative. The fruits are edible but not tasty. Was thought to be a Florida native, but it's probably not.

GUMBO-LIMBO

Bursera simaruba
Torchwood family: Burseraceae

HARDINESS–Zones 10-11

NATIVE RANGE–Florida, Mexico, Caribbean, Central America, and northern South America

COLOR(S)–Red to silver-red peeling bark

PEAK SEASON–Loses then regrows leaves in late winter and early spring. Dark-red fruit takes a year to ripen.

MATURE SIZE–30 to 40-plus feet x 20-plus feet (9 to 12-plus m x 6-plus m)

WATER NEEDS–Water established trees during drought; keep mulched

CARE–Once established, the fast-growing gumbo-limbo needs little care. Trees can be started from branch cuttings. Keep root zone and branch watered.

PROBLEMS–No problems.

USES AND SELECTIONS–This native is often found in river and coastal areas of the warmer parts of Florida. For light, high shade, a mature tree makes a beautiful specimen, especially older trees with a large girth. Low under-plantings of ferns and bromeliads show off the almost sculptural trunks. When planted on the south side of a home, this deciduous tree allows winter sun to come through the branches for energy-conscious plantings.

HOLLY

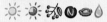

Ilex spp. There are 12 native species in Florida.
Holly family: Aquifoliaceae

HARDINESS–Zones 8-10

NATIVE RANGE–Florida and widespread across the globe

COLOR(S)–Red or black berries; green leaves

PEAK SEASON–Fall and winter berries

MATURE SIZE–5 to 40 feet x 3 to 25 feet (1.5 to 12 m x 1 to 7.5 m)

WATER NEEDS–Most hollies like well-drained acid soils and are drought tolerant once established. Water during droughts. A few, including dahoon holly (*I. cassine*), grow in damp sites.

CARE–Feed in March for first 3 years. Minimize trimming so limbs can develop berries. Hollies are dioecious, with male and female trees. Be sure to include one male plant in the region, so fruit can develop.

PROBLEMS–The leaf drop in late winter signals the coming new growth and is not a problem.

USES AND SELECTIONS–The adaptable hollies are good for view barriers, hedges, and accents. Hollies can be shrubs or trees. Attractive with acid-loving plants like azaleas, camellias, and gardenias. 'East Palatka' holly (*I. x attenuata*), a naturally occurring hybrid, has many berries and is great for attracting wildlife.

LADY PALM

Rhapis spp.
Palm family: Arecaceae

HARDINESS–Zones 9b-11

NATIVE RANGE–Southeast Asia

MATURE SIZE–6 to 15 feet x 15 feet (183 cm to 4.5 m x 4.5 m)

WATER NEEDS–Water daily for a few weeks, then gradually taper off, but keep root ball moist. After the first growing season, lady palms can withstand fairly dry conditions. Reduce watering to a minimum except in drought.

CARE–Use compost or palm fertilizer in March for the first 2 years after planting. Grow in protected areas of Central Florida; in colder areas grow in containers.

PROBLEMS–When hungry or in full sun, the leaves turn yellow.

USES AND SELECTIONS–The pliable and forgiving lady palm brings a sense of grace to landscapes. It serves as a screen and hedge when grown as a middle layer between a ground cover and taller palms. It is also used in containers. Two species work well in Florida. *Rhapis excelsa slowly grows to 12 or 14 feet (3.5 to 4 m). R. humilis is taller, with more drooping leaves, and it takes more cold.*

LIGNUM VITAE

Guaiacum sanctum
Caper-bean family: Zygophyllaceae

HARDINESS–Zones 10b-11

NATIVE RANGE–South Florida, Caribbean, and Central America

COLOR(S)–Blue-violet flowers; golden pods

PEAK SEASON–Blooms spring to summer; evergreen leaves

MATURE SIZE–15 to 20 feet x 10 to 15 feet (4.5 to 6 m x 3 to 4.5 m)

WATER NEEDS–Keep root ball moist after planting. Once established, is drought tolerant.

CARE–Needs good drainage. Use half-strength fertilizer weekly for new seedlings and compost or slow-release fertilizer every 3 to 4 months for 2 years after planting.

PROBLEMS–It takes several years for the tree to produce the incomparable blue flowers.

USES AND SELECTIONS–Plant this very slow-growing tree where small flowers can be seen near patio, home entrance, or in a mega-container. Use lignum vitae as a specimen tree. The tree has extremely heavy hard wood and black heartwood, which doesn't float. Now prized for wood turners, it was once used for boat and submarine construction. The United States Navy harvested trees from the Florida Keys, where it occurs naturally. The few left today are endangered.

LIVE OAK

Quercus virginiana
Beech family: Fagaceae

HARDINESS–Zones 8-11

NATIVE RANGE–All of Florida, and Southeast states from Virginia to Texas

PEAK SEASON–Leaves drop in spring before new growth

MATURE SIZE–50 or more feet x 80 feet (15 or more m x 24 m)

WATER NEEDS–Drought tolerant once established

CARE–Takes a wide range of soils. Mulch or plant with shallow-rooted ground cover. Although once thought to be slow growing, fertilizer, water, and mulch bring faster growth.

PROBLEMS–Select locations with lots of room for limbs, which naturally grow low and horizontal. Hanging Spanish moss and resurrection ferns may grow on the tops of the horizontal branches. These epiphytes add character and are not harmful.

USES AND SELECTIONS–Whether grouped with other trees or alone, this strong and long-lived tree is ruggedly handsome. It is highly prized as a shade tree. Orchids grow wonderfully in it, as do bromeliads. Use ferns and bromeliads beneath. In Florida there are specimen live oaks that are hundreds of years old. The sand live oak (*Q. geminata*) is smaller and suitable for smaller landscapes. In addition, there are a dozen other oaks native to Florida. They all are suitable additions to your yard.

MAHOGANY

Swietenia mahagoni
Mahogany family: Meliaceae

HARDINESS–Zones 10–11. Use only in frost- and freeze-free locations.

NATIVE RANGE–South Florida and Caribbean

PEAK SEASON–Leaves drop in spring before new growth begins.

MATURE SIZE–45 feet x 40 feet (14 x 12 m)

WATER NEEDS–Water new plantings, gradually tapering off watering. Established trees are drought tolerant. Irrigate during severe drought.

CARE–Add compost 4 to 6 weeks after planting. Add more compost in March for 2 or 3 years. Prune in winter to keep straight trunk and develop even branching.

PROBLEMS–None.

USES AND SELECTIONS–Combine with other small trees and greenery. Suitable for shade, to plant street-side, or to frame the home. The strong wood, salt tolerance, and wind resistance make mahogany suitable for coastal landscapes. Add the tropical look with hibiscus, bird-of-paradise, and bananas. Mahogany's Central American relative is used for timber.

PIGEON PLUM

Coccoloba diversifolia
Smartweed family: Polygonaceae

HARDINESS–Zones 9b–11

NATIVE RANGE–South Florida, Caribbean, Mexico, Central America, and northern South America

COLOR(S)–White flowers; fallen leaves turn golden

PEAK SEASON–Blooms around March; evergreen foliage

MATURE SIZE–30 to 50 feet x 15 to 20 feet (9 to 15 m x 4.5 to 6 m)

WATER NEEDS–Water young trees. Once established, they take drought well.

CARE–Add compost for first few years. If growing in a group, it grows tall and narrow; it grows shorter and fatter in sun.

PROBLEMS–None.

USES AND SELECTIONS–Pigeon plum is plentiful in coastal hammocks from the center of Florida to the Keys. It has dense upright growth and pretty bark, which make it useful in the landscape or for street planting. Use in coastal plantings, along a wall, in large planters, or in a native habitat. This versatile tree can blend with wild coffee, beautyberry, and other coastal woodland plants. It tolerates harsh conditions, taking wind and salt spray well. Female trees have somewhat edible berries that attract wildlife.

PINDO PALM

Butia capitata
Palm family: Arecaceae

HARDINESS–Zones 8–10

NATIVE RANGE–Eastern South America

COLOR(S)–Blue-green fronds

PEAK SEASON–Spring flowers

MATURE SIZE–15 feet x 15 feet (4.5 x 4.5 m)

WATER NEEDS–Keep new plantings moist and do not allow it to dry out for several growing seasons. Drought tolerant once established.

CARE–Add container-grown plants at any time. Plant field-dug palms during spring and summer. To encourage growth and maintain best color, fertilize once in March with palm fertilizer. Somewhat salt tolerant.

PROBLEMS–Susceptible to leaf spots and trunk rots

USES AND SELECTIONS–Pindo or jelly palm is one of Florida's finest landscape plants. It is often planted as a focal point or to line streets. There is plenty of room for ground cover plantings beneath this large palm. Use ornamentals that repeat the needle-like look, including junipers, liriope, or iris.

PINE

Pinus spp. There are 7 species of pine native to Florida.
Pine family: Pinaceae

HARDINESS–Zones 8–11

NATIVE RANGE–All of Florida and more

PEAK SEASON–Evergreen

MATURE SIZE–To 100 feet x 50 feet (to 30.5 m x 15 m)

WATER NEEDS–Water daily for first few weeks, then gradually taper off. Drought tolerant once established.

CARE–Plant in well-drained soil. Apply compost 4 to 6 weeks after planting and again the next March. Once established, grows quite rapidly. Too frequent watering and fertilizing of established trees can cause decline.

PROBLEMS–Pests include caterpillars and borers. Keep vehicles away from trees to prevent root damage.

USES AND SELECTIONS–Underplant with acid-loving azaleas, camellias, and blueberries. Can also be clustered as a backdrop for home sites and in wildlife areas. Some native pines include: sand pine (*P. clausa*), yellow pine (*P. echinata*), slash pine (*P. elliottii*), spruce pine (*P. glabra*), longleaf pine (*P. palustris*), pond pine (*P. serotine*), and loblolly pine (*P. taeda*). Japanese black pine (*P. thunbergii*) is also sold in Florida.

PLUMERIA

Plumeria spp.
Dogbane family: Apocynaceae

HARDINESS–Zones 10–11 and warmer areas of 9b

NATIVE RANGE–Caribbean, Mexico, Central America, and northern South America

COLOR(S)–Red, white, yellow, pink, multihued flowers

PEAK SEASON–Blooms summer through fall; deciduous foliage

MATURE SIZE–20 to 25 feet (6 to 7.5 m)

WATER NEEDS–Drought tolerant. Requires well-drained soil.

CARE–Add compost in the spring for 2 or 3 years after planting. Long narrow leaves grow only at ends of stubby branches, which can be pruned for multiple trunks. Has some salt tolerance.

PROBLEMS–All parts of the plant are poisonous. Branches susceptible to breaking. Poor drainage can cause root rot. Must be protected from freezing. Control of rust fungus may be needed.

USES AND SELECTIONS–Use plumeria (also called frangipani) where its beauty and fragrance can be appreciated–near decks, patios, and entryways. Plant for a tropical look. There are countless species and cultivars.

PYGMY DATE PALM

Phoenix roebelenii
Palm family: Arecaceae

HARDINESS–Zones 10–11 and warmer areas of 9b

NATIVE RANGE–Southeast Asia

MATURE SIZE–10 feet x 8-plus feet (3 m x 2.5-plus m)

WATER NEEDS–Keep the root zone of newly planted date palms moist during the first growing season. This has more need for water than other palms.

CARE–Use palm fertilizer with micronutrients to prevent deficiencies in March, June, and October. May show potassium deficiencies and need additional applications of potassium sulfate with manganese sulfate. Protect from cold in Central and North Florida. Pygmy date palm is small enough to grow in large containers.

PROBLEMS–The spines at the base of Phoenix palm fronds warrant care when trimming and handling.

USES AND SELECTIONS–This versatile tree is useful for entrances, small accent trees, and containers for pool and patio areas. Multi-trunked specimens are especially attractive. Other date palms (*Phoenix* spp.) have also been planted in South Florida. They are dioecious, so if you are planning to harvest fruit, make sure a male palm is in the vicinity.

RED MAPLE

Acer rubrum
Soapberry family: Sapindaceae

HARDINESS–Zones 8–10

NATIVE RANGE–Most of eastern North America, including all of southernmost Florida

COLOR(S)–Small red flowers and seeds; green leaves turn red and orange in fall before dropping

PEAK SEASON–Spring blooms are followed by new leaves

MATURE SIZE–40 to 50 or more feet x 30 feet (12 to 15 or more m x 9 m)

WATER NEEDS–Tolerates some extended flooding but prefers slightly drier areas or periodically wet, acidic soils.

CARE–Get trees with a single leader to prevent future splitting. Avoid dry, sandy soils. Once established, little care is required if properly located.

PROBLEMS–Borers may be a problem. The wide-spreading and shallow roots can interfere with in-ground infrastructure and can displace lawn areas, so plant only where there is enough room.

USES AND SELECTIONS–This big handsome tree is adapted to wet areas, such as rain gardens or lakefronts. The beauty of changing fall leaves is possible in Florida with this native. Plant with cabbage palms, sweet bay magnolia, dahoon holly, and wax myrtle. There are four other maples (*Acer* spp.) also native to Florida, but the red maple has the widest natural range.

REDBERRY STOPPER

Eugenia confusa
Myrtle family: Myrtaceae

HARDINESS–Zones 10-11

NATIVE RANGE–South Florida and the Caribbean

COLOR(S)–White flowers; glossy dark-green foliage

PEAK SEASON–Blooms spring

MATURE SIZE–20 feet x 10 feet (6 x 3 m)

WATER NEEDS–Drought tolerant once established

CARE–Plant from beginning of rainy season through midsummer. Mulch to retain moisture. Adapted to rocky soil. Once established, needs little care.

PROBLEMS–None.

USES AND SELECTIONS–This slow-growing native is a durable and dependable small tree that should be planted more often. This beautiful columnar tree can be useful for townhouses where space is tight. Three other stopper species are also native to Florida. Red stopper (*E. rhombea)* is one of Florida's rarest native trees. Spanish stopper *(E. foetida*) and white stopper (*E. axillaris*) are both salt tolerant.

REDBUD

Cercis canadensis
Legume family: Fabaceae

HARDINESS–Zones 8-9

NATIVE RANGE–Most of eastern North America, including North and north Central Florida

COLOR(S)–Purple-pink flowers

PEAK SEASON–Blooms in spring before foliage; foliage deciduous

MATURE SIZE–20 to 30 feet x 15 to 25 feet (6 to 9 m x 4.5 to 7.5 m)

WATER NEEDS–Drought tolerant, although it grows best with some moisture and tolerates brief periods of standing water.

CARE–It's a legume, so it fixes nitrogen in the soil and can do well in lousy soil. Transplant in spring or fall. Plant container-grown trees any time. Tends to grow multiple trunks, with drooping outer branches. If desired, can be pruned to have a single trunk.

PROBLEMS–Branches susceptible to breakage. Scale can be controlled with horticultural oil sprays. Borers and webworms may also occur.

USES AND SELECTIONS–Plant redbud as a shade tree or understory tree, or use near a patio. This flowering tree makes a beautiful specimen and works well when planted as a shrub border. The leaves turn yellow before falling in winter. There are numerous cultivars. However, this Florida native is the one predominantly planted.

REDCEDAR

Juniperus virginiana
Cypress family: Cupressaceae

HARDINESS–Zones 8-11

NATIVE RANGE–Eastern North America, including all of Florida

COLOR(S)–Green leaves; blue-green fruits

MATURE SIZE–40 to 50 feet x 10 to 20 feet (12 to 15 m x 3 to 6 m)

WATER NEEDS–Water until established, then forget about it. Very drought tolerant. Does not like soggy roots.

CARE–Thrives in any well-drained soil. Carefree. Lower branches are sometimes pruned for visibility, but it's better to allow them to remain for the conical shape. Is a dioecious conifer with male and female plants, so make sure there is at least one male tree in the area to produce fruit.

PROBLEMS–No serious pests

USES AND SELECTIONS–Once the most common tree in the eastern United States, it's also called southern redcedar. Florida was once filled with these tough, long-lived trees. Cedar Key was named for them, and its port shipped fragrant cedar lumber to northern factories to make pencils and hope chests. Plant them as specimens, screens, and windbreaks. They also are suitable as bonsai, for Christmas trees, and in wildlife gardens. Birds, especially cedar waxwings, relish the blue-green fruit.

ROYAL PALM

☀ Ⓝ 🐝 🌴

Roystonea regia
Palm family: Arecaceae

HARDINESS–Zones 10-11

NATIVE RANGE–South Florida, Caribbean, southern Mexico, and Central America

MATURE SIZE–50 feet x 30 feet (15 x 9 m)

WATER NEEDS–Newly planted royal palms should be kept moist until roots begin to grow out. Make sure soil does not thoroughly dry out for several growing seasons. Mulch new plantings to retain moisture. Once established, water weekly or whenever soil begins to dry, especially during drought.

CARE–Looks and grows best when fertilized once in March with compost and/or palm fertilizer.

PROBLEMS–Brace new plantings to prevent wind damage. In some soils they can exhibit nutrient deficiencies. Old fronds that drop from the tree can weigh up to 40 pounds (18 kg), so plant where that won't be a problem.

USES AND SELECTIONS–Plant these tall, fast-growing palms alone or in clusters of three or more. Use as accents or in rows along wide streets. The long area of smooth green trunk at the top catches attention. Add ornamentals that complete the tropical look, including bougainvillea, crotons, allamanda, gingers, and philodendrons.

ROYAL POINCIANA

☀ 💧 🌴

Delonix regia
Legume family: Fabaceae

HARDINESS–Zones 10b-11

NATIVE RANGE–Madagascar

COLOR(S)–Cerise, scarlet, and yellow flowers

PEAK SEASON–Blooms spring to summer; often but not always deciduous

MATURE SIZE–25 to 40 feet x 40 feet (7.5 to 12 m x 12 m)

WATER NEEDS–After planting, keep root zone moist throughout first growing season. While young, water in dry season. Drought tolerant when established.

CARE–Plant in large, open space; it requires a big landscape. Apply compost in early spring. Prune out deadwood. Remove lawn from under this tree.

PROBLEMS–This tree is too large for a small yard. Roots can uplift asphalt. Aggressive roots and long pods create a grass cutter's nightmare, so replace lawn around these trees with shrubs, ferns, and ground covers.

USES AND SELECTIONS–The cascading canopy of brilliant color makes a flowering royal poinciana stop traffic. After the enormous initial showing in spring, flowers linger throughout summer. The doubly compound leaves have a ferny look and provide dappled shade. Golf courses, parks, and wide boulevards are best for this large, spreading tree.

RUFFLED FAN PALM

☀ ☀ ☀ 🐝 🌿 🌴

Licuala grandis
Palm family: Arecaceae

HARDINESS–Zones 10-11

NATIVE RANGE–Santa Cruz Islands (east of Australia)

MATURE SIZE–To 9 feet x 5- to 6-foot crown (to 274 cm x 152- to 183-cm crown)

WATER NEEDS–This rainforest palm likes plenty of moisture. Water thoroughly, twice weekly in dry season, to encourage roots to penetrate deep into soil. Mulch well.

CARE–These palms are difficult to transplant. A low area with a humid microclimate protected from winds and hot sun is best. Shrubs, trellises, or other garden devices can be used for protection. Growth is slow, but leaves stay on a long time. Use compost to enrich the soil in March.

PROBLEMS–Falling fruit or branches from overhead may damage the large leaves.

USES AND SELECTIONS–The round, pleated leaves of these fan palms are so different and attractive that even non-palm-fanciers admire them. The palms look good in groups. These palms can be planted in containers–use a saucer to keep the root ball wet.

SATINLEAF

Chrysophyllum oliviforme
Sapodilla family: Sapotaceae

HARDINESS–Zones 10-11. Will freeze back if unprotected.

NATIVE RANGE–South Florida, Caribbean, and eastern Mexico

COLOR(S)–White flowers; green leaves with coppery backs

PEAK SEASON–Blooms spring

MATURE SIZE–30 to 40 feet x 15 feet (9 to 12 m x 4.5 m)

WATER NEEDS–Keep roots moist throughout first growing season. Fairly drought tolerant when established.

CARE–Add compost in the spring until plant becomes established. Seedlings may proliferate and can be dug at any time.

PROBLEMS–None.

USES AND SELECTIONS–Few other trees have leaves as beautiful as the native satinleaf. Group several trees or plant as a specimen tree. The copper undersides are clearly visible when wind blows or when you're beneath it. The dark-purple fruits attract birds. If landscaping for wildlife, use with wild coffee, pigeon plum, sea grape, and other fruit-bearing natives that offer birds and small animals food and shelter. The flowers are sweetly scented.

SOUTHERN MAGNOLIA

Magnolia grandiflora
Magnolia family: Magnoliaceae

HARDINESS–Zones 8-10

NATIVE RANGE–Southeastern states and North and Central Florida

COLOR(S)–White flowers; glossy green leaves

PEAK SEASON–Blooms May through July; Evergreen but sheds most leaves in late winter and spring, before new growth begins.

MATURE SIZE–80 to 90 feet x 30 to 40 feet (24 to 27 m x 9 to 12 m)

WATER NEEDS–New plantings are moisture sensitive. Keep soil moist with frequent waterings. Apply mulch. Once established, is drought tolerant in enriched soils.

CARE–Apply compost in March for first 3 years.

PROBLEMS–Leaf drop all year long makes it a maintenance problem when located in a lawn. Scale and black sooty mold can be ignored or controlled with oil spray.

USES AND SELECTIONS–Magnolias represent the South. They're ideal to frame a home, for shade, or to serve as a backdrop. It's often difficult to find plants to grow under magnolias, so leave the lower branches in place so that's not a problem. Use bromeliads and ferns. 'Little Gem' cultivar is smaller and an early bloomer with extended flowering.

SWEETBAY MAGNOLIA

Magnolia virginiana
Magnolia family: Magnoliaceae

HARDINESS–Zones 8-11

NATIVE RANGE–Eastern states from Massachusetts to Texas, all of Florida, and Cuba

COLOR(S)–White flowers; green leaves

PEAK SEASON–Blooms summer; evergreen to semi-evergreen foliage

MATURE SIZE–50 feet x 20 feet (15 x 6 m)

WATER NEEDS–Tolerates wet soil. Grows best in moist, fertile soils. Grows in sandy soils if provided adequate water. Water new plantings daily for first few weeks, then gradually taper off.

CARE–Add compost 4 to 6 weeks after planting and again in March for first 2 or 3 years only. Prune older trees in late winter if needed to keep trunk straight and develop even branching.

PROBLEMS–None.

USES AND SELECTIONS–Plant this narrow shade and accent tree in damp areas and for naturalistic plantings. Use with other moisture-loving trees and shrubs, such as bald cypress and wax myrtle. Nighttime blooms are highly fragrant.

SWEET GUM

Liquidambar styraciflua
Sweetgum family: Altingiaceae

HARDINESS–Zones 8-10a

NATIVE RANGE–Massachusetts through to Texas, including North and Central Florida; Mexico and Central America

COLOR(S)–Fall foliage colorful before leaves drop

MATURE SIZE–50 feet x 25 feet (15 x 7.5 m)

WATER NEEDS–Water daily for first few weeks, then gradually taper off. Established trees are drought tolerant.

CARE–Apply compost 4 to 6 weeks after planting, then again in March for 2 or 3 years. Established trees do not need additional feedings. Prune in late winter if needed for a straight trunk and even branching.

PROBLEMS–Some years the gum ball drop is prolific and can create hazardous footing. Older limbs often produce a corky ridge. This is a normal growth.

USES AND SELECTIONS–The sweet gum is a truly reliable native tree with a good shape that won't get too tall for average landscapes. It is upright and pyramidal in habit. The lobed leaves have a star-like appearance and are great for fall color.

TEXAS WILD OLIVE

Cordia boissieri
Borage family: Boraginaceae

HARDINESS–Zones 8b-11

NATIVE RANGE–Texas through Central America

COLOR(S)–White flowers

PEAK SEASON–Blooms and foliage year-round

MATURE SIZE–About 20 feet x 10 to 15 feet (about 6 m x 3 to 4.5 m)

WATER NEEDS–Keep root zone moist for first growing season and gradually allow nature to take over. Is drought tolerant and prefers well-drained soils.

CARE–Takes wide range of soils. Apply compost 4 to 6 weeks after planting. These little trees require little care and may flower at an early age, even at 1 foot (30 cm) high.

PROBLEMS–Avoid areas that flood or are near sprinklers. No major pruning is necessary. Remove dead wood and rubbing or diseased branches in late winter or early spring.

USES AND SELECTIONS–This little flowering tree is also called white olive and white geiger. Its good behavior and blooms are suitable in a front yard, near an entryway, or as a specimen tree. Plant with other drought-tolerant plants. Not as sensitive to cold like its cousin, the geiger tree.

TRUMPET TREE

Tabebuia spp. Caribbean trumpet tree (T. caraiba) & pink trumpet tree (T. rosea)
Bignonia family: Bignoniaceae

HARDINESS–Zones 10-11

COLOR(S)–Golden yellow or pink flowers

PEAK SEASON–Leaves drop just before flowers appear in spring.

MATURE SIZE–25 to 40 feet x 40 feet (7.5 to 12 m x 12 m)

WATER NEEDS–Water daily for first few weeks, then gradually taper off. Established trees are drought tolerant. Water during severe drought.

CARE–Add compost 4 to 6 weeks after planting and again in March for only 2 or 3 years. Prune crossed or dead limbs after flowering. In mid-Central Florida, plant in warmest landscape location. Areas near a lake are best. Frozen trees grow back but need training to keep central trunk.

PROBLEMS–None.

USES AND SELECTIONS–The trumpet trees make good small specimen trees. Their month-long bloom is spectacular, and fallen blossoms produce a yellow or pink carpet. Also prized for their gnarled trunks. Other yellow species grow in warmer parts of zone 9b.

WINGED ELM

Ulmus alata
Elm family: Ulmaceae

HARDINESS–Zones 8-9

NATIVE RANGE–Southeastern states, including North Florida

COLOR(S)–Flowers not showy

PEAK SEASON–Late-summer flowers; semi-evergreen foliage

MATURE SIZE–35 to 40 feet (10.5 to 12 m)

WATER NEEDS–Keep soil moist for first year or two. Thereafter, they are quite drought tolerant.

CARE–Plant at least 20 feet (6 m) from buildings. Add compost topdressing a few months after planting and again in March the following year or two. Maintain central leader until 6 to 8 feet (183 to 244 cm) tall, then prune periodically to keep sagging limbs above sidewalks and patios.

PROBLEMS–The Dutch elm disease is usually not a problem in Florida.

USES AND SELECTIONS–Grow as specimen tree to showcase the interesting winged branches. Also suitable for an understory tree or general landscape use. Plant with other drought-tolerant selections. Use shade-tolerant underplantings including beautyberry. Other native elms are: American elm (*U. Americana*); cedar elm (*U. crassifolia*); and slippery elm (*U. rubra*). Also, Chinese elm (*U. parvifolia*) is often sold.

PALMS

NAME	AREA OF FLORIDA	HEIGHT (FEET)	LIGHT NEEDED	GROWTH HABIT	BEST USES
Areca	S	10–20	Sun, filtered sun	Multi-stemmed	Accent, patios
Australian Fan	CS	40–50	Sun	Single trunk	Clusters
Bismarck	CS	40–70	Sun	Single trunk	Accent, street
Butia	NCS	10–20	Sun	Single trunk	Accent, patios
Cabbage	NCS	30–40	Sun	Single trunk	Clusters, streets
California Washingtonia	NCS	50–60	Sun	Single trunk	Clusters, streets
Canary Island Date	NCS	30–40	Sun	Single trunk	Accent, streets
Chinese Fan	CS	20–30	Sun	Single trunk	Clusters, patios
Date	NCS	40–50	Sun	Single trunk	Accent, streets
Dwarf Palmetto	NCS	3–6	Sun	Single trunk	Accent, natural areas
European Fan	NCS	6–8	Sun, filtered sun	Multi-stemmed	Accent, patios
Florida Silver	S	15–20	Sun, filtered sun	Single trunk	Accent, patios
Gru-Gru	S	30–40	Sun	Single trunk	Clusters, streets
Jamaica Thatch	S	10–20	Sun	Single trunk	Clusters
Lady	CS	8–10	Filtered sun	Multi-stemmed	Foundations, patios
Licuala	S	6–8	Filtered sun	Single trunk	Accent, patios
MacArthur	S	20–25	Sun, filtered sun	Multi-stemmed	Accent, patios
Malayan Dwarf Coconut	S	40–60	Sun	Single trunk	Clusters, street
Mexican Washingtonia	NCS	80–90	Sun	Single trunk	Streets
Needle	NCS	4–5	Light shade	Multi-stemmed	Accent, natural areas
Paurotis	CS	15–20	Sun, light shade	Multi-stemmed	Accent, patios
Puerto Rico Hat	CS	40–50	Sun	Single trunk	Clusters
Pygmy Date	S	8–10	Sun, filtered sun	Single trunk	Accent, patios
Royal Palm	S	80–90	Sun	Single trunk	Clusters, streets
Saw Palmetto	NCS	4–6	Sun, filtered sun	Multi-stemmed	Accent, natural areas
Senegal Date	S	20–25	Sun	Multi-stemmed	Accent, patios
Solitaire	S	15–20	Sun, filtered sun	Single trunk	Accent, patios
Windmill	NC	10–15	Sun, filtered sun	Single trunk	Accent, patios

N = North Florida   C = Central Florida   S = South Florida

TREES

NAME	AREA OF FLORIDA	H/W (FEET)	SOIL TYPE	FLOWERS/ SEASON	FRUITS/SEASON	BEST USES
African Tuliptree	S	50/50	Average	Orange, yellow/ Winter, spring	Not showy	Accent, shade
American Holly	NC	40/20	Average	White/Spring	Red/Fall	Accent, street, shade
Attenuate Holly	NC	30/15	Average	White/Spring	Red/Fall	Street, shade
Bald Cypress	NCS	80/30	Wet or dry	Inconspicuous	Green/Summer	Street, shade
Black Olive	S	40/40	Average	Inconspicuous	Black/Fall	Shade, street
Cherry Laurel	NC	35/30	Average	White/Spring	Black/Fall	Shade, street
Chickasaw Plum	NC	20/20	Average	White/Spring	Reddish/Summer	Accent, shade, street
Chinese Elm	NC	35/40	Average	Greenish/Fall	Not showy	Shade, street
Chinese Pistache	NC	25/25	Average	Greenish/Spring	Orange/Fall	Shade, street
Crape Myrtle	NC	20/20	Average	Various/Summer	Brown/Fall	Accent, shade, street
Dahoon Holly	NCS	25/10	Moist	White/Spring	Red/Fall	Accent
Dogwood	NC	30/20	Moist	White/Spring	Red/Fall	Accent, shade
Fringe Tree	NC	12/10	Average	White/Spring	Not showy	Accent, understory
Geiger Tree	S	25/25	Average	Orange/Spring	Not showy	Accent, shade, street
Golden Shower Tree	S	40/40	Average	Yellow/Summer	Pod/Fall	Accent, shade, street
Italian Cypress	NCS	30/10	Average	Inconspicuous	Not showy	Accent, hedge
Jacaranda	CS	40/50	Average	Purple/Spring	Not showy	Accent, shade
Jerusalem Thorn	NCS	20/20	Average	Yellow/Summer	Not showy	Accent
Laurel Oak	NCS	60/50	Average	Inconspicuous	Acorn/Fall	Shade, street
Lignum Vitae	S	15/10	Average	Blue/Year-round	Yellow/Year-round	Accent
Live Oak	NCS	60/100	Average	Inconspicuous	Acorn/Fall	Shade, street
Loblolly Bay	NC	40/15	Moist	White/Summer	Not showy	Accent, shade
Loquat	NCS	25/20	Average	White/Fall	Orange/Fall, winter	Shade, fruit
Mahogany	S	50/50	Average	Green/Spring	Brown/Fall	Shade, street
Pigeon Plum	S	30/20	Average	White/Spring	Red/Fall	Accent, shade, street
Pines	NCS	60/40	Average	Inconspicuous	Cone	Shade
Plumeria	S	20/20	Average	White, pink/ Summer	Not showy	Accent, street

N = North Florida   C = Central Florida   S = South Florida

TREES

NAME	AREA OF FLORIDA	H/W (FEET)	SOIL TYPE	FLOWERS/ SEASON	FRUITS/SEASON	BEST USES
Queen's Crape Myrtle	S	30/30	Average	Purple/Summer	Not showy	Accent, shade, street
Redbud	NC	25/20	Average	Pink/Spring	Not showy	Accent, shade, street
Redcedar	NCS	50/20	Average	Inconspicuous	Not showy	Accent, hedge
Red Maple	NCS	40/30	Moist	Red/Winter	Reddish/Spring	Shade, street
River Birch	NC	40/30	Moist or dry	Inconspicuous	Not showy	Accent, shade, street
Royal Poinciana	S	40/50	Average	Orange, red/ Summer	Not showy	Accent, shade, street
Saucer Magnolia	NC	25/20	Average	Pink/Spring	Not showy	Accent
Sea Grape	CS	20/12	Average	White/Spring	Purple/Summer	Accent, shade, street
Shumard Oak	NC	60/60	Average	Inconspicuous	Acorn/Fall	Shade, street
Silver Buttonwood	S	15/15	Average	Inconspicuous	Not showy	Accent, shade, street
Southern Magnolia	NCS	80/40	Moist or dry	White/Summer	Green pod/Summer	Accent, shade, street
Southern Juniper	NCS	30/30	Average	Inconspicuous	Blue/Fall	Shade, street, hedge
Sugarberry	NC	50/50	Moist	Inconspicuous	Red/Fall	Shade, street
Sweet Acacia	CS	15/20	Average	Yellow/Year-round	Brown/Year-round	Accent, street
Sweetbay Magnolia	NCS	40/20	Moist	White/Spring	Not showy	Shade
Sweet Gum	NC	60/30	Moist or dry	Inconspicuous	Brown/Fall	Shade, street
Sycamore	NC	80/60	Average	Inconspicuous	Brown/Fall	Shade, street
Trumpet Tree	CS	25/25	Average	Yellow, pink/Spring	Not showy	Accent, shade
Tuliptree	NC	80/30	Average	Yellowish/Spring	Not showy	Shade, street
Water Oak	NCS	50/60	Average	Inconspicuous	Acorn/Fall	Shade, street
Wax Myrtle	NCS	15/20	Moist or dry	Inconspicuous	Blue/Fall	Accent, street
Weeping Fig	S	50/70	Average	Inconspicuous	Not showy	Shade
Winged Elm	NC	30/25	Average	Inconspicuous	Not showy	Shade, street
Yaupon Holly	NC	20/15	Average	White/Spring	Red/Fall	Accent, street
Yellow Poinciana	CS	50/50	Average	Yellow/Summer	Not showy	Accent, shade
Yew Podocarpus	NCS	40/20	Average	Cream/Spring	Purple/Summer	Accent, hedge

N = North Florida   C = Central Florida   S = South Florida

FLORIDA TREES & PALMS CARE: BY THE MONTH

JANUARY

❏ Trees can be planted now, but palm plantings should wait until warmer weather. Plant dormant bare-root trees shortly after receipt and keep soil moist. In fact, Arbor Day in Florida is the third Saturday of this month.

❏ Do not top trees. Start pruning dead limbs, suckers, lanky growth, and crisscrossed limbs. Trim old seed stalks and declining fronds from palms. Don't perform major pruning of fruiting or spring-flowering trees, or crape myrtle.

❏ Few established trees and palms need special waterings. However, most new plantings should be watered daily for first few months. The larger the tree, the longer watering is needed before the tree is left on its own.

❏ Shade tree and palm feedings should be delayed until March.

FEBRUARY

❏ When purchasing trees, look for disease-free ones with straight, untopped trunks and good branching. Avoid twin trunks and branches with sharp "V" angles. Rootbound trees have been in containers too long and may take extra time to become established. A younger tree will establish much faster than a larger one. Transport new trees carefully or arrange for delivery.

❏ Maintain a 3- to 4-inch (7.5- to 10-cm) mulch layer around trees and palms, but not touching the trunk.

❏ Keep soil of new trees thoroughly moist for several months.

❏ Feed trees (not palms) for their first 3 years. Apply compost either now or next month. Apply fertilizer over the ground with a spreader or use tree spikes, liquid fertilizer, or composted manure.

❏ Caterpillars may start appearing. Most can be ignored, especially if you want butterflies and birds. Also look for aphids, scales, and thrips. Seldom are controls applied except for small trees.

MARCH

❏ When choosing container-grown trees and palms, look for those with good root systems. When ready to plant, rinse all the growing medium and place it in a shallow planting hole with no amendments. Straighten out coiling roots and arrange roots radiating out in all directions. Water well when planting and every day for at least 2 or 3 weeks. Gradually taper off as tree adjusts. Do not prune trees for at least a year after planting.

❏ Make sure younger trees maintain a straight trunk. Remove all limbs that may compete with central leader. Once shade trees are above head high, branching is allowed to develop a rounded tree. Palms need little guidance. Keep buds of nursery-dug plants covered with leaves for about 60 days.

❏ Keep up water schedule for new plantings since March is a dry month.

❏ Spread the compost on top of the soil in a circle outside the planting hole. For palms apply "palm special" under the fronds' spread. Where possible, use slow-release product. Unlike trees, palms need regular annual feedings.

❏ Stressed trees may be susceptible to borers. Palms may be affected by the palmetto weevil. Contact your local Extension Service for control recommendations.

APRIL

❏ The time for planting bare-root trees is over, but you can still add balled-and-burlapped and container-grown trees. Most balled-and-burlapped trees and palms are planted by nursery employeesn these days. Homeowners usually plant container specimens. Be sure to stake trees against wind damage.

❏ Check new trees regularly for possible problems. Do not provide corrective pruning for at least a year after planting.

❏ Keep up regular waterings for new plantings. Older trees and palms can exist with seasonal rains.

❏ Feeding time is over for most trees.

❏ Treehoppers may appear in some trees, but damage is usually minimal. Caterpillars may be extra heavy this month, but most can be ignored and they provide the perfect food for birds. The oak leaf blister is caused by a fungus that must be controlled before infection occurs, in winter or early spring.

MAY

❏ There is still plenty of planting time. Nursery inventory will be reduced for summer. If you get trees home but can't plant them yet, keep them at landscape light levels. Check daily for water needs. If stored for a long time, apply compost to the soil. Now is the ideal time to add palms.

❏ Continue grooming all trees and palms. Remove limbs and fronds that interfere with landscape maintenance. Adjust ties on staked trees so they don't cut into trunks.

❏ Keep watering on regular schedule.

❏ Feed palms with compost or slow-release fertilizer.

❏ Powdery mildew fungus loves spring months. It will not cause major decline, but may cause contorted and smaller leaves. Active pests are borers, caterpillars, thrips, palm leaf skeletonizers, and scale. It is normal for magnolias to drop their leaves during spring.

JUNE

❏ The beginning of our wet season. Prevent potential damage from storms and hurricanes. Check for weak or insect-damaged branches. Consider older trees that could affect buildings or neighboring property. Palms are wind-resistant; remove only completely dead fronds and coconuts.

❏ Planting never stops. Add container-grown trees or palms. All palm plantings are best done at this time.

❏ With a little luck, Mother Nature will help with watering. Provide daily soaking of new plantings if necessary. No fertilizer for trees or landscape during the wet season.

❏ Pest damage is minimal and seldom are sprays needed. Look for aphids, borers, mites, oak leaf blister, powdery mildew, and scale. In palms, check for skeletonizers and leaf spots.

JULY

❏ Summer pruning can be made on trees that flower during winter. But don't delay much longer, since buds are formed during summer. Don't forget to remove dead or declining limbs.

❏ Check palm fronds and remove only dead fronds, but not the green ones, which are needed for food production.

❏ Summer rains should do most of the watering. Make sure new plantings stay thoroughly watered.

❏ Lacewings emerge in the summer and both the larvae and adults feed on aphids, small caterpillars, and scales.

AUGUST

❏ Rains make planting easier and provide some waterings. Decide now where you need additional palms or shade trees.

❏ Continue summer pruning of unwanted or damaged limbs, competing shoots, out-of-bounds branches, and old palm fronds and seed stalks. Do not apply paints or wound coverings.

❏ Make sure root balls of new plantings get completely wet.

❏ No tree feeding is recommended until the dry season.

❏ Grasshoppers, katydids, or beetles may chew tree leaves. Unless trees are small, the damage is minimal and will not affect their growth. Hand pick on young trees. On trees, look for lacewings that will prey on aphids, thrips, scale, and whiteflies. Palms may have skeletonizers and leaf spots.

SEPTEMBER

❏ Tree and palm planting can continue with container-grown material. Provide good care while transporting home. If you cannot move them properly, ask for delivery.

❏ Eliminate competition from weeds, grass, and shrubs around the tree base. Coverings can encourage foot rot and give insects a hiding place. Don't use weed trimmers around trees because they damage the trunk.

❏ If you have new trees and palms, keep up daily waterings.

❏ Damage from tree borers is usually ignored. Where possible, prune them from trees to eradicate the population. Twigs dropped from twig girdler activity should be destroyed. Some active insects are caterpillars, scales, and whiteflies.

OCTOBER

❏ Planting gets easier during cooler weather. Add several stakes for support if affected by winds. Allow the trunk a little freedom to move.

❏ Tree and palm care begins to wind down in fall. Continue checking for storm-damaged limbs and fronds and declining portions. These can be removed anytime. In colder parts of the state, try to complete major pruning. Where possible, the planting should be dormant or growth slowed.

❏ You do not need to be as conscientious about watering new trees and palms this month, but it's best if they remain moist until established.

❏ Pests slow their feeding habits with cooler weather and damage is generally ignored. Pests include caterpillars and twig girdlers, which provide food for birds.

NOVEMBER

❏ Adding trees to the landscape never stops in Florida, thanks to container production. As weather turns cooler, it becomes easier to move balled-and-burlapped and bare-root trees. Planting techniques are about the same. Late fall and winter are not the best time to add palms to the landscape.

❏ Taller trees and those with large canopies could be staked for up to a year. Don't stake a tree if it's not needed. The natural movement of the trunk produces a sturdier tree.

❏ It's drier but cooler, so watering is not quite as necessary as during hotter weather. Make sure the soil stays moist with newer trees.

❏ Spanish and ball moss, lichens, and peeling bark on trees are normal and do not hurt trees.

DECEMBER

❏ Delay all palm plantings until warmer weather, March through midsummer. If transplanting a tree, make sure the soil is moist when digging.

❏ Make sure the area under trees and palms remains weed-free. Even though winter arrives this month, Florida has winter weeds. Pull weeds by hand and renew mulches as needed to maintain moist soil and help control weeds.

❏ Most trees and palms are dormant and have received all the nutrients needed for growth. The next feeding time for trees up to 3 to 5 years of age is February or March. Palm feeding time begins in March. Make sure all leftover fertilizer is stored in a sealed bag to keep it from clumping and becoming difficult to spread.

❏ Most pests are not very active at this time of year.

TROPICAL PLANTS
for Florida

outh Florida is considered tropical even though the Tropic of Cancer is 70 miles (113 km) south of Key West. Many people like to grow tropical plants and tropical-looking plants, because then their landscapes resemble beautiful, paradise-like tropical vacation spots. Tropical plants bring wonderful foliage patterns and colors, beautiful flowers, and an intriguing way of life with them.

Many tender tropical plants require extra care and are not recommended for Central or North Florida unless they can be grown in pots that can be moved inside in winter. Most tropical plants prefer well-drained, enriched soil with plenty of moisture. Like many rainforest plants, they like water but also good drainage. Compost or slow-release fertilizer is practical in order to keep a flow of nutrients available throughout the growing season. If foliage yellows, apply periodic foliar sprays of micronutrients or add fish emulsion to keep tropical plants performing well.

Keep tropical plants that prefer moist soil together with other water-thirsty plants to avoid over-watering the entire landscape just to water them. Areas in wind and sun will require more frequent waterings.

ORCHIDS

The splendor of orchids is almost impossible to resist, and with more than 20,000 species and untold numbers of hybrids, orchids have become hugely popular in the last decade, with phalaenopsis orchids topping the charts. One reason is the long-lasting spray of flowers, which can remain pretty for 2 months. Some orchids are marketed for their fragrance. Cattleyas and oncidiums, for example, may give off rich chocolate or vanilla aromas.

HOW ORCHIDS GROW

Many orchids, such as cattleyas, are air plants, or epiphytes (epi means "upon"; phyte means "plant"). They grow on other plants, most often tree branches, expanding into clumps by means of a rhizome, or a stem from which roots grow downward and shoots grow up. They are not parasites—they take no nutrients away from the trees where they are perched.

To germinate in nature, orchid seeds have to be infected with a fungus, a fact not known until the turn of the century. Today, most orchids are produced using tissue culture and are cloned in labs, making them more accessible. They are enjoyed by people in every walk of life.

The epiphytic orchids most easily grown in South Florida are the cattleyas, vandas, oncidiums, phalaenopsis, and dendrobiums. Growing in trees, epiphytic orchids have developed special roots that are photosynthetic, yet covered with a silver-gray coating of cells that absorbs water and protects against desiccation. These roots cling tightly to tree bark or clay pots. Pseudobulbs are water-storage organs.

Orchids with pseudobulbs, such as cattleyas and oncidiums, require a bit less water than do those without. (More orchids die from over-watering than under-watering.)

ALOE

Aloe vera
Asphodel family: Asphodelaceae

HARDINESS–Zones 9b-11

NATIVE RANGE–Arabian Peninsula

COLOR(S)–Gray-green leaves; reddish inflorescence on flower stalk

PEAK SEASON–Bloom in late spring to early summer

MATURE SIZE–1 to 2 feet x 2 to 3 feet (30 to 61 cm x 61 to 91 cm)

WATER NEEDS–Drought tolerant, but needs well-drained soil

CARE–This succulent is easy to grow and requires very little maintenance. Aloe grows slowly, forming clumps.

PROBLEMS–Do not overwater. The thick leaves are edged with short spines.

USES AND SELECTIONS–Aloe's clear, gel-like sap helps burns and other wounds heal faster. This drought-tolerant plant can be used for xeriscape and rock gardens, as well as in planters, as a ground cover, or in mass plantings. It is also used as a small accent or as a border planting. Grow in containers in colder locations.

ANGEL'S TRUMPET

Brugmansia spp.
Nightshade family: Solanaceae

HARDINESS–Zones 9b-11

NATIVE RANGE–South America

COLOR(S)–Orange, white, yellow, pink, or two-toned

PEAK SEASON–Blooms most of year; foliage evergreen

MATURE SIZE–To 15 feet x 15 feet (to 4.5 m x 4.5 m)

WATER NEEDS–Water well to establish, then can tolerate some drought. Flowers best with water during dry periods.

CARE–Fast-growing brugmansia can be left untrimmed with branches drooping to the ground. Or it can be pruned into an upright tree or overhead canopy to better display flowers. Frost kills them back to roots, but they come back.

PROBLEMS–Shield from winds to protect blooms. All parts are poisonous or narcotic when eaten.

USES AND SELECTIONS–The abundant hanging flowers, up to 12 inches (30 cm) long, create a dramatic and exotic effect. For maximum impact, plant as a free-standing specimen to show off blooms without crowding from other plants. Can also be used as a border or in containers. Use near decks or patios to enjoy the fragrance.

ANTHURIUM

Anthurium spp.
Arum family: Araceae

HARDINESS–Zones 10-11

NATIVE RANGE–Caribbean, Mexico, Central & South America

COLOR(S)–Generally grown for foliage

PEAK SEASON–Evergreen foliage

MATURE SIZE–Varies with species

WATER NEEDS–Plants in terra cotta pots or mounted in trees dry faster, especially in windy weather. Check moisture levels closely and water daily if necessary. Once established, rain will be sufficient except in dry seasons.

CARE–Plant terrestrial anthuriums in shady beds with other tropicals, in pots, or as specimens throughout the garden. Good drainage is the key. Epiphytic ones can be attached and grown in trees. Anthuriums do well with slow-release fertilizer, supplemented with occasional foliar sprays. Feed those in trees with mesh bags filled with slow-release fertilizer.

PROBLEMS–None.

USES AND SELECTIONS–Anthuriums have dramatic foliage and most have unique spathes at the base of the flower spikes. They add distinction to a tree trunk, garden path, or bed, and complement bromeliads, ferns, and even boulders. Anthuriums may be used as summer flowers in Central or North Florida, or grown in containers.

AUSTRALIAN TREE FERN

Sphaeropteris cooperi
Tree fern family: Cyatheaceae

HARDINESS–Zones 9b–11

NATIVE RANGE–Eastern Australia

COLOR(S)–Green foliage on russet trunk

PEAK SEASON–Evergreen

MATURE SIZE–12 to 18 feet x 8 to 15 feet (3.5 to 5.5 m x 2.5 to 4.5 m)

WATER NEEDS–Requires regular moisture.

CARE–This slow-growing fern prefers fertile, well-drained soils. Plant in area protected from wind. Fertilize lightly regularly during growing season.

PROBLEMS–Do not allow to completely dry out. The hair on the trunk and undersides of fronds can be irritating; handle with gloves.

USES AND SELECTIONS–Ideal as a specimen along shady entryways and around patios or pools. Underplant with small ferns or other low-growing tropicals. For an exotic look, attach orchids to the trunk. Although this fern provides a soothing tropical feel, it is hardier than it looks. It can briefly take freezing weather and still come back. When provided with plenty of moisture, can withstand almost full sun.

BIRD-OF-PARADISE

Strelitzia reginae
Bird of paradise family: Strelitziaceae

HARDINESS–Zones 9–11

NATIVE RANGE–South Africa

COLOR(S)–Flowers orange and white with blue

PEAK SEASON–Most blooms in summer and fall

MATURE SIZE–3 to 4 feet x 4 feet (91 to 122 cm x 122 cm)

WATER NEEDS–Water well then let dry

CARE–Bird-of-paradise forms clumps and has tuberous roots, which should be set just at soil surface. Add compost or slow-release fertilizer in March. Remove dying leaves to allow light into center of clump.

PROBLEMS–Over-crowded, unfertilized plants will not produce flowers.

USES AND SELECTIONS–Plant as an eye-catching accent, in front of tall hedges, or in foundation plantings. Bird-of-paradise can be used with its relatives: the traveler's trees and heliconias. This plant provides texture and color outside and cut flowers for inside. There are several selections, including giant bird-of-paradise, which grows to 30 feet (9 m).

BIRD'S NEST FERN

Asplenium nidus
Spleenwort family: Aspleniaceae

HARDINESS–Zones 9b–11

NATIVE RANGE–Australia and Pacific islands

COLOR(S)–Green foliage

MATURE SIZE–To 4 feet (122 cm)

WATER NEEDS–An epiphyte, so it gains all its moisture from the air. Does best with regular moisture. Only allow to dry slightly between waterings.

CARE–Provide them with well-drained non-soil plus an area protected from drying winds and cold temperatures. Feed in the spring with diluted fertilizer or fish emulsion. The fern is slow growing and does not require much care if the basics are provided. This epiphytic fern naturally grows in jungle trees.

PROBLEMS–Hand pick any snails.

USES AND SELECTIONS–This showy, vase-shaped fern has thick, undivided fronds. It is an excellent specimen plant that quickly captures attention. It has a strong tropical flavor and can be used as an accent or in clusters as ground covers in shady gardens, perhaps under a tree fern. Also suitable for containers, but don't use soil, just pine bark chunks. There are cultivars with ruffled edges.

BROMELIAD

Aechmea, Billbergia, Guzmania, Neoregelia, Tillandsia spp.
Bromeliad family: Bromeliaceae

HARDINESS–Zones 9b-11

NATIVE RANGE–Tropical regions of the world. Some are native to Florida.

COLOR(S)–Varies with genus and species

PEAK SEASON–Varies

MATURE SIZE–Few inches to several feet

WATER NEEDS–Keep bromeliad cups filled with water

CARE–Fertilize ¼ strength fish emulsion twice a year. Off-shoots can be removed and planted. Bromeliads grown outdoors in Central and North Florida must be removed or covered during freezing weather.

PROBLEMS–Flush water in cups every few days to kill the mosquito larvae. When working with spiny bromeliads, use beekeeper's or rose gloves. Scale may appear in overcrowded conditions.

USES AND SELECTIONS–Bromeliads can be selected for almost anything from ground covers to specimens and from Pineapples to Spanish Moss.Some genera grow in trees, others under them. Use as accents or mass plantings. Their often brilliant colors have tropical flare, plus some produce inflorescences lasting many months.

CATTLEYA

Laelia spp. (Cattleya is no logger the accepted genus of this orchid.)
Orchid family: Orchidaceae

HARDINESS–Zones 10b-11. Takes low-40s (about 4°C to 7°C) temperatures for short periods.

NATIVE RANGE–Cuba, Mexico, Central & South America

COLOR(S)–White, lavender, purple

PEAK SEASON–Varies

MATURE SIZE–20 to 40 inches (51 to 101 cm)

WATER NEEDS–Water every 2 or 3 days, allowing medium to become almost dry. Likes high relative humidity.

CARE–Plant in February or March. Use quick-draining orchid-growing mix. Position four or five "back" bulbs with new growth toward pot's center. Anchor with pot clip. Use diluted fish emulsion 2 or 3 times per year.

PROBLEMS–Plants that don't bloom usually need more light. To prevent fungus, don't overcrowd.

USES AND SELECTIONS–This queen of orchids is extraordinarily tough and makes a good beginner plant. Tie or wire to trees with rough bark in 50 percent light. Or plant in pots to bring inside when flowers are glorious. North and Central Florida gardeners can keep orchids outdoors in trees or shade houses in warmer months.

CHINESE EVERGREEN

Aglaonema spp.
Arum family: Araceae.

HARDINESS–Zones 10-11

NATIVE RANGE–Southeast Asia and Papua New Guinea

COLOR(S)–Small white flowers; green foliage with patterns of ivory, red, pink, and more

PEAK SEASON–Summer blooms

MATURE SIZE–2 to 3 feet x 1 to 4 feet (61 to 91 cm x 30 to 122 cm)

WATER NEEDS–After established, let soil become medium-dry between watering.

CARE–They prefer shade, although morning sun is fine, particularly for silvery leaves. They thrive in well-drained soil. Protect plants from cold.

PROBLEMS–In dry weather, mites may appear. Mealybugs may occur if brought indoors for winter. Wipe with rubbing alcohol.

USES AND SELECTIONS–Display these plants next to paths or in raised beds as ground covers. In containers, they can beautify patio and townhouse gardens. Give vitality to the "floor" of shade gardens with groups of complementary colors. New varieties from Thailand come in myriad colors and patterns.

COPPERLEAF

Acalypha wilkesiana
Spurge family: Euphorbiaceae

HARDINESS–Zones 9-11

NATIVE RANGE–Bismarck Archipelago in the Pacific

COLOR(S)–Coppery leaves mottled in bronze, green, purple, red, pink

PEAK SEASON–Evergreen foliage

MATURE SIZE–8 to 12 feet x 6 to 8 feet (2.5 to 3.5 m x 2 to 2.5 m)

WATER NEEDS–Somewhat drought tolerant. Prefers regular watering during drought.

CARE–Plant in any well-drained soil. Does best with enriched soil. This fast-growing shrub may need occasional trimming to look tidy and to cut off any drooping side branches. A late-winter pruning can remove portions affected by freezes.

PROBLEMS–Aphids, mites, and scale may be problems.

USES AND SELECTIONS–This colorful shrub with large leaves makes a wonderful specimen with showy year-round color. Copperleaf comes in different multi-hued cultivars that provide a rainbow of colors, which explains its other common name, Joseph's coat. It looks best planted amid mixed-green-foliage plants. Plant it as a hedge, view barrier, border, or accent.

CROTON

Codiaeum variegatum
Spurge family: Euphorbiaceae

HARDINESS–Zones 9b-11. In colder areas, plant in containers and protect from frosts and freezing.

NATIVE RANGE–Pacific island nations and Australia

COLOR(S)–Green, pink, yellow, red foliage

PEAK SEASON–Year-round foliage

MATURE SIZE–3 to 8 feet x 3 feet (1 to 3.5 m x 1 m)

WATER NEEDS–Relatively drought resistant. Water during periods of extended drought.

CARE–Does well in sandy soils. Does better with compost, applied in March. Looks best when protected from midday sun. For compact plants with colorful shoots, prune periodically.

PROBLEMS–Scale, thrips, and mites may occur.

USES AND SELECTIONS–These relatively narrow plants are ideal for cramped gardens and small spots between house and sidewalk. Also good for hedges and screens. Great accent plant for containers or beds. A rainbow of color combinations is available, in a wide range of leaf shapes. Some selections tolerate lower light, although colors may be subdued.

CROWN OF THORNS

Euphorbia milii
Spurge family: Euphorbiaceae

HARDINESS–Zones 9b-11. Damaged by freezes.

NATIVE RANGE–Madagascar

COLOR(S)–Pink, red, orange, salmon, yellow, and bi-colors

PEAK SEASON–Year-round blooms

MATURE SIZE–1 to 3 feet (30 to 91 cm)

WATER NEEDS–Very drought tolerant

CARE–This tough, slow-growing plant requires little maintenance, blooming year-round in heat, sun, drought, and seaside conditions that would kill other plants. Requires well-drained soil. Too much shade or over fertilization will reduce the number of blooms. Although the flower is actually small, it is surrounded by colorful showy bracts.

PROBLEMS–Do not overwater. Milky sap may cause skin irritation or be poisonous if eaten.

USES AND SELECTIONS–Recent interest in the tough but thorny crown of thorns has resulted in many new hybrids. It is good for xeriscape or rock gardens. The dwarf varieties have more attractive foliage.

CUT-LEAF PHILODENDRON

Monstera deliciosa
Arum family: Araceae

HARDINESS–Zones 9b–11

NATIVE RANGE–Central America

COLOR(S)–Green foliage; white spathe

PEAK SEASON–Evergreen foliage

MATURE SIZE–To 50 feet x 2-foot leaf width (to 15 m x 61-cm leaf width)

WATER NEEDS–Requires regular watering

CARE–This plant grows quickly in almost any soil, although it prefers well-drained, enriched soil. It will clamber over rocks or up trees. To speed growth, apply compost in March. May require trimming.

PROBLEMS–Usually pest free, although in dry seasons the lubber grasshopper may consume leaves. All parts of the plant except for the ripe fruit can be poisonous.

USES AND SELECTIONS–Although its common names include cut-leaf philodendron or split-leaf philodendron, it is not a philodendron. Also called the Swiss cheese, fruit salad plant, or ceriman plant, this vine produces an edible fruit that requires about a year to ripen and is said to taste like canned fruit salad.

DANCINGLADY ORCHID

Oncidium spp.
Orchid family: Orchidaceae

HARDINESS–Zones 10–11

NATIVE RANGE–Florida, Caribbean, Mexico, Central & South America

COLOR(S)–Yellow with brown, maroon, or olive

PEAK SEASON–Spring blooms

MATURE SIZE–3 inches to 2 feet (7.5 to 61 cm)

WATER NEEDS–Keep evenly moist, except for miniatures, which like to dry between waterings.

CARE–These are epiphytic orchids. Attach with florist's tape, wire, or cloth strap to tree limbs or trunks of trees and palms. In pots, use a fast-draining mix. Once or twice during warm growing season fertilize with diluted water-soluble fertilizer. Consistency is key. Oncidiums can be acclimated to tolerate sun. North and Central Florida growers must bring them in or provide protection when temperatures drop below 50°F (10°C).

USES AND SELECTIONS–These orchids consistently provide cascades of flowers with little care, tolerating all kinds of awful weather, except freezes. Numerous varieties come in all the spots, stripes, and bright colors you could want, plus fragrance variety too. The Florida dancinglady (*O. ensatum*) is the only one native to Florida.

DENDROBIUM

Dendrobium spp.
Orchid family: Orchidaceae

HARDINESS–Zones 10–11

NATIVE RANGE–India, Southeast Asia, Australia

COLOR(S)–White, yellow, lavender, rose, maroon

PEAK SEASON–Blooms fall, spring, summer

MATURE SIZE–6 inches to 4 feet (15 to 122 cm)

WATER NEEDS–Water generously during spring. During winter, allow plant to dry out between waterings.

CARE–Plant in spring on cork pieces, in pots with quick-draining medium, or on trees. Attach to cork or trees with florist's tape or wire. Prefers 50 to 70 percent shade. In pots, put oldest growth against sides. Spray every month or two in spring with diluted fish emulsion. Reduce fertilizer in winter.

PROBLEMS–When overwatered, offshoots may be produced, which can be cut off and potted.

USES AND SELECTIONS–The orchids in this genus are diverse, including miniatures. North and Central Florida growers can keep them in trees or shade houses during warm months, but protection is needed when temperatures drop below 50°F (10°C).

DRACAENA

Dracaena spp.
Asparagus family: Asparagaceae

HARDINESS–Zones 10b-11. Some species tolerate more cold.

NATIVE RANGE– Central America, Africa, India, Southeast Asia, Australia

COLOR(S)–Leaves solid green or striped with ivory, yellow, or red

MATURE SIZE–Varies by species

WATER NEEDS–Needs good drainage. Can stay fairly dry for long periods.

CARE–Not fussy and does well despite neglect. However, it prefers acidic soil and enriched soil to stay rich green. Compost with other landscape plants in spring. When top of branch is cut off, new buds and heads of leaves form. Tops can be rooted for new plants.

PROBLEMS–None.

USES AND SELECTIONS–Use dracaena when narrow, vertical elements are needed. It is useful as an accent or for screening. Clusters with plants of differing heights are especially effective. In Central and North Florida, grow in containers and protect from temperatures below 40°F (4°C). There are approximately 120 dracaena species, many used as interior plants because they tolerate low light and stay the same size for years.

ELEPHANT EAR

Alocasia spp.
Arum family: Araceae

HARDINESS–Zones 9-11 Damaged by cold in northern regions and during prolonged cold in South Florida.

NATIVE RANGE–India, Southeast Asia, Australia

COLOR(S)–Green and dark green, often with colored veins

PEAK SEASON–Evergreen foliage

MATURE SIZE–2 to 12 feet tall x 8 feet wide (61 cm to 3.5 m x 2.5 m)

WATER NEEDS–Provide plenty of water in spring. Water twice weekly if it doesn't rain.

CARE–Use compost, which could be supplemented with fish emulsion if leaves turn yellow. Prune away damaged leaves in early spring.

PROBLEMS–Leaves may fade in full sun all day.

USES AND SELECTIONS–The enormous elephant ear leaves proclaim tropical in a garden and produce dramatic effects. Also attractive in pots and ponds. Varieties come in all sizes and venation patterns. Taro (*Colocasia esculenta*) is sometimes called elephant ear and is not recommended because it's a Category I invasive in all of Florida.

FIG

Ficus spp.
Mulberry family: Moraceae

HARDINESS–Zones 9b-11. Damaged by freezes.

NATIVE RANGE–Tropical and subtropical areas around the world, including Florida.

COLOR(S)–Foliage green with occasional red or variegation

PEAK SEASON–Evergreen

MATURE SIZE–Few inches to 40 feet (5 cm to 12 m)

WATER NEEDS–Drought tolerant once established. Needs regular watering in containers.

CARE–Usually fast growing without any fertilizer. If used as hedges, needs frequent pruning to maintain shape because those hedge plants are full-sized trees.

PROBLEMS–Ficus roots are strong and may grow above the soil. Don't plant near sidewalks and structures.

USES AND SELECTIONS–This diverse genus ranges from the small creeping fig to the enormous banyan tree, with many shrubs and trees in between. Their glossy green leaves and ability to tolerate a wide range of conditions (except hard freezes) makes them ubiquitous in South Florida, especially as tightly pruned hedges of weeping fig trees (*F. benjamina*). There are several figs native to Florida, so choose those when possible. Use in containers, as patio plants, borders, hedges, and shade trees.

GINGER

Shell gingers: *Alipinia spp.; true gingers: Zingiber spp.; hidden gingers: Curcuma spp.; ginger lilies: Hedychium* spp.
Ginger family: Zingiberaceae

HARDINESS–Zones 9-11

NATIVE RANGE–India, Southeast Asia, Australia

COLOR(S)–Red, pink, purple, white flowers

PEAK SEASON–Blooms summer; foliage evergreen

MATURE SIZE–3 to 15 feet (1 to 4.5 m) x various

WATER NEEDS–Requires good soil moisture

CARE–Locate in high shade, allowing room to grow. Gingers are fast growers and prefer to be well fertilized. They will spread and form big clumps. Maintain by cleaning out old, brown stems. In Central and North Florida, use in containers, protected from chilling winds.

PROBLEMS–Too much light may cause yellowing.

USES AND SELECTIONS–These useful plants say "Welcome to the tropics." There are about 1,000 species. The flowers are lovely amid the broad tropical foliage. A popular pink ginger contrasts nicely with the red. Use mass plantings of dwarf and variegated forms in understory beds and as ground covers.

HELICONIA

Heliconia spp.
Heliconia family: Heliconiaceae

HARDINESS–Zones 9-11. In North Florida, they may die back to the ground after a frost, but they resprout in warmer weather.

NATIVE RANGE–Mexico, Central & South America, Melanesia

COLOR(S)–Yellow, orange, scarlet flowers

PEAK SEASON–Blooms spring and summer

MATURE SIZE–2 to 15 feet (61 cm to 4.5 m) x various

WATER NEEDS–Once established, keep somewhat damp. In sunny or windy conditions, water more often.

CARE–Requires good drainage and some protection from cold and wind. Leaves get yellow on hungry plants. To feed their big appetites, use slow-release fertilizer combined with compost. If grown in in clumps, the outer stems may lean. Stake from within so flowers can show.

PROBLEMS–May be susceptible to fungal root and stem rot.

USES AND SELECTIONS–These fascinating plants have become important tropical plants in Florida. Use at gardens' edges, as specimen plants, along walls, and plant for accents or in mass plantings. Use dwarf varieties in containers, especially in colder areas. There are hundreds of cultivars.

MOTH ORCHID

Phalaenopsis spp.
Orchid family: Orchidaceae

HARDINESS–Zones 10-11

NATIVE RANGE–India, Southeast Asia, Pacific island nations, and Australia

COLOR(S)–White, yellow, pink, peach, bronze, orange, and spots

PEAK SEASON–Blooms winter to spring

MATURE SIZE–8 to 16 inches (20 to 41 cm)

WATER NEEDS–It's an epiphyte and prefers to have roots moist but not wet. They like to dry slowly, but never completely dry out.

CARE–Keep in shady areas or shade house, between 70 to 50 percent shade. Pot in loose-draining mix with sphagnum to retain moisture. Use diluted organic fertilizer once a month or so during growing season. Toward the end of October switch to bloom-booster fertilizer and add 1 tablespoon (14 g) of epsom salts to strengthen flower spike. In North and Central Florida keep outside in shade houses during warm months, but protect when temperatures drop below 55°F (13°C).

PROBLEMS–Don't let water remain in crown, which can lead to crown rot.

USES AND SELECTIONS–For grace, sophistication, and elegance, the popular moth orchids are the best. Flowers can stay unblemished for weeks, and varieties come in all colors.

MUSSAENDA

Mussaenda philippica
Madder family: Rubiaceae

HARDINESS–Zones 9-11

NATIVE RANGE–Philippines

COLOR(S)–Pink, white, yellow

PEAK SEASON–Year-round blooms with more in summer

MATURE SIZE–9 to 10 feet x 6 feet (2.5 to 3 m x 183 cm)

WATER NEEDS–Keep soil moist.

CARE–Plant in full sun for best color. Prefers acidic soil. Flowers and showy bracts form on branch ends, so spring pruning will encourage more branches. Prune after bracts fade to encourage more flowering in same season. If shrubs grow too large or leggy, cut back quite hard. Grow in containers in Central and North Florida because it is vulnerable to damage below 45°F (7°C).

PROBLEMS–Fungal leaf spot can affect some plants.

USES AND SELECTIONS–Plant in mixed border so shorter shrubs conceal leggy trunks. Plant with purple foliage plants to complement the pink varieties. Mussaenda is not for the everyday duty of planting along a fence. Its lusciousness is best in smaller doses.

NIGHT BLOOMING CEREUS

Selenicereus undatus
Cactus family: Cactaceae

HARDINESS–Zones 9b-11

NATIVE RANGE–Mexico

COLOR(S)–White blooms

PEAK SEASON–Blooms summer; evergreen foliage

MATURE SIZE–Climbs to 30 feet (9 m); stems are triangular, about 3 inches (7.5 cm) across

WATER NEEDS–This cactus is drought tolerant once established.

CARE–Attach with florist's tape to start the vine, until plant starts producing its own aerial roots. Grows quickly, branching frequently. Add compost in the spring and augment with fish emulsion at the beginning of summer for maximum blooms.

PROBLEMS–Handle stems with care to avoid spines.

USES AND SELECTIONS–Climbs masonry walls, palm trunks, and up onto tree branches. It has fragrant nocturnal blooms up to 12 inches (30 cm) long and across. Some varieties are grown for edible fruit, which is prized in Thailand and called dragon fruit or pitaya. This unusual plant is salt tolerant and can be found growing wild in South and Central coastal Florida. Several cacti have the same common name.

PEACE LILY

Spathiphyllum spp.
Arum family: Araceae

HARDINESS–Zones 10-11

COLOR(S)–White flowers; deep-green, shiny foliage

PEAK SEASON–Blooms summer

MATURE SIZE–12 inches to 4 feet (30 to 122 cm)

WATER NEEDS–Likes moisture in regular amounts, with good drainage. Don't overwater.

CARE–Choose shady location with some protection against cold. In too much shade, the plants will grow but not flower. Add compost at least once a year.

PROBLEMS–All parts of this plant are toxic to humans and pets.

USES AND SELECTIONS–Peace lily sizes go from petite to huge. They make wonderful potted specimens for both indoors and out. Consider them for shady patios. Combine with tree ferns for interesting texture contrast. Testing in the 1990s showed that the peace lily was a top performer in removing indoor air pollutants and alleviating sick building syndrome.

PEACOCK PLANT

Calathea spp.
Arrowroot family: Marantaceae

HARDINESS–Zones 10-11

NATIVE RANGE–Southern Mexico, Central & South America

COLOR(S)–Foliage in shades of green, white, pink, silver, and combinations

MATURE SIZE–Varies with species, to 5 feet tall x 4 feet wide (152 x 122 cm)

WATER NEEDS–Keep moist

CARE–Plant in beds enriched with organic material. Use compost or slow-release fertilizer. Does well with early morning or late afternoon, but not midday sun. Use as houseplant in Central and North Florida to protect from cold.

PROBLEMS–Hand pick any snails.

USES AND SELECTIONS–Peacock (or rattlesnake) plants are among the most ornate plants, with beautifully patterned leaves on short stems. Markings usually follow the central vein, with endless combinations. The undersides are frequently red or wine colored. Inconspicuous flowers are produced inside bracts. Calatheas are wonderful in beds beneath canopy trees, such as oaks. Also does well in containers on shady patio or deck.

PEPEROMIA

Peperomia spp.
Pepper family: Piperaceae

HARDINESS–Zones 10-11

NATIVE RANGE–Tropical and subtropical regions around the world, including Florida

COLOR(S)–Green, or variegated foliage with cream or burgundy

MATURE SIZE–12 to 18 inches x 4 inches (30 to 46 cm x 10 cm)

WATER NEEDS–Requires well-drained soil. Mulch to keep evenly moist.

CARE–Add compost in the spring. Some plants clump up or mound slightly. Cuttings can be easily rooted or planted directly in the ground.

PROBLEMS–Hand pick snails.

USES AND SELECTIONS–Often seen as houseplants. In your garden, peperomias can easily serve as ground covers or potted plants for the patio. Also make a pretty hanging basket, particularly those with variegated leaves. Use tree stumps left in the garden or decorative logs as a place to get them started. Too tender for widespread use in Central and North Florida, unless grown in containers. South Florida is home to several native species.

PERSIAN SHIELD

Strobilanthes dyerianus
Acanthus family: Acanthaceae

HARDINESS–Zones 9b-11

NATIVE RANGE–Myanmar

COLOR(S)–Leaves iridescent dark-green with silvery purple on top and purple underneath

PEAK SEASON–Evergreen

MATURE SIZE–3 to 4 feet x 2 to 3 feet (91 to 122 cm x61 to 91 cm)

WATER NEEDS–During growing season prefers moisture. With enriched soil and mulch, it has slight drought tolerance. In dormant season, reduce watering.

CARE–Grows best with morning sun and afternoon shade. In colder areas, it dies back to roots with frost. However, it may return in spring even in Zone 8.

PROBLEMS–To prevent it from getting too tall, pinch back to stimulate branching.

USES AND SELECTIONS–Persian shield's textured showy leaves add drama, even through the winter. It provides unique color in shady gardens where flowering plants don't thrive. Use it as an accent in mass plantings or in containers.

PONYTAIL PALM

Beaucarnea recurvata
Asparagus family: Asparagaceae

HARDINESS–Zones 9b-11

NATIVE RANGE–Mexico

COLOR(S)–Green foliage, whitish flower

PEAK SEASON–Blooms in spring; evergreen leaves

MATURE SIZE–12 to 18 feet x 10 to 15 feet (3.5 to 5.5 m x 3 to 4.5 m)

WATER NEEDS–Very drought tolerant. Water deeply, but then allow to dry out.

CARE–This slow grower requires little care, although indoor plants must be gradually acclimated to the garden. Provide room to grow up and out. Mature plants may withstand light freezes and are somewhat salt tolerant. Large plants may flower.

PROBLEMS–To prevent root rot, use well-drained soil and don't mulch close to base.

USES AND SELECTIONS–While called ponytail palm, this is not a palm but a succulent related to yucca. Its spindly branches rise from a swollen base and are topped with tufts of long droopy leaves. Use this unique plant as an attention-getter. It does well in containers, xeriscape plantings, and low-maintenance or rock gardens.

SHRIMP PLANT

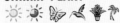

Justicia brandegeeana
Acanthus family: Acanthaceae

HARDINESS–Zones 9-11

NATIVE RANGE–Mexico and Central America

COLOR(S)–White flowers within overlapping copper, red, yellow, lime-green bracts

PEAK SEASON–Blooms almost year-round; foliage evergreen

MATURE SIZE–3 to 6 feet x 3 feet (91 to 183 cm x 91 cm)

WATER NEEDS–Keep soil moist, especially during hot weather

CARE–Likes fertile, well-drained soil. It is adaptable and easy to grow. Add compost in March. It dies back to the ground in hard frosts but comes back with warm weather. Can also be grown as an annual in northern range.

PROBLEMS–Branches sometimes get spindly. Keep tip pruned to increase bushiness and promote flowering.

USES AND SELECTIONS–This exotic sprawling shrub can be used wherever color masses are needed. Group together in mass plantings or plant in mixed perennial beds and borders. Since the 6-inch (15-cm) long showy flower spikes attract butterflies and hummingbirds, use in wildlife gardens. Varieties come in several flower colors and one with white foliage variegation.

SPIRAL GINGER

Costus spp.
Spiral ginger family: Costaceae

HARDINESS–Zones 9b-11

NATIVE RANGE–Tropical areas of Central & South America, Africa, and Asia

COLOR(S)–Yellow, orange, white flowers

PEAK SEASON–Blooms summer

MATURE SIZE–4 to 8 feet x 4 to 5 feet (122 to 244 cm x 122 to 152 cm)

WATER NEEDS–Keep moist, with less water in winter

CARE–Locate in high, light shade where shallow-rooted Costus can clump and spread. Mulch and use acid-forming fertilizer. Once stems have flowered and bracts faded, cut out parent stem. Every few years, it benefits from digging and refreshing the beds with organic material. Grow in protected areas or containers in cold-sensitive areas.

PROBLEMS–Tends to look haggard in winter.

USES AND SELECTIONS–Use as an accent, as a screen, in containers, or as mass plantings. Try beneath oaks with stands of red and pink gingers. *C. speciosus* is 8 or 9 feet (2.5 to 3 m) tall with white flowers from red bracts. There is a variety with variegated leaves.

STAGHORN FERN

Platycerium spp.
Polypody family: Polypodiaceae

HARDINESS–Zones 9b-11

NATIVE RANGE–Tropical areas of Central & South America, Africa, Asia, and Australia

COLOR(S)–Both green and brown fronds

MATURE SIZE–2 to 6 feet across (61 to 183 cm)

WATER NEEDS–Water thoroughly, then allow to dry out. Do not overwater this epiphyte or place where constantly wet.

CARE–There are both basal fronds and antler-shaped (fertile) foliage fronds. Once established, staghorns need minimal care. Feed in late spring with diluted fish emulsion fertilizer. Provide good air circulation. Can be mounted onto a board or tree, with sphagnum moss or coconut coir behind the fern. Attach with florist's tape or cloth strap, which new shield fronds will cover.

PROBLEMS–Beginners often overwater staghorns. If in doubt, wait until the green fronds become limp before watering. The fuzzy brown growths on the back of fronds are spores and are normal.

USES AND SELECTIONS–This unusual epiphytic fern is striking as a wall decoration, mounted on trees, or when hanging from branches. *P. bifurcatum* is the easiest to grow and handles temperatures down to 25°F (-4°C).

TI PLANT

Cordyline fruticosa
Asparagus family: Asparagaceae

HARDINESS–Zones 10b–11

NATIVE RANGE–Australia and Papua New Guinea

COLOR(S)–Green foliage, or green, cream, and red combinations

MATURE SIZE–6 feet x 20 inches (183 x 51 cm)

WATER NEEDS–Keep moist for summer; let dry slightly in fall and winter.

CARE–Plant in high shade with bright, indirect light. Their best color comes in fall and winter. Too much light or fertilizer can bleach the foliage. Do not over-fertilize cordyline growing in shade. Organic fertilizer, such as compost or fish emulsion, is gentle, and slow-release is fine. Tip cuttings easily develop roots. These tender plants are suitable for container culture in Central and North Florida, especially miniature hybrids.

PROBLEMS–Watch for mealybugs, scale, and thrips, plus spider mites in winter. Often ends up looking straggly or spindly. Trim it back to 1 or 2 feet (30 to 61 cm) high every few years to keep it full.

USES AND SELECTIONS–Use colorful ti plants between billowy shrubs for flair, contrast a group of dark burgundy ones with variegated ginger, and use the tricolor for bringing color to palm and aroid plantings. They are exclamation points.

TRAVELER'S TREE

Ravenala madagascariensis
Bird-of-paradise family: Strelitziaceae

HARDINESS–Zones 10–11

NATIVE RANGE–Madagascar

COLOR(S)–White flowers

PEAK SEASON–Blooms summer

MATURE SIZE–40 feet x 25 feet (12 x 7.5 m)

WATER NEEDS–Likes plenty of water during summer, less in winter

CARE–Plant in area large enough to accommodate large head of leaves. Add compost in March for 2 or 3 years after planting. As natives of high altitudes, they can withstand more cold than most tropicals. In smaller gardens, remove suckers from the base.

PROBLEMS–For best appearance, remove wind-tattered leaves.

USES AND SELECTIONS–Often called traveler's palms, they are not related to palms, but to the bird-of-paradise. These handsome wonders of botanical geometry are attention-getters when pruned so their fan shows off, especially when young and closer to eye level. A mature traveler's tree can be a stunning sculptural element where low plants suddenly give way to exuberance. When inappropriately used, these impressive specimens can overpower the rest of the garden. The bases of the 10- to 12-foot (3- to 3.5-m) leaves fill with water, which was handy for travelers.

JANUARY

❏ Cut some anthuriums or other tropical flowers for indoor winter beauty.

❏ January and February are the coldest months. If you have cold-sensitive tropical plants in northern or central parts of Florida, protect them from north winds and low temperatures. Move container plantings to a safe location and cover in-ground tropical plants with cloths or blankets. Do not use plastic, which provides no cold protection and can cook plants if not removed during the day. Be sure covers reach to the ground to trap warmth of surrounding soil. Pay close attention to plants with large or thin leaves, like elephant ear.

❏ In South Florida, tropical plants can be planted most times of the year, but the cold and dry months are the worst times to do so.

❏ Tropicals have slowed their growth and need less moisture. Water only when needed.

❏ Mites may appear with the drier weather. Mealybugs may also be a problem.

FEBRUARY

❏ February is often the coldest month of the year. Be prepared for any unusually low temperatures, even in the warmer areas of the state. Cover sensitive tropicals or move them to sheltered parts of the landscape. For cold-sensitive ground covers that cannot be moved, thoroughly wet the soil before the freeze. Cold winds can damage delicate ferns. Move at-risk ferns and other hanging baskets to protected locations or cover carefully with blankets.

❏ Some tropical plants that are damaged by cold may regrow once warmer weather returns. Cut off any unsightly dead leaves, but wait until spring for trimming.

❏ Water when needed.

❏ Mites may continue to be a problem with the drier weather. Scale may also be more noticeable this time of year as plant growth remains slow.

MARCH

❏ Some tropical plants can be propagated from now until summer.

❏ As plants start to grow, they will need more moisture. Water regularly and renew the layer of mulch to retain moisture. Begin watering orchids more frequently now.

❏ Prune cold-damaged tropical plants.

❏ Enrich the soil around your tropicals with applications of compost. You could apply fish emulsion monthly for hungry plants. Orchids do best with a special fertilizer blend, and now is the time to start applying it. Some prefer to use a low dose with every watering. Make sure to soak all the leaves and roots.

❏ Aphids may start to appear on new growth.

APRIL

❏ This is a good month to plant many tropicals, when the coming spring rains will provide natural irrigation. The weather outside is still cool, so planting is stress-free.

❏ Move container tropical plants back outside in colder parts of the state.

❏ Bring a pot of blooming phalaenopsis orchids inside for a month or more of display. Place in a bright spot and do not overwater while indoors.

❏ Prune cold- and wind-damaged foliage to make room for new growth.

❏ Many tropical plants prefer to dry out between waterings. They cannot tolerate constantly wet roots and must have good drainage. Check any plantings that may be a problem when the rains return. Move those plants to a better location, build raised beds with good drainage, or plant in containers.

❏ As new growth appears, pests may become more active.

MAY

❏ As the rainy season approaches, this is the best time to plant most tropicals, both terrestrial and epiphytic species. Orchids can be tied on with florist tape and bromeliads can be glued on with a waterproof construction adhesive.

❏ Remove suckers from the base of traveler's tree when they're still small. Also, begin watching fast-growing tropical plants like gingers for overgrowth that may need to be trimmed.

❏ Until the rainy season arrives at the end of the month, water regularly, especially new plantings.

❏ Use slow-release fertilizer with micronutrients to provide a steady supply of nutrients to any heavy feeders.

❏ Mealybugs and scale may occur.

JUNE

❏ June is the beginning of Florida's wet season and is the best time to add new tropical plants. They grow best when organic material is added to the soil and plantings are topped with a mulch layer to retain moisture. Group tropicals together so the entire landscape does not need to be watered whenever they need moisture.

❏ Cuttings and divisions may be made now, while the plants are making fast growth and nature is providing the irrigation.

❏ Mother Nature is probably doing the watering. However, continue to monitor new plantings for moisture levels and provide any waterings that are needed, especially if the rains fail.

❏ Tropical plants are in full growth mode now and using nutrients at a rapid rate. If leaves yellow, apply a micronutrient foliar spray.

JULY

❏ Tropical plants are the source of many exotic flowers in arrangements. Periodically, cut a few blooms and bring them indoors. As an example, bird-of-paradise blossoms are even more beautiful when displayed close up.

❏ Keep tropical shrubs, including croton and copperleaf, trimmed so they stay full and bushy. Some that may become leggy, like mussaenda, may need hard pruning.

❏ Watering should not be necessary this month, but continue to check new plantings to make sure they have enough moisture.

❏ Orchids should get their regular feedings.

❏ Snails and slugs may be active, as well as caterpillars and grasshoppers. If plant foliage is too wet and air circulation poor, fungal leaf spots may occur.

AUGUST

❏ Be prepared to move or protect wind-sensitive tropical plants if a hurricane or storm approaches. Pruning damaged plants may be required afterward.

❏ As tropicals make lots of growth, they may need pruning to allow for flowers and new growth. Plants like dracaena can be topped to force new leaf heads. Others like the gingers can have old stems removed.

❏ Make sure summer rains aren't flooding any tropical. Don't allow standing water.

❏ Check that bromeliad cups are regularly flushed to keep out mosquitoes. Or treat with a *Bacillus thuringiensis* product formulated to kill their larvae.

❏ Snails, slugs, caterpillars, and grasshoppers may be active.

SEPTEMBER

❏ Cut off any bromeliad pups once they are about a third of the size of the parent plant, then plant. They may appear at any time of the year. Wear long gloves to protect your arms from spiny varieties. Other tropicals can still be planted. Once the rains subside, you will need to provide the waterings. Start checking all plants regularly for moisture levels, especially new plantings.

❏ September and October are usually the height of hurricane season. Be prepared to move or protect wind-sensitive tropical plants if a hurricane or storm approaches. Pruning damaged plants may be required after it passes.

❏ Prune excessive growth as needed to control and to shape tropical plants.

❏ Snails and slugs are very active, as well as caterpillars and grasshoppers. As the weather begins to dry, mites may make an appearance.

OCTOBER

❏ Tropical plants can still be added to the landscape. However, tropicals will now need your ongoing attention so they stay moist.

❏ September and October are usually the height of the hurricane season. Be prepared to move or protect wind-sensitive tropical plants if a hurricane or storm approaches. Pruning damaged plants may be required after it passes.

❏ Renew mulch layers. Use soaker hoses or micro sprinklers wherever possible.

❏ Continue orchid feedings. In the northern part of the state, this may be the season's last feeding to make certain new growth can mature before the damaging cold weather. Add a compost topdressing to all container plantings to refresh the soil.

❏ Snails and slugs are very active, as well as caterpillars and grasshoppers. Mites occur as the weather becomes drier.

NOVEMBER

❏ Although the weather is cooler and plant growth has slowed, continue to monitor the water needs of all tropical plants, especially new plantings. Spray foliage with water regularly to discourage pests and to make up for lack of rainfall.

❏ Bring blooming orchids indoors for maximum enjoyment. Don't overwater.

❏ As weather turns dry, watch for mites, mealybugs, or other pests, especially on leaf undersides.

DECEMBER

❏ Be prepared to cover sensitive tropicals if you are unable to move them. A sheet or blanket is the best material to use if draped directly on top of the plants. If growing in containers, move tropicals indoors when first frost or freeze is forecast.

❏ Make sure tropical plants are pest free before bringing inside. Carefully and thoroughly wash all leaves, especially nooks and crannies. Use alcohol to wipe away lingering insects.

❏ Scale and mites can be controlled with oil spray, if applied when temperatures are above 40°F (4°C). Insects and sooty mold slowly flake off after a month or more.

VINES
for Florida

My, how they get around, these vines. Shameless climbers, stealthy twiners, exuberant clingers, superlative sprawlers, midnight ramblers . . . cling to me like a vine, we say, and mean every word at the time.

VINE USES

The ability to camouflage may be a vine's most useful characteristic in the landscape. Vines can hide a concrete block wall in just one or two seasons. Other vines that have clusters of hanging flowers, such as the jade vine or bleeding heart, make a beautiful trellis plant. Pergolas and trellises can be used to create outdoor rooms or walkways, with vines adding colorful, natural decoration. Grow philodendrons on a tree or stump, flame vine on a lamppost, or bridal wreath on porch lattice . . . your garden will benefit from their unique qualities.

PLANNING

Nature gave vines the ability to reach for the sun and very few really like the shade. Vines grow best when given some support, usually a trellis or a wire or wood support. They can be trained to be freestanding or attached to a wall. Vines tend to grow quickly during the warmer months. Plant vines as accent features. Use the flowers and fruits to attract attention. Vines are ideal where you have limited space but need some height. They can grow in a container and still climb a wall or trellis.

PLANTING

Vines aren't very particular about planting sites. Most like a well-drained soil, but it can be sandy, clayey, or peaty. Care is made a lot easier if the soil is enriched with organic matter, but in fact you can pop these plants in the ground just about anywhere. When their roots systems become established, many are drought tolerant.

It is important to learn a little about the plant to be added to the landscape. If you are going to use more than one vine, give them adequate room to grow. Make sure you learn which is going to spread out and will need more room. Most of this information is found on plant labels or can be obtained from garden center employees. Now you can put the plants in the ground: see page 224.

CARE

Primary care involves guiding the growth of the new plants and keeping older plants in-bounds. Periodically check the new growths from beginning vines to make sure they are filling the trellis. If needed, pinch back ends to cause branching and new growth. Vines may need periodic trimming to stay in-bounds. Check these plantings monthly for errant growth during warm weather. Cut them back hard after flowering or in early spring before they shoot out.

WATERING

Vines are a hardy bunch. Once established, most can exist primarily with seasonal rains. After planting, however, you should give each enough water to establish a root system and begin growth out into the surrounding soil.

FERTILIZING

Enriched soil is needed to encourage growth during the establishment period, so apply compost around the planting hole. After the vines fill a trellis, little fertilizer is needed.

PEST CONTROL

Many vines grow pest free. Seldom do you have to spray, as they can tolerate the few leaf spots and holes made by insects. See the appendix on page 224 for more on pests and what actions to take.

ALLAMANDA

Allamanda cathartica
Dogbane family: Apocynaceae

HARDINESS–Zones 9b-10

NATIVE RANGE–Central & South America

COLOR(S)–Yellow flowers

PEAK SEASON–Spring, summer, fall blooms; foliage evergreen

MATURE SIZE–5 feet (1.5 m); vining

WATER NEEDS–Once established, are fairly drought tolerant, but may need weekly watering in dry season.

CARE–Grows vigorously in enriched soil. Apply fertilizer with micronutrients in spring and fall. Cut back hard in early spring to remove intertwined stems. In Central Florida, prune after warm weather returns.

PROBLEMS–The milky white sap is somewhat toxic to humans and pets. Few insects bother allamanda, except aphids in spring. Use ladybugs or horticultural oil spray.

USES AND SELECTIONS–Allamanda doesn't have tendrils to cling, but it sprawls and reaches with gusto, needing a strong support. Use to wrap chain-link fences in large yellow flowers and glossy leaves. Tie against a wooden privacy fence and allow shoots to cascade down. Or lean it on a picket fence. There are purple, pink, and bronze cultivars.

BLEEDING HEART VINE

Clerodendrum thomsoniae
Mint family: Lamiaceae

HARDINESS–Zones 9-11

NATIVE RANGE–Tropical west Africa

COLOR(S)–White with red flowers

PEAK SEASON–Blooms summer; evergreen foliage

MATURE SIZE–To 15 feet (4.5 m)

WATER NEEDS–Prefers moist, but not soggy, soil

CARE–This vine grows by twining, but it can be pruned into a shrub. When provided with support, it can be grown as a somewhat restrained vine. It is slightly salt tolerant.

PROBLEMS–In colder areas, plant bleeding heart in a container so it can be protected when temperatures drop below 45°F (7°C).

USES AND SELECTIONS–Since bleeding heart is less vigorous than other vines, it is best planted in limited areas like a trellis or a garden arch. Save the more spirited vines for covering fences and arbors. The beautiful and unusual flower clusters have interior crimson petals. After they fall, the surrounding showy white calyces remain. It is also called glorybower, and bleeding glory bower.

BOUGAINVILLEA

Bougainvillea spp.
Four o'clock family: Nyctaginaceae

HARDINESS–Zones 9-11

NATIVE RANGE–South America

COLOR(S)–Small white flowers surrounded by bracts in all colors

PEAK SEASON–Spring through fall blooms; foliage evergreen

MATURE SIZE–6 to 20 feet (1.5 to 6 m)

WATER NEEDS–Once established, irrigate then allow to dry before watering again. Will not flower well if it receives too much regular water.

CARE–Not fussy about soil, but it blooms better with enriched soil. Apply compost in March each year. Tolerant of some cold; comes back from the ground if frozen. Prune and shape in September.

PROBLEMS–Small moth caterpillars may attack the leaves. Let the cycle run its course. Be careful of thorns, which are more prominent on young plants.

USES AND SELECTIONS–The stunning color of the papery bracts is dazzling. A good fence plant. Supremely beautiful when colors are mixed. Can be grown in large containers. The semi-thornless varieties are good container plants for patios or balconies. The purple *B. spectabilis* is somewhat more cold tolerant than others.

BOWER VINE

Pandorea jasminoides
Crossvine family: Bignoniaceae

HARDINESS–Zones 10-11

NATIVE RANGE–Eastern Australia

COLOR(S)–White-pink flowers
PEAK SEASON–Spring and summer

MATURE SIZE–To 6 feet (183 cm)

WATER NEEDS–Water daily for first few weeks. Gradually taper off to an as-needed schedule. This vine is drought tolerant. However, when growth is desired, water weekly.

CARE–Tolerates sandy soils but grows best in enriched soil. Apply compost 4 to 6 weeks after planting and again the next March. Prune when it begins to grow out of bounds. After years of growth, may need renewal pruning during late winter. Freezing will cause major damage. Remove damaged sections before spring growth begins. Mulch well to protect the basal buds during winter months.

PROBLEMS–Pest problems are few.

USES AND SELECTIONS–Can be used on trellises, fences, or similar supports.

BRIDAL WREATH

Stephanotis floribunda
Dogbane family: Apocynaceae

HARDINESS–Zones 10-11

NATIVE RANGE–Madagascar

COLOR(S)–White flowers; glossy dark-green leaves

PEAK SEASON–Blooms summer; evergreen foliage

MATURE SIZE–To 15 feet (4.5 m)

WATER NEEDS–Prefers to be moist, but not wet. Let dry between waterings.

CARE–Plant in sun or part shade in enriched, well-drained soil. This vine climbs by means of twining. Train over trellises and keep pruned. Apply compost in March to keep soil rich.

PROBLEMS–Grow in containers in frost-prone areas to move indoors for protection against cold.

USES AND SELECTIONS–The clusters of long-lasting white flowers are often used for wedding bouquets, which explains some of its many common names: Madagascar jasmine, bridal bouquet, Hawaiian wedding flower, and wax flower. Plant in areas where the strong fragrance can be appreciated–over mail boxes, near patios, and by entryways. While the white variety is considered very attractive against the thick dark-green leaves, a variegated form is also available.

CAPE HONEYSUCKLE

Tecoma capensis
Crossvine family: Bignoniaceae

HARDINESS–Zones 9-11

NATIVE RANGE–Southern Africa

COLOR(S)–Bright orange-red flowers

PEAK SEASON–Blooms spring through winter; evergreen foliage

MATURE SIZE–To 10 feet x 5 feet (3 x 1.5 m) as shrub; to 25 feet (7.5 m) long as vine

WATER NEEDS–Moderately drought tolerant once established

CARE–Plant in any well-drained soil. Blooms best in full sun, but tolerates light shade. This vine is more like a sprawling shrub that likes to wander. To use as a vine, it must be tied in place. Prune regularly to train as a shrub or hedge. It is salt tolerant.

PROBLEMS–It takes root where branches droop down to contact the ground.

USES AND SELECTIONS–Use cape honeysuckle as a shrub, hedge, view barrier, or climbing vine. This tough plant is especially useful in seaside conditions where it stands up to heat, wind, and salt. The clusters of tubular flowers attract hummingbirds. A yellow cultivar and a more compact cultivar with orange flowers are available.

CAROLINA YELLOW JESSAMINE

Gelsemium sempervirens
Jessamine family: Gelsemiaceae

HARDINESS—Zones 8-9

NATIVE RANGE—Virginia through to Honduras including North and Central Florida

COLOR(S)—Yellow flowers

PEAK SEASON—Blooms early winter

MATURE SIZE—20-plus feet (6-plus m); climbing

WATER NEEDS—Water daily for first few weeks; gradually taper off to as-needed. Drought tolerant.

CARE—Grows well in sandy soils. Makes lots of growth, so allow adequate room. Apply compost 4 to 6 weeks after planting. Prune when plants begin to grow out of bounds.

PROBLEMS—No major pests affect this native vine. All portions are poisonous if eaten by humans or livestock.

USES AND SELECTIONS—Plant as a space divider or backdrop for a patio or garden opening. Stage other flowers in front, including pentas, salvia, gaillardia, and caladiums. Use to hide fences or cover walls.

CLEMATIS

Clematis spp.
Crowfoot family: Ranunculaceae

HARDINESS—Zones 8-9

NATIVE RANGE—Cosmopolitan across the world, including Florida

COLOR(S)—A rainbow of flower colors

PEAK SEASON—Blooms summer, fall; deciduous foliage

MATURE SIZE—15 feet (4.5 m) or more

WATER NEEDS—Native species are drought tolerant once established.

CARE—Plant in well-drained soil. Grows best when plant is in sun or partial shade, but root zone is cool. Use mulch or overplant the roots. Add compost 4 to 6 weeks after planting and again the following March.

PROBLEMS—The stems are somewhat fragile and can be easily broken.

USES AND SELECTIONS— There are six species of clematis native to Florida and hundreds of cultivars and hybrids, including the Jackman group of clematis hybrids, which have single or double flowers up to 7 inches (18 cm) across. Grow clematis vines on fences, walls, and trellises. The Jackman Clematis won an award from the Royal Horticultural Society.

CONFEDERATE JASMINE

Trachelospermum jasminoides
Dogbane family: Apocynaceae

HARDINESS—Zones 8-10

NATIVE RANGE—Eastern Asia, Korea, and Japan

COLOR(S)—White flowers

PEAK SEASON—Blooms early winter; foliage evergreen

MATURE SIZE—10-plus feet (3-plus m); climbing

WATER NEEDS—Water daily for first few weeks. Gradually taper off to watering as needed. Drought tolerant.

CARE—Grows well in sandy Florida soils. Add compost 4 to 6 weeks after planting and again the following March. Prune when it begins to grow out of bounds. To renew growth, every few years prune in spring after flowering.

PROBLEMS—None.

USES AND SELECTIONS—A great plant for trellises under oak, pine, and similar trees. With just a little support, it forms a dense view barrier or attractive vertical accent. Fragrant flowering lasts a month. Small-leaf confederate jasmine (*T. asiaticum*) is an ideal wall covering for small gardens or a turf substitute in hard-to-mow areas. 'Variegatum' has green and cream-colored foliage.

CORAL HONEYSUCKLE

Lonicera sempervirens
Honeysuckle family: Caprifoliaceae

HARDINESS—Zones 8-10

NATIVE RANGE—Eastern United States including North and Central Florida

COLOR(S)—Reddish-orange and yellow blooms; red berries

PEAK SEASON—Spring through summer blooms; evergreen foliage

MATURE SIZE—20 feet (6 m) or more; climbing

WATER NEEDS—Water daily for first few weeks after planting. Gradually taper off to an as-needed schedule. Vines are drought tolerant.

CARE—Add compost 4 to 6 weeks after planting and again during March the following year. Prune when it grows out of bounds. Give renewal pruning in late spring every 5 years or so. Grows best where plants receive some chilling winter weather.

PROBLEMS—Usually pest-free

USES AND SELECTIONS—A Florida native, it attracts hummingbirds and butterflies. Use for fences, masonry walls, and trellises. Selections come in yellow and red.

DUTCHMAN'S PIPE

Aristolochia spp.
Dutchman's pipe family: Aristolochiaceae

HARDINESS—Zones 8-11

NATIVE RANGE—Cosmopolitan in much of the world, including Florida

COLOR(S)—Purple flowers

PEAK SEASON—Blooms summer; evergreen foliage except in northern areas

MATURE SIZE—15 or 20 feet (4.5 to 6 m)

WATER NEEDS—Water daily until established. Then water regularly.

CARE—Plant in partial shade in enriched soil, with a support. Leaves wilt if too dry, so some midday shade is best. Use compost in March, plus a fish emulsion spray at the beginning of summer to boost blooming. Grows quickly.

PROBLEMS—These vines are toxic to humans. The calico flower (*A. elegans*) is invasive in Florida, so don't plant it and pull it out if you have it.

USES AND SELECTIONS—Marsh's Dutchman's pipe (*A. pentandra*), Virginia snakeroot (*A. serpentaria*), and wooly pipevine (*A. tomentosa*) are native to various regions of Florida. Their dense twining foliage makes good screens, even on chain-link fences. The large, unusual flowers are showy. These plants lure butterflies and provide food for butterfly larva.

FLAME VINE

Pyrostegia venusta
Crossvine family: Bignoniaceae

HARDINESS—Zones 9-11

NATIVE RANGE—Mexico, Central & South America

COLOR(S)—Bright orange flowers

PEAK SEASON—Winter blooms

MATURE SIZE—Indeterminate

WATER NEEDS—Drought tolerant once established

CARE—Plant on a fence or trellis in full sun, in enriched soil to keep it vigorous. Add compost in the spring for a year or two after planting. After the blooms have dropped, cut the vine back hard. Flowers grow at the terminals of new shoots, so pruning will earn you more flowers. If temperatures hit 32°F (0°C), it dies back to the ground, but will grow back rapidly.

PROBLEMS—None.

USES AND SELECTIONS—It can be dazzling with little care. Use to cover fences and trellises.

GARLIC VINE

Bignonia aequinoctialis
Crossvine family: Bignoniaceae

HARDINESS–Zones 9–11

NATIVE RANGE–Caribbean, Mexico, Central & South America

COLOR(S)–Flowers start purple then fade to almost white

PEAK SEASON–Blooms spring, fall

MATURE SIZE–To 12 feet (3.5 m)

WATER NEEDS–Needs average water. Mulch to retain moisture.

CARE–Plant in well-drained soil. Unlike many other vines, garlic vine has only a moderate growth rate. Prune the plant after flowers are gone, since buds form on new growth. Can be planted in containers to move indoors for protection against freezing temperatures.

PROBLEMS–None.

USES AND SELECTIONS–The leaves smell like garlic when crushed. The clusters of funnel-shaped flowers have several different colors, from purple to almost white. Attractive for hiding a chain-link or other fence or planted on a trellis.

JADE VINE

Strongylodon macrobotrys
Legume family: Fabaceae

HARDINESS–Zones 10b–11

NATIVE RANGE–The Philippines

COLOR(S)–Blue-green flowers

PEAK SEASON–Blooms winter and spring

MATURE SIZE–Indeterminate

WATER NEEDS–Keep roots well irrigated to get established. Drought tolerant once established.

CARE–Add compost a few weeks after planting and then again the next March. In late fall use diluted fish emulsion to help flower development. Jade vine needs a pergola or an arbor that is as burly as this aggressive vine, which can get a stranglehold on whatever it clutches.

PROBLEMS–Cold sensitive.

USES AND SELECTIONS–The aquamarine flowers grow on chains up to 3 feet (91 cm) long. The exotic color is memorable.

MANDEVILLA

Mandevilla spp. and hybrids
Dogbane family: Apocynaceae

HARDINESS–Zones 9–11. In Zone 8, it regrows after cold damage.

NATIVE RANGE–Texas, New Mexico, Mexico, Central & South America

COLOR(S)–Pink, yellow, white, red flowers

PEAK SEASON–Blooms summer; foliage evergreen

MATURE SIZE–To 10 feet (3 m)

WATER NEEDS–Withstands brief droughts. Do not overwater.

CARE–Plant in enriched, well-drained soil. Grow in full sun, preferably with midday shade. Add compost in March and diluted fish emulsion at the beginning of summer to maximize blooms. With regular trimming, this twining vine can be kept bushy. Has moderate salt tolerance. Plant in containers and bring indoors for cold protection.

PROBLEMS–Stressed plants may get mealybugs, scale, or whiteflies.

USES AND SELECTIONS–Use this showy vine near entryways and patios to enjoy the large flowers. Use over arbors, trellises, or mailbox posts. It makes colorful screens to hide unsightly fences or sheds. Once called pink allamanda because it only came in pink. The pink hybrid 'Alice du Pont' is still popular. Now, there are yellow, white, and red selections.

PAINTED TRUMPET

Bignonia callistegioides
Crossvine family: Bignoniaceae

HARDINESS–Zones 8-11

NATIVE RANGE–South America

COLOR(S)–Pale lavender flowers; dark-green foliage

PEAK SEASON–Blooms spring; evergreen foliage

MATURE SIZE–20 feet (6 m) or more

WATER NEEDS–Is drought tolerant. When given plenty of moisture, it grows more aggressively.

CARE–Will grow in any well-drained soil, although it's more compact and less rampant in sandy soils. This robust and carefree grower climbs using tendrils that tightly grab things in its path.

PROBLEMS–Virtually pest free. The vine may need to be restrained. Seeds pods are large and prickly.

USES AND SELECTIONS–The showy flowers put on a large, beautiful display in spring and may continue into summer. Use this fast grower where there is plenty of room to spread. It is not suitable for smaller gardens. Plant on arbors, over pergolas, and as screens to block unwanted views. Other common names are violet trumpet vine and Argentine trumpet vine.

PASSION VINE

Passiflora spp.
Passion vine family: Passifloraceae

HARDINESS–Zones 9-11. Killed to ground by severe frost, but grows back.

NATIVE RANGE–Eastern states including Florida; also Mexico, Central & South America, Southeast Asia, Pacific island nations, and eastern Australia

COLOR(S)–Blue, purple, white, red, crimson flowers

PEAK SEASON–Blooms spring and summer

MATURE SIZE–20 feet (6 m) or more

WATER NEEDS–Somewhat drought tolerant once established, but blooms better with regular waterings

CARE–Plant in any well-drained soil. Easy to grow.

PROBLEMS–Passion vines can get out of control. If necessary, prune severely to keep it in-bounds. The two-flowered variety (*P. bicolor*) is invasive in Florida.

USES AND SELECTIONS–Grow these natural climbers on fences, arbors, walls, or trellises. Can be used to cover up unsightly features like chain-link fences. They attract lots of butterflies by providing both nectar and larval food. For maximum benefit in butterfly gardens, do not use insecticides. There are six native Florida passion vines.

PHILODENDRON

Philodendron spp.
Arum family: Araceae

HARDINESS–Zones 10b-11

NATIVE RANGE–Caribbean, Mexico, Central & South America

COLOR(S)–White spathe; foliage green

PEAK SEASON–Intermittent blooms; foliage evergreen

MATURE SIZE–To top of trees

WATER NEEDS–Water daily until vine produces new leaves and roots, then gradually reduce watering.

CARE–Apply compost 4 to 6 weeks after planting. Philodendrons, like other aroids, are sensitive to cold, but some survive cold and drought unscathed by growing beneath trees. They may withstand cold, but not freezes. Prune vigorous climbers.

PROBLEMS–Hand pick snails.

USES AND SELECTIONS–Philodendrons are extremely agile at surviving in their native rain forests. They can survive in the dim areas or climb for the light. This makes them suitable for gardens and easier to contain than some other vines. In fact, some are even suitable for containers. There are several cold-tolerant species.

QUEEN'S WREATH

Petrea volubilis
Verbena family: Verbenaceae

HARDINESS–Zones 10b-11

NATIVE RANGE–Caribbean, Mexico, Central & South America

COLOR(S)–Blue-purple flowers

PEAK SEASON–Spring blooms

MATURE SIZE–To 35 feet (10.5 m)

WATER NEEDS–Water twice a week in summer; bi-weekly in winter.

CARE–This vigorous vine must be supported by a pergola or arbor. Without tendrils, the vine twines and does best on craggy surfaces. Add compost in March. Cut back hard after flowering or in late winter. In Central Florida, plant this tender vine in a sunny area.

PROBLEMS–Has few pests, although spider mites can be a problem in dry weather. Give the affected areas a hard spray of water.

USES AND SELECTIONS–Because it is so strongly seasonal, the vine shows off when it finally does flower. Using it at an arching front gate, or on a pergola or trellis of some sort, is ideal. Give it a place to show off. With age, the vine develops a thick trunk.

RANGOON CREEPER

Combretum indicum
White mangrove family: Combretaceae

HARDINESS–Zones 10-11

NATIVE RANGE–Tanzania, Tropical & Subtropical Asia to North Australia

COLOR(S)–Flowers start white, then change to pink, then red

PEAK SEASON–Blooms summer; evergreen foliage

MATURE SIZE–Over 40 feet (12 m)

WATER NEEDS–Water regularly during growing season, less during winter.

CARE–Plant in well-drained soil. Rangoon creeper starts as a bush and then becomes an energetic vine, using its spiny stems to hold as it twines. It grows lush quickly.

PROBLEMS–Handle with care because of the thorny stems. Keep an eye on this vine so that it doesn't get out of control. Prune when necessary.

USES AND SELECTIONS–Rangoon creeper can appear to be different plants. A cluster of flowers will have several colors at once as individual blossoms age. Its appropriate botanical name means "who" (*quis*) and "what" (*qualis*). This rampant grower needs a strong support to hold the long, glossy leaves and to showcase the drooping fragrant flowers. Plant on arbors, trellises, arches, fences, and pergolas.

TRUMPET CREEPER

Campsis radicans
Crossvine family: Bignoniaceae

HARDINESS–Zones 8-9

NATIVE RANGE–Eastern states from Maine to Texas, including North and Central Florida

COLOR(S)–Orange flowers

PEAK SEASON–Blooms summer; foliage evergreen

MATURE SIZE–30 or more feet (9 or more m)

WATER NEEDS–Water daily for first few weeks after planting. Gradually taper off to an as-needed schedule. Vines are quite drought tolerant and only need weekly watering during drought. This native also adapts to moist conditions.

CARE–Grows in most Florida soils, but does best in enriched soil. Apply compost 4 to 6 weeks after planting. Needs a trellis, fence, or similar support.

PROBLEMS–None.

USES AND SELECTIONS–The large blooms are borne in clusters and attract hummingbirds. Plant this native to hide a sunny wall or fill a trellis. Use with other natives–ornamental grasses, shrubs, and saw palmettos. Suitable as a space divider or backdrop for other plantings. There is a yellow selection.

VINES

NAME	AREA OF FLORIDA	CLIMBING HEIGHT (FEET)	FOILAGE TYPE	FLOWER COLOR/SEASON	LIGHT NEEDED
Allamanda, Purple	CS	Variable	Evergreen	Purple/Summer-fall	Sun
Allamanda, Yellow	CS	Variable	Evergreen	Yellow/Year-round	Sun, light shade
Bengal Clock Vine	CS	20–30	Evergreen	White, blue/Summer	Sun
Bleeding Heart	CS	12–15	Evergreen	White & red/ Spring–fall	Sun, light shade
Bougainvillea	CS	10–20	Evergreen	Numerous/ Year-round	Sun
Bower Vine	CS	15–20	Evergreen	White & pink/Spring	Sun, light shade
Bridal Wreath	S	10–15	Evergreen	White/Summer	Sun, light shade
Cape Honeysuckle	CS	6–10	Evergreen	Orange/Summer-fall	Sun
Cat's Claw Vine	NCS	20–30	Evergreen	Yellow/Spring	Sun, light shade
Confederate Jasmine	NCS	15–20	Evergreen	White/Spring	Sun, shade
Coral Vine	CS	30–40	Evergreen	Pink/Spring-fall	Sun
Dutchman's Pipe	CS	12–15	Evergreen	White & brown/ Summer	Sun, light shade
Flame Vine	CS	30–40	Evergreen	Orange/Winter	Sun
Garlic Vine	CS	20–30	Evergreen	Lavender, pink, white/Spring-fall	Sun, light shade
Japanese Clematis	NC	10–15	Evergreen	White/Summer	Sun
Mandevilla	CS	15–20	Evergreen	Pink/Spring-fall	Sun
Mexican Flame Vine	CS	15–20	Evergreen	Orange/Spring-summer	Sun, light shade
Monstera	CS	15–20	Evergreen	Green/Summer	Light shade, shade
Ornamental Sweet Potato	CS	2–6	Evergreen	Inconspicuous	Sun, light shade
Painted Trumpet	NCS	15–20	Evergreen	Lavender/Spring	Sun
Passion Flower, Red	CS	15–20	Evergreen	Red/Spring-summer	Sun
Queen's Wreath	S	20–30	Evergreen	Purple/Spring-summer	Sun, light shade
Rangoon Creeper	CS	15–25	Evergreen	White, red/Summer	Sun, light shade
Showy Combretum	CS	15–20	Evergreen	Red/Fall-spring	Sun
Trumpet Creeper	NC	20–30	Deciduous	Orange/Summer	Sun
Trumpet Honeysuckle	NC	15–25	Evergreen	Orange, yellow/ Spring–summer	Sun
Yellow Jessamine, Carolina	NC	20–30	Evergreen	Yellow/Winter	Sun, light shade

N = North Florida   C = Central Florida   S = South Florida

JANUARY

❏ When planting vines, choose a site near a support. Determine the maximum width and space plants will need so shoots grow together at maturity.

❏ Vines may need grooming. Trim dead and declining plant portions. Remove extra-long shoots growing out of bounds. Plants that flower during late winter or early spring usually have pruning delayed until after blossoms fade.

❏ In South Florida, plants may begin growth, and spring feedings can begin. Apply compost around base of plant. In Central and North Florida, wait until February or March to add compost.

❏ Most insects do not become active until growth begins. However, scale can appear at any time. Control with oil spray if temperatures are above 40°F (4°C). Insects and sooty mold slowly flake off after a month or more.

FEBRUARY

❏ This is the most stress-free planting time of year. The weather is warming and garden centers are filling. Most vines are tough and need very little site preparation. However, results are more certain with good planting procedures.

❏ Water new plantings daily for a week or two. For the next few weeks, water every few days. Hand water to make sure moisture runs through the root system. Use soaker hoses or micro sprinklers where possible. Except during drought, established vines usually do not need waterings.

❏ Some gardeners keep vines off trees and provide trellises or arbors instead.

❏ Many vines get nutrients from decomposing mulches. However, a diluted fish emulsion in the spring feeding may boost the blooming.

❏ Some aphid presence can be ignored on new growth. When populations are high, spray with water. Skip the sprays if beneficial insects are present. Other problems this month are mites, mealybugs, scale, and powdery mildew.

MARCH

❏ Vines need guidance as they begin growing. Direct them onto a trellis so they can form a complete wall covering or create a solid view barrier. Some may need regular trimming to keep them in-bounds. Pinching back the vines just above buds will cause branching and produce additional shoots.

❏ This is the dry season, so make sure new plantings have adequate moisture. The first month or two is the critical period. Established plants only need water during drought or when plants wilt.

❏ If you missed the spring feeding, apply compost this month.

❏ Mites are often a problem during drier months. Other problems include aphids, caterpillars, powdery mildew, and scale.

APRIL

❏ Adding vines can continue throughout the year, though it's best to buy vines early in the season. They can become entangled while waiting at the nursery. If you do obtain a vine later in the season, try to find one on a trellis so the shoots can be easily switched to your growing area.

❏ Check vines to make sure they are filling the trellis or climbing the wall properly. Position or tie shoots if necessary. Trim back shoots that are too vigorous.

❏ Established plantings can often go a week or two without irrigation. Make sure new plantings have adequate moisture.

❏ Plants in containers should receive a top dressing of compost a few times each year to keep the soil alive.

❏ Some insects are becoming active. Check for grasshoppers, mealybugs, mites, powdery mildew, and scale.

MAY

❏ Once the new vines are in the ground, controlling weeds will help them grow better. Add a layer of mulch, apply a pre-emergence weed-control product, and remember that hoeing and pulling are still good ways to control weeds.

❏ This is the last full month of dry weather. Keep up regular watering of newly planted vines. Once established, make periodic checks for adequate moisture levels.

❏ Delay all feedings until next spring.

❏ Caterpillars may be active at this time of year. Wait for those butterflies.

JUNE

❏ Check vines that may be growing out of control. The start of the rainy season is when you can expect a flush of new shoots. Keep plants off nearby shrubs and out of trees.Control weeds.

❏ Most plantings make good growth as the rainy season returns. You may not have to do any waterings of even newly established plantings. However, continue to check the moisture levels of recently added plants.

❏ With the summer rains comes the chance of rot problems. are often a minor problem. Summer pests include aphids, caterpillars, grasshoppers, and scale.

JULY

❏ If you don't have a lot of room but still want to enjoy vines, use a small area or plant in containers. Vines are especially useful as screens in containers on patios or balconies. Let vines trail over the edges of walls.

❏ Keep up with the growth of vines. There is always trimming to do to keep them in-bounds.

❏ Mother Nature is probably helping with the watering. Continue to check the more recent plantings for water needs or possible overwatering. Very few established plants need special watering.

❏ For container gardens, apply compost as a topdressing.

❏ Most plantings can tolerate some defoliation from caterpillars. Scale may also be active. Hand pick the grasshoppers.

AUGUST

❏ Don't let the hot summer months keep you from adding plants. Just be sure you have a well-prepared site before planting. Add organic material to help hold moisture. After planting, thoroughly moisten and add a mulch layer.

❏ This is the last pruning time for bougainvillea. Trim to keep them in-bounds and then let them form buds for winter bloom. Other vines that bloom during spring should get their last trimming of the year.

❏ Regular rains should provide lots of water, but continue to check new plantings to make sure they are moist.

❏ Mealybugs may be found on tropical plants. Other pests and problems include grasshoppers, caterpillars, scale, leaf spots, and root rot.

SEPTEMBER

❏ With cooler weather it's easier to work outdoors. Any vines can be planted now.

❏ Sometimes vines get completely out of control and need major pruning. The best time for rejuvenation pruning is after they flower, but you can actually trim any time the plants are making growth. Heavy pruning may delay flowering for a year. Try to trim so the new growth will reach maturity before severe winter weather in central and northern portions of the state.

❏ If the rainy season ends early, you must provide water for new plantings and container plants.

❏ Caterpillars are often heavy in fall. Wait for those butterflies, because many vines are larval food sources. Other active pests include grasshoppers, leaf spots, mites, and scales.

OCTOBER

❏ There is no excuse not to get outdoors and enjoy the landscape; complete all needed trimming this month.

❏ Check new plantings regularly for needed moisture. Make sure the water is wetting the root balls.

❏ Gardeners may begin noticing many leaf spots on deciduous vines during fall. Some are getting ready for winter, and leaf spotting as the leaves begin to drop is normal. Even some evergreen types, including mandevilla, are not as vigorous during fall and may develop brown to yellow patches. This is normal. Pests you might be concerned about are caterpillars, grasshoppers, mites, and scale insects.

NOVEMBER

❏ It continues to be a good time for planting. If only adding one or two plants, soil preparation is not needed.

❏ Most landscape plant growth is slowing. If it's not the cool weather, it's the shorter days that reduce growth. Your job is to remove vine growth that may be interfering with landscape movement or affecting other plantings. Continue to control weeds.

❏ Cool weather means slower growth and less waterings. Continue to check new plantings to make sure soil is moist. Established plants seldom need watering, except in containers.

❏ For containers, apply compost to the soil to keep soil alive.

❏ Mites can remain a pest during fall. Luckily vines are fairly resistant. Mealybugs may develop, especially in shady spots. Use water for both mites and mealybugs. Caterpillars and grasshoppers may still be around.

DECEMBER

❏ Little care is needed this month. Very little pruning is needed except for vines that may blow off a trellis or arbor.

❏ Continue to check all plantings for adequate water. Water as needed to maintain moist soil for new plantings. Older plantings can usually go weeks between waterings. Container plantings can usually skip a day or two. This is also a good time to check the irrigation system.

❏ If you have container plantings, stretch the compostings to 4 to 6 weeks. Skip if plants are dormant.

❏ Scale insects might be quite evident. Cooler months are a good time to control with oil spray, as long as the temperatures are above 40°F (4°C). Coat all portions of the plant. In warmer locations of the state where plants continue to grow, check for aphids, mealybugs, and mites that may need control.

INVASIVE PLANTS IN FLORIDA

Plants from other regions of the world are determined to be invasive when they have overtaken wild areas in the state. Not all non-native plants are invasive, just those that can rapidly and uncontrollably reproduce. Seeds may be spread by the wind, by birds, by water, or by other wildlife.

Control of invasive plants is important for several reasons. Invasives choke out or displace native plants, which reduces the habitat for wildlife. They also interfere with plant and animal life in bodies of water and impede navigation and flood control. The control of invasive exotics is expensive, with millions of dollars (both private and public funds) being spent in Florida. Progress is being made in some public natural areas, but the work is neverending.

How a plant behaves in your yard is not important in our discussion of what is invasive and what is not. The invasiveness of a plant is declared only after careful study of the damage it's doing in the wild parts of Florida. Category I invasives have already done significant damage, while Category II invasives have done some damage with the potential to do more significant damage in the future. The Florida Exotic Plant Pest Council (www.fleppc.org) maintains a list of plants that have adverse effects on Florida's biodiversity and plant communities. It is updated every 2 years and also includes plants on the Federal and State of Florida lists.

As gardeners, we can do our part. Whenever possible we should avoid planting any invasive exotics in our yards and communities, and remove those that are growing there. Unfortunately, at this point, garden centers still sell known invasive plants. There are countless beautiful Florida natives and non-invasive exotics that can be used in their place.

FLORIDA'S PESTS

We have no shortage of pests in Florida, but we also have a vast number of predators of those pests. So not everything that is crawling on your plants is a pest, and even if caterpillars are eating your plants, some of them will become beautiful butterflies. And, even more of them will become bird food. So what is a gardener to do? Practice Integrated Pest Management (IPM) using the least amount of synthetic chemical pesticides as possible, using physical barriers such as cardboard collars to protect seedlings, learning to identify the "good bugs," and hand-picking the bad ones.

Except for your crop plants, learn to tolerate some amount of damage, knowing that if something is eating your plants, then it's playing a valuable role in your yard's ecosystem. For further references on IPM, go to the Florida Agriculture Extension's website for this topic: https://ipm.ifas.ufl.edu/

APHIDS are small pear-shaped insects, variously colored, that feed only on new growth. Look for them in buds and new leaves. They suck sap from plants, and their excreta attract ants and encourage growth of black sooty mold fungus. A water spray is usually all that is needed for control. If lady beetles and other predatory insects are present, let Nature be the control.

BLACK SPOT produces dark spots, often with a yellow halo, on roses; affected leaves drop and plant vigor is affected. You can help keep this disease under control by watering only during early-morning hours to allow foliage to dry during the day. Control with fungicides as needed, especially during rainy weather.

BORERS are insects or insect larvae that feed in the woody parts of plants. Borers may be an indication of more severe problems. Check for sap or sawdust around the trunks of trees and dying branches. If only minor, the damage from borers can be ignored–the plant may have the problem under control. When borer activity appears severe, some control can be achieved with sprays. Follow label instructions. Look for major causes of plant stress and correct while controlling the borer attacks. If borers persist, have the plants checked by a specialist. Severe damage or infections may make plant removal necessary.

BROWN PATCH is a turf disease caused by a fungus living in most soils. The fungus is active during warmish late-fall and early-spring weather in moist soils and locations with poor air movement. The disease causes large, brown, somewhat circular areas to develop. Control with a fungicide if severe or skip the poisons and fill in the spot with a mowable ground cover.

CATERPILLARS are the larvae of moths or butterflies. They chew plant foliage, stems, or flowers, and are of varying sizes and colors. Unless they attack crops, most gardeners allow caterpillars to feed on their plants, as many turn into attractive moths or butterflies. When the damage is heavy, they are best handpicked and destroyed, or the plants can be treated with *Bacillus thuringiensis*–a natural insecticide.

CHINCH BUGS are common in St. Augustine grass and cause yellow spots in the lawn that gradually enlarge. Adults are 1/5 inch (1/2 cm) long, and black with white crossed wings. Immature stages are red and the size of a pinpoint. Check sunny warm areas for small yellowing patches that start to turn brown and enlarge. Look for the chinch bugs at the edge of a yellow-and-green area. They overwinter in all areas of Florida and begin mounting large populations in spring. When the insects are damaging the turf, treat just the affected areas and a few feet around them with a lawn insecticide labeled for chinch bugs. The damage usually continues for 2 weeks after the pests are under control due to toxins placed in the runners by the bugs. Replace severely damaged turf.

CUTWORMS are the larvae of various moths. They feed on and destroy a wide variety of plants, often chewing through stems of seedlings near the ground as if cutting them off. Check for cutworms when preparing new beds. If present, hand pick from the beds or treat the soil with a general insecticide labeled for preplant application. A paper or cardboard collar placed at the plant base around the stem can also help control cutworms.

DEER can wreak havoc in garden beds. Exclude with fencing or apply repellents available from garden centers. Plant varieties which are deer resistant.

DOLLAR SPOT is a fungal disease that can attack any lawn but is often seen in Bermudagrass. It's often an indication of weak turf affected by drought or pest problems. Usually a fertilizer application helps the grass outgrow the fungus.

GARDEN FLEAHOPPERS are 1/16-inch- (1.5-mm-) long black insects that suck juices from marigolds, verbenas, and similar flowers, plus some vegetables and herbs. The damage resembles mite injury, so look for the little black bugs. Use a general garden insecticide for piercing and sucking-type insects labeled for your plants.

GRASSHOPPERS are large-legged brown to bright-green insects up to 3 inches (7.5 cm) long that chew plant foliage. Some damage can be ignored. Otherwise, hand pick them. After hatching, eastern lubber grasshoppers are black with yellow and red lines and are also easier to control than adults. The adults are large with orange and brown markings.

GRUBS are the immature stage of beetles and damage some turf. The grubs are white with a brown head and three pairs of legs at the front of the body. They live underground feeding on roots. Look for grass that is yellowing in patches. Dig up a layer of sod an inch or two (2.5 to 5 cm) below the surface. Sometimes the sod just rolls back when affected. Look for the grubs. If two or more are present per square foot (30 cm) of turf, you need a control. Apply a granular or liquid insecticide labeled for grubs.

LAWN CATERPILLARS chew grass blades, making a lawn look closely mowed. Several types might be active. Most of the time, they can be ignored. The three most common are the sod webworm, armyworm, and grass looper. Check the grass blades—if they appear to be chewed, you most likely have a lawn caterpillar. Armyworms and grass loopers feed on the blades during the day and sod webworms at night. During the day, sod webworms hide in the grass near the ground. When damage is significant, try *Bacillus thuringiensis*. Synthetic pesticides for lawn caterpillar control are also available. Treat only the infested area and a few feet (30 to 61 cm) around it. Keep damaged areas moist and the grass will usually grow back.

LEAFMINERS are the immature stages of a moth or fly that tunnel between the leaves of plants. Some damage should be tolerated. Some control can be obtained by hanging sticky boards near plantings in flower, vegetable, or herb gardens.

LEAF SPOTS are various-shaped yellow to brown spots caused by fungal activity on leaves. Many are normal and can be ignored, as the fungus may attack older foliage as it declines and drops. Where new and healthy leaves are infected and the fungus is affecting the quality of the plant, control with a copper-containing fungicide or synthetic fungicide according to label directions for your plants. Pittosporums are notorious for having fungal problems.

MEALYBUGS are white insects about 1/8 inch (3 mm) or smaller, often found in buds and leaf angles of plants. They suck juices from plants and encourage growth of sooty mold. Look for a general decline in plant vigor. Wash off with water.

MITES are small pinpoint-sized spider relatives that are prevalent during warm, dry weather or on plants kept inside. They suck juices from plant foliage. Damage is often first noted as a yellowing to browning of foliage. You need a hand lens to see these pests but can often spot transparent skins on leaves with the unaided eye. Check for mites under leaves. They are often found near the veins of the leaves at first and then they spread out. They may be clear or orange in color; some make webs. Control with a strong stream of water.

MOLE CRICKETS are often found in all lawns but are especially damaging to bahiagrass and Bermudagrass. The adult mole crickets lay eggs that start hatching in May. When the ground begins to feel soft under the grass, it's the first hint the insects may be present. Monitor the populations in your lawn with a soap flush starting in May. Mix 1½ tablespoons (22 ml) of a mild dish detergent in 2 gallons (7.5 l) of water, and sprinkle over 4 square feet (122 cm) of turf. If young crickets are present, they will scramble to the soil surface in a matter of minutes. When two or more mole crickets are spotted in a square foot of lawn, it's time to apply a control. Apply a mole cricket bait or liquid control, following label instructions.

MUSHROOMS and TOADSTOOLS may produce fruiting bodies on the surface of the soil during damp weather. They cause no harm and can be picked from a lawn and garden or knocked over to shrivel. Some are poisonous, so it's best to remove them when children or pets might be in the area.

PALMETTO WEEVILS are large beetle-like insects that usually attack transplanted cabbage palms and some other palm species, causing death. Contact your local Extension Service office to obtain the latest control recommendations.

POWDERY MILDEW is a common disease of many landscape plants that can be seen as a white covering on the surface of foliage and buds. The disease affects the appearance of the plants, reduces vigor, and can distort growth. Most plants are susceptible to this powdery-looking fungus, but only a few, including roses and gerbera, have a real problem. Try a copper fungicide or one of the synthetic fungicides available at local garden centers if the problem is severe.

RABBITS can wreak havoc in garden beds. Exclude with fencing or apply repellents available from garden centers. Plant varieties which are not a favorite food of rabbits.

ROOT KNOT NEMATODES are microscopic roundworms that feed on plant roots. Nematodes reduce plant vigor and cause the plants to decline. Many vegetables and annual flowers are affected. Try planting nematode-resistant varieties or practicing soil solarization during the summer. A cover crop of French marigolds (*Tagetes patula*) planted in the summer and turned into the soil is an effective treatment.

SCALES are yellow, green, or dark-colored insects that have a waxy coating and cluster on leaves and stems. They range in size from a pinhead to a dime. Most can be easily scraped off with a fingernail to reveal the insect under the covering. They are often hard to see and may be hidden under foliage. Some contribute to a black sooty mold. Wash off with water or oil. When using oils, make sure you cover all portions of the plant and especially under the leaves. Winter is a good time to use oil sprays for scale insect control. The products are of low toxicity and are very effective at eliminating scale populations.

SLIME MOLD is a fungus-like organism that can grow on turf, compost, or other damp locations, usually in late spring or early summer. It is scary-looking, producing a gray covering over the surface of the leaves, but it is harmless. Just use a broom to sweep it off, or wash it away with water.

SLUGS and SNAILS are slimy pests. They love leafy crops and come out during warm, moist weather to chew holes in plant leaves. Look for slime trails in the morning, then hunt for them at night. Hand pick from the plants, lure into shallow containers of beer, or use a synthetic snail and slug bait, following label instructions. Learn to identify the rosywolf snail (*Euglandina rosea*), a carnivore that preys on other snails and slugs.

SOOTY MOLD is a gray to black fungus associated with aphids, mealybugs, scale, and other piercing/sucking insects. Loosen with a soap spray or treat with a horticultural oil spray to control the pests associated with the sooty mold, following label instructions for your plant type.

STEM CANKERS appear on plant stems as gray to brown dead areas. Sometimes the bark is loose or cracked in the affected areas. This is where the fungus is living and causing the stem to decline. Prune out all canker portions, cutting back into healthy growth. Sterilize your pruning shears between cuts. Apply a fungicide made for your plant after pruning.

TAKE-ALL ROOT ROT is a fungus that affects stressed lawns. No fungicides have been found effective, and the disease may run rampant during the summer months. Lawns that receive too much water are very susceptible. The best way to fight this disease is to mow the lawn at highest setting. If take-all root rot is diagnosed, apply light but frequent liquid fertilizer applications. When turf declines due to the disease, remove the old grass, till the soil deeply, and re-establish new sod. Or replace this part of the lawn with a grove of trees or a wildflower meadow garden.

THRIPS are very small insects, about the size of a thread, that attack flowers and some plant foliage. Your first hint of damage may be buds not opening properly and developing brown edges. Thrips are real spoilers of gardenias and roses. Remove a flower and pull it apart to see the very small clear to brownish thrips. Select an insecticide labeled for thrip control to treat the flower buds and foliage as needed.

WHITEFLIES are small fly-like insects, snow-white in color, that live among foliage. They have a yellowish immature stage that forms on the leaf undersides. Control with a water or oil spray according to label instructions for your plants. Repeat sprays are usually needed.

GLOSSARY

ACID SOIL: soil with a pH less than 7.0, sometimes called "sour" soil. Sulfur is typically added to the soil to make it more acidic.

ALKALINE SOIL: soil with a pH greater than 7.0, often called "basic" or "sweet" soil. It lacks acidity, often because it has limestone in it. Lime is typically added to soil to make it more alkaline.

ALLELOPATHIC: when a plant produces biochemicals that inhibit the germination and/or growth of other plants.

ALL-PURPOSE FERTILIZER: powdered, liquid, or granular fertilizer with the three key nutrients–nitrogen (N), phosphorus (P), and potassium (K). It is suitable for maintenance nutrition for most plants. Many fertilizers now contain zero or little phosphorus, where this nutrient is adequate.

AMENDMENT: components added to soil to improve fertility, water retention, or structure.

ANNUAL: a plant that lives its entire life in one season. It is genetically determined to germinate, grow, flower, set seed, and die the same year. Some plants that are perennial in their native habitats, but not hardy in another region, can also be used as annuals.

BALLED AND BURLAPPED: describes a tree or shrub grown in the field whose soilball was wrapped with protective burlap and twine when the plant was dug up to be sold or transplanted.

BARE ROOT: describes plants that have been packaged without any soil around their roots. (Often young shrubs and trees purchased through the mail arrive with their exposed roots covered with moist peat or sphagnum moss, sawdust, or similar material, and wrapped in plastic.)

BENEFICIAL INSECTS: insects or their larvae that prey on pest organisms and their eggs. They may be flying insects, such as ladybugs, parasitic wasps, praying mantids, and soldier bugs, or soil dwellers such as predatory nematodes, spiders, and ants.

BERM: a narrow, raised ring of soil around a tree, used to hold water so it will be directed to the root zone.

BRACT: a modified leaf structure on a plant stem just below its flower, resembling a petal. Often it is more colorful and visible than the actual flower, as in dogwood or poinsettia.

Bt: abbreviation of *Bacillus thuringiensis*, an organism that attacks a certain stage in the life cycle of some pests. Forms of Bt can be created to target a particular species. Used as a natural pest control for caterpillars and mosquitoes.

BUD UNION: the place where the top of a plant was grafted to the rootstock; usually refers to roses.

CANOPY: the overhead branching area of a tree, usually referring to its extent including foliage.

COCONUT COIR: made from coconut husks, it's a sustainable and non-acidic organic material to add water-retaining humus to soil. There are also coir pots and coir liners for hanging baskets. Use this for general garden use instead of the non-sustainable sphagnum peat moss.

COLD HARDINESS: the ability of a plant to survive the winter cold in a particular area.

COMPLETE FERTILIZER: containing all three major components of fertilizers–nitrogen (N), phosphorus (P), and potassium (K), although not necessarily in equal proportions. An incomplete fertilizer does not contain all three elements.

COMPOST: organic matter that has undergone progressive decomposition by microbial activity until it is reduced to a spongy, fluffy texture. Added to soil of any type, it improves the soil's ability to hold air and water and to drain well. It also adds microbes to bring life to the soil.

CORM: the swollen, energy-storing structure, analogous to a bulb, under the soil at the base of the stem of plants such as crocus and gladiolus.

COVER CROP: A crop of a specific plant that is grown primarily for the benefit of the soil rather than the crop yield. Cover crops are commonly used to suppress weeds, manage soil erosion, help build and improve soil fertility and quality, control diseases and pests, and promote biodiversity. Normally, the crop is turned into the soil at the end of the cycle.

CROWN: the base of a plant at, or just beneath, the surface of the soil where the roots meet the stems; the head of a palm.

CULTIVAR: a CULTIvated VARiety. It is a naturally occurring form of a plant that has been identified as special or superior and is purposely selected for propagation and production.

DEADHEAD: a pruning technique that removes faded flower heads from plants to improve their appearance, abort seed production, and stimulate further flowering.

DECIDUOUS PLANTS: unlike evergreens, these trees and shrubs lose their leaves in the fall.

DESICCATION: drying out of foliage tissues, usually due to drought or wind.

DIOECIOUS: plants that maintain male and female reproductive structures on separate individuals. The result is male and female plants where at least one male plant should be in the area to ensure the development of fruit.

DIVISION: the practice of splitting apart perennial plants to create several smaller-rooted segments. The practice is useful for controlling the plant's size and for acquiring more plants; it is also essential to the health and continued flowering of certain ones.

DORMANCY OR DORMANT PERIOD: time during which no growth occurs because of unfavorable environmental conditions. For some plants it is in winter, and for others summer. Many plants require this time as a resting period.

DROUGHT TOLERANT: plants able to tolerate dry soil for varying periods of time. However, plants must first be well established before they are drought tolerant.

ESTABLISHED: the point at which a newly planted tree, shrub, flower, or grass begins to produce new growth, either foliage or stems. This is an indication that the roots have recovered from transplant shock and have begun to grow and spread.

EVERGREEN: perennial plants that do not lose their foliage annually with the onset of winter. Needled or broadleaf foliage will persist and continues to function on a plant through one or more winters, aging and dropping unobtrusively in cycles of 3 or 4 years or more.

FLORET: a tiny flower, usually one of many forming a cluster that comprises a single blossom. An example are the disc florets in the center of a sunflower and the ray florets around the rim of the flower head that look like petals.

FOLIAR: of or about foliage–usually refers to the practice of spraying foliage, as in fertilizing or treating with insecticide; leaf tissues absorb liquid directly for fast results, and the soil is not affected.

FUNGICIDE: a pesticide material for destroying or preventing fungus on plants.

GENUS: a distinct botanical group within a family, typically containing several species. Plural form is "genera," referring to more than one genus.

GRAFT (UNION): the point on the stem of a woody plant with sturdier roots where a stem from a highly ornamental plant is inserted so that it will join with it. Roses are commonly grafted.

GRUBS: fat, off-white, wormlike larvae of some beetles. They reside in the soil and feed on plant roots until summer when they emerge as adult beetles.

HARDSCAPE: the permanent, structural, non-plant part of a landscape, such as walls, sheds, pools, patios, arbors, and walkways.

HEAT TOLERANCE: the ability of a plant to withstand the summer heat in a particular area.

HERBACEOUS: plants having fleshy or soft stems; the opposite of woody.

HUMUS: partially decomposed organic matter.

HYBRID: a plant that is the result of intentional or natural cross-pollination between two or more plants of the same species or genus.

INVASIVE: when a non-native plant has such a vigorous growth habit that it has killed off native plants in wild areas. A plant is determined to be invasive by Florida Exotic Plant Pest Council, a nonprofit organization that maintains an invasive list at: www.fleppc.org

MICRONUTRIENTS: elements needed in small quantities for plant growth. Sometimes called "minor elements." Sometimes a soil will be deficient in one or more of them and require a particular fertilizer formulation.

MULCH: a layer of material over bare soil to protect it from erosion, to discourage weeds, and to retain moisture. It may be organic (wood chips, bark, pine needles, chopped leaves) or inorganic (gravel, fabric), which is rarely recommended in Florida.

NECTAR: the sweet fluid produced by glands on flowers that attract pollinators such as hummingbirds and bees, which use it as a source of energy.

NODE: structure on a stem from which leaves, roots, and branches arise.

NON-SELECTIVE: herbicides that have the potential to kill or control any plant to which they are applied.

ORGANIC MATERIAL/MATTER: any material or debris that is derived from plants or animals. It is carbon-based material capable of undergoing decomposition and decay.

OVERSEEDING: distributing new grass seed on an established lawn to thicken the grass coverage or introduce another type of grass to extend the green season.

PATHOGEN: the causal organism of a plant disease.

PEAT MOSS: organic matter from peat sedges (United States) or sphagnum mosses (Canada) that can never be sustainably harvested. The extreme acidity of sphagnum peat moss makes the nutrients unavailable to most plants. Use coconut coir as a replacement to add water-retaining humus to soils.

PERENNIAL: a flowering plant that lives for 2 or more years. Many die back with frost, but their roots survive the winter and generate new shoots in the spring.

pH: a measurement of the relative acidity (low pH) or alkalinity (high pH) of soil or water based on a scale of 1 to 14, 7 being neutral. Individual plants require soil to be within a certain range so that nutrients can dissolve in moisture and be available to them.

PINCH: to remove tender stems and/or leaves by pressing them between thumb and forefinger. This pruning technique encourages branching, compactness, and flowering in plants, or it also removes aphids clustered at growing tips.

PLUG: piece of sod used in establishing a new lawn. Plugs can also be grown or purchased in small cells or pots within a flat, sometimes referred to as trays.

POLLEN: the yellow, powdery grains in the center of a flower. A plant's male sex cells, they are transferred to the female plant parts by means of wind or animal pollinators to fertilize them and create seeds.

POST-EMERGENT: an herbicide applied to already germinated and actively growing weeds to kill or control them.

PRE-EMERGENT: an herbicide applied to the soil surface to prevent weed seed from germinating, such as corn gluten.

RAIN GARDEN: (aka bio-swale or bio-retention swale) a low spot in the landscape designed to collect runoff from impervious urban areas like roofs, driveways, and parking lots. The retained stormwater is absorbed by plants and soaks into the soil, which reduces the total urban/suburban runoff into the nearby waterways and thus improves the water quality.

RHIZOME: a horizontal stem structure in the soil. New plants that grow from rhizomes are clones of the parent plant and can be at some distance away. Similar stems that grow along the surface of the soil are called stolons. Some rhizomes are similar to bulbs and are swollen energy-storing structures with roots emerging from the lower surface and growth shoots from a growing point at or near its tip, as in iris.

ROOTBOUND (OR POTBOUND): the condition of a plant that has been confined in a container too long, its roots having been forced to wrap around themselves and even swell out of the container. Successful transplanting or repotting requires untangling and trimming away of some of the matted roots.

ROOT FLARE: the transition at the base of a tree trunk where the bark tissue begins to differentiate and roots begin to form just before entering the soil. This area should not be covered with soil when planting a tree. Trees grown from cuttings will not have a distinct root flare.

RUNOFF: when water moves across the landscape without being absorbed. This can be caused by steep slopes, water volume exceeding the soil's absorption capacity, compacted soil, or impenetrable surface material. Runoff from areas with applied chemicals can cause problems in the bodies of water ultimately receiving the runoff.

SELECTIVE: herbicides and other pesticides that target a particular type of weed or pest, such as broad-leaf herbicides used in lawns to kill off non-grasses.

SELF-SEEDING: the tendency of some plants to sow their seeds freely around the yard; can create many seedlings the following season that may or may not be welcome.

SEMI-EVERGREEN: tending to be evergreen in a mild climate but deciduous in a rigorous one.

SHEARING: the pruning technique whereby plant stems and branches are cut uniformly with long-bladed pruning shears (hedge shears) or powered hedge trimmers. It is used when creating and maintaining hedges and topiary.

SLOW-ACTING FERTILIZER: fertilizer that is water insoluble and therefore releases its nutrients gradually as a function of soil temperature, moisture, and related microbial activity. Typically granular, it may be organic or synthetic. Other names are slow-release, time release, and controlled-release fertilizers.

SOLARIZE: A summer soil treatment, usually for vegetable garden beds, to kill weeds, kill grubs and other soil insects, and reduce nematodes, including root-knot nematodes. Clear away plants, smooth the soil, and then lay a clear plastic sheet over the bed and bury and secure all the edges so that it can't blow away. Leave it in place for 6 weeks. Time this procedure so that when done, it's planting time.

SPECIES: a group of fundamentally identical plants within a genus.

SUCCULENT GROWTH: fleshy, water-storing leaves or stems.

SUCKER: a new-growing shoot. Underground plant roots produce suckers to form new stems and spread by means of these suckering roots to form large plantings, or colonies. Some plants produce root suckers or branch suckers as a result of pruning or wounding.

THATCH: layer of decaying grass found between the soil surface and the living grass blades. Dethatching is the raking of this material from the lawn.

TUBER: a type of underground storage structure in a plant stem, analogous to a bulb. It generates roots below and stems above ground (example: dahlia).

VARIEGATED: having various colors or color patterns. The term usually refers to plant foliage that is streaked, edged, blotched, or mottled with a contrasting color—often green with yellow, cream, or white.

WINGS: (a) the corky tissue that forms edges along the twigs of some woody plants such as winged elm; (b) the flat, dried extension of tissue on some seeds, such as maple, that catch the wind and help them disseminate.

BIBLIOGRAPHY

Bar-Zvi, David, Chief Horticulturist, and Elvin McDonald, series editor. *Tropical Gardening*. New York: Pantheon Books, Knopf Publishing Group, 1996.

Batchelor, Stephen R. *Your First Orchid*. West Palm Beach: American Orchid Society, 1996.

Bechtel, Helmut, Phillip Cribb, and Edmund Launert. *The Manual of Cultivated Orchid Species, Third Edition*. Cambridge, MA: The MIT Press, 1992.

Bell, C. Ritchie and Byron J. Taylor. *Florida Wild Flowers and Roadside Plants*. Chapel Hill, NC: Laurel Hill Press, 1982.

Berry, Fred and W. John Kress. *Heliconia, An Identification Guide*. Washington and London: Smithsonian Institution Press, 1991.

Black, Robert J. and Kathleen C. Ruppert. *Your Florida Landscape, A Complete Guide to Planting & Maintenance*. Gainesville, FL: Cooperative Extension Service, Institute of Food and Agricultural Sciences, University of Florida, 1995.

Blackmore, Stephen and Elizabeth Tootill, eds. *The Penguin Dictionary of Botany*. Middlesex, England: Penguin Books, Ltd., 1984.

Blombery, Alec and Tony Todd. *Palms*. London, Sydney, Melbourne: Angus & Robertson, 1982.

Bond, Rick and editorial staff of Ortho Books. *All About Growing Orchids*. San Ramon, CA: The Solaris Group, 1988.

Boning, Charles R. *Florida's Best Fruiting Plants*. Sarasota, FL: Pineapple Press, 2009.

Brookes, John. *The Book of Garden Design*. New York: Macmillan Publishing Co. and London: Dorling Kindersley Ltd., 1991.

Broschat, Timothy K. and Alan W. Meerow. *Betrock's Reference Guide to Florida Landscape Plants*. Cooper City, FL: Betrock Information Systems, Inc., 1991.

Brown, Deni. *Aroids, Plants of the Arum Family, Second Edition*. Portland, OR: Timber Press, 2000.

Bush, Charles S. and Julia F. Morton. *Native Trees and Plants for Florida Landscaping*. Gainesville, FL: Florida Department of Agriculture and Consumer Services, 1968.

Calkins, Carroll C., ed. *Reader's Digest Illustrated Guide to Gardening*. Pleasantville, NY and Montreal: The Reader's Digest Association, Inc., 1978.

Campbell, Richard J., ed. *Mangos: A Guide to Mangos in Florida*. Miami: Fairchild Tropical Garden, 1992.

Courtright, Gordon. *Tropicals*. Portland, OR: Timber Press, 1988.

Dade County Department of Planning, Development and Regulation. *The Landscape Manual*. 1996.

Dunn, Teri and Walter Reeves. *Jackson & Perkins Selecting, Growing, and Combining Outstanding Perennials, Southern Edition*. Nashville, TN: Cool Springs Press, 2003.

Editors of Sunset Books and Sunset Magazine. *Sunset National Garden Book*. Menlo Park, CA: Sunset Books, Inc., 1997.

Gerberg, Eugene J. and Ross H. Arnett, Jr. *Florida Butterflies*. Baltimore: Natural Science Publication, Inc., 1989.

Gilman, Edward F. *Betrock's Florida Plant Guide*. Hollywood, FL: Betrock Information Systems, 1996.

Graf, Alfred Byrd. *Tropica*. East Rutherford, NJ: Roehrs Co., 1978.

Hillier, Malcolm. *Malcolm Hillier's Color Garden*. London, New York, Stuttgart, Moscow: Dorling Kindersley, 1995.

Holttum, R.E. and Ivan Enock. *Gardening in the Tropics*. Singapore: Times Editions, 1991.

Hoshizaki, Barbara Joe. *Fern Growers Manual*. New York: Alfred A. Knopf, 1979.

Kilmer, Anne. *Gardening for Butterflies and Children in South Florida*. West Palm Beach: The Palm Beach Post, 1992.

Kramer, Jack. *300 Extraordinary Plants for Home and Garden*. New York, London, Paris: Abbeville Press, 1994.

Lamp'l, Joe. *The Green Gardener's Guide*. Franklin, TN: Cool Springs Press, 2007.

Lessard, W.O. *The Complete Book of Bananas*. Miami, 1992.

MacCubbin, Tom and Georgia Tasker. *Florida Gardener's Guide, Revised Edition*. Franklin, TN: Cool Springs Press, 2002.

MacCubbin, Tom. *Florida Home Grown: Landscaping*. Sentinel Communications, Orlando, Florida, 1989.

MacCubbin, Tom. *Florida Lawn Guide*. Franklin, TN: Cool Springs Press, 2007.

MacCubbin, Tom. *Month-by-Month Gardening in Florida, Revised Edition*. Franklin, TN: Cool Springs Press, 2005.

Mathias, Mildred E., ed. *Flowering Plants in the Landscape*. Berkeley, Los Angeles, London: University of California Press, 1982.

Meerow, Alan W. *Betrock's Guide to Landscape Palms*. Cooper City, FL: Betrock Information Systems, Inc., 1992.

Morton, Julia F. *500 Plants of South Florida*. Miami: E.A. Seemann Publishing, Inc., 1974.

Myers, Ronald L. and John J. Ewel, eds. *Ecosystems of Florida*. Orlando: University of Central Florida Press, 1991.

The National Gardening Association. *Dictionary of Horticulture*. New York: Penguin Books, 1994.

Neal, Marie. *In Gardens of Hawaii*. Honolulu: Bishop Museum Press, 1965.

Nelson, Gil. *Florida's Best Native Landscape Plants*. Gainesville, FL: University Press of Florida. 2003.

Nelson, Gil. *The Trees of Florida, A Reference and Field Guide*. Sarasota: Pineapple Press, Inc., 1994.

Perry, Frances. *Flowers of the World*. London, New York, Sydney, Toronto: The Hamlyn Publishing Group, Ltd., 1972.

Rawlings, Marjorie Kinnan. *Cross Creek*. St. Simons Island, GA: Mockingbird Books, 1942. Seventh Printing, 1983.

Reinikka, Merle A. *A History of the Orchid*. Portland, OR: Timber Press, 1995.

Rittershausen, Wilma and Gill and David Oakey. *Growing & Displaying Orchids, A Step-by-Step Guide*. New York: Smithmark Publishers, Inc., 1993.

Scurlock, J. Paul. *Native Trees and Shrubs of the Florida Keys*. Pittsburgh: Laurel Press, 1987.

Stearn, William T. *Stearn's Dictionary of Plant Names for Gardeners*. New York: Sterling Publishing Co., Inc., 1996.

Stevenson, George B. *Palms of South Florida*. Miami: Fairchild Tropical Garden, 1974.

Stibolt, Ginny. *The Art of Maintaining a Florida Native Landscape*. Gainesville, FL: University Press of Florida, 2015.

Stibolt, Ginny. *Sustainable Gardening for Florida*. Gainesville, FL: University Press of Florida, 2009.

Stibolt, Ginny and Melissa Contreras. *Organic Methods for Vegetable Gardening in Florida*. Gainesville, FL: University Press of Florida, 2013.

Tasker, Georgia. *Enchanted Ground: Gardening with Nature in the Subtropics*. Kansas City: Andrews and McMeel, 1994.

Tasker, Georgia. *Wild Things: The Return of Native Plants*. Winter Park, FL: The Florida Native Plant Society, 1984.

Tomlinson, P.B. *The Biology of Trees Native to Tropical Florida*. Allston, MA: Harvard University, 1980.

Vanderplank, John. *Passion Flowers, Second Edition*. Cambridge, MA: The MIT Press, 1996.

Walker, Jacqueline. *The Subtropical Garden*. Portland, OR: Timber Press, 1992.

Warren, William. *The Tropical Garden*. London: Thames and Hudson, Ltd., 1991.

Watkins, John V. and Thomas J. Sheehan. *Florida Landscape Plants, Native and Exotic, Revised Edition*. Gainesville, FL: The University Presses of Florida, 1975.

Workman, Richard W. *Growing Native*. Sanibel, FL: The Sanibel-Captiva Conservation Foundation, Inc., 1980.

PHOTO CREDITS

COOL SPRINGS PRESS WOULD LIKE TO THANK THE FOLLOWING CONTRIBUTORS TO *The Florida Gardener's Handbook, 2nd Edition*

André Viette, Bruce Asakawa, Bruce Holst, Charles Mann, Dency Kane, David Price, Georgia B. Tasker, iStockphoto and its artists, Jackson & Perkins, Jerry Pavia, Jupiter Images, Kirsten Llamas, Langeveld Bulb Company, Liz Ball and Rick Ray, Lorenzo Gunn

Michael Dirr, Mark Turner, Nan Sterman, Paula Biles, Pam Harper, Photo courtesy of Proven Winners, Stephen G. Pategas/Hortus Oasis, Robert Bowden, Roger Hammer, Ralph Snodsmith

Sacbee, Shutterstock and its artists, Ginny Stibolt, Thomas Eltzroth, Tom Koske, Tom MacCubbin, W. Atlee Burpee & Co., William Adams

ABOUT THE AUTHORS

TOM MACCUBBIN is known to gardeners in Florida through his radio, television, and newspaper contributions. He retired from his position as an extension environmental horticulturist with the University of Florida in Orange County after 36 years and was promoted to the distinguished position of Extension Agent Emeritus with the University of Florida. Readers are familiar with Tom's question-and-answer gardening columns and feature articles for *The Orlando Sentinel, while others may recognize him as a co-host of Orange County Gardening* on cable television and weekly horticulture reports on Central Florida News 13. His radio program, *Better Lawns & Gardens*, is broadcast over twenty Florida stations.

The National Association of County Agriculture Agents has recognized his media contributions with numerous awards, including awards for the best state personal column, best news photo story, best news column, and best television program. Most recently, his *Better Lawns & Gardens radio program was judged best in the nation for 1998 & 2000; in 1999, he was presented the AT&T Communications Award in the Best Videotape/Television category as a regional winner for his role as co-host of Orange County Gardening*; in 2001 he received an Award of Excellence for work as a county horticulture agent and for effective involvement with media programming from the National Council of State Garden Clubs, Inc. He has been honored with the Best Horticulture Writer Award by the Florida Nurserymen and Growers Association, and was granted the Garden Communicators Award by the American Nurserymen's Association. In June 2007 Tom was recognized nationally as Teacher of the Year by the American Horticultural Society. MacCubbin has authored more than eight gardening books for Florida including the *Florida Gardener's Guide, Month-by-Month™ Gardening in Florida, My Florida Garden: A Gardener's Journal, and The Florida Lawn Guide* with Cool Springs Press. Active in their community, MacCubbin and his wife, Joan, live near Apopka.

GEORGIA TASKER was the garden writer for the *Miami Herald* for more than 30 years. Recognized frequently for her outstanding work, Tasker was a Pulitzer Prize finalist for her writing on tropical deforestation, and the Florida Nurserymen and Growers Association named her Outstanding Horticultural Writer. Following the destruction of Hurricane Andrew, Tasker was given the Media Award of Greatest Merit by the Florida Urban Forestry Council for her work to help save trees in areas devastated by the storm. She has also received Fairchild's highest honor, the Barbour Medal, and a lifetime achievement award from Tropical Audubon Society. Georgia currently writes and blogs for the Fairchild Tropical Botanic Garden, and is an avid photographer, gardener, and traveler. In addition to being co-author of the *Florida Gardener's Guide* with Tom MacCubbin, Tasker is the author of *Wild Things: The Return of Native Plants and Enchanted Ground: Gardening with Nature in the Subtropics*. Georgia lives in Coconut Grove.

ROBERT BOWDEN is currently the Executive Director of Leu Gardens in Orlando. He served in this capacity at Atlanta Botanical Gardens and as Director of Horticulture at the Missouri Botanical Garden. His photographs and fun-filled essays have appeared in such magazines as *Garden Design, Traditional Home, Southern Accents, and The New York Times.* He appears regularly on a variety of nationally syndicated television shows, including *Victory Garden on PBS, Discovery Channel's Home Matters,* HGTV's *Way To Grow! and Rebecca's Garden.* He travels extensively in the U.S. and Caribbean talking about growing vegetables, perennials, tropical and sub-tropical plants, flowering vines, trees, and shrubs.

JOE LAMP'L, aka joe gardener®, is the host of two national television shows: *GardenSMART on PBS, and DIY Network's Fresh from the Garden.* His latest project includes producing and hosting a series on PBS, *Growing a Greener World. He's also a syndicated columnist and author of books, including his latest, The Green Gardener's Guide: Simple, Significant Actions to Protect & Preserve Our Planet.* Joe's passion and work related to gardening, sustainable living, and environmental stewardship through multiple media platforms has positioned him as one of the most recognized personalities in the "green" sector today. Find out more information about Joe and his work online at www.joegardener.com.

A

Abelmoschus esculentus, 84
Acalypha hispida, 148
Acalypha wilkesiana, 199
Acer rubrum, 179
Achillea millefolium, 137
Acrostichum danaeifolium, 130
Aechmea, 198
Agapanthus africanus, 42
Agave spp., 127
Ageratum houstonianum, 22
Aglaonema spp., 198
Ajuga reptans, 111
Alcea rosea, 25
Alipinia spp., 202
Allamanda cathartica, 214
Allium cepa, 84
Allium schoenoprasum, 82
Alocasia spp., 201
Aloe vera, 196
Alstroemeria spp., 47
Amelia patens, 149
Ananas comosus, 68
Anethum graveolens, 83
Anthurium spp., 196
Antirrhinum majus, 29
Aristida stricta, 117
Aristolochia spp., 217
Artocarpus heterophyllus, 65
Asclepias spp., 133
Asian persimmon, 67
Aspidistra elatior, 111
Asplenium nidus, 197
Averrhoa carambola, 69
Axonopus fissifolius, 100

B

Beaucarnea recurvata, 205
Bignonia aequinoctialis, 218
Bignonia callistegioides, 219
Billbergia, 198
Bismarckia nobilis, 173
Bougainvillea spp., 214
Brassica oleracea, 80, 81
Brugmansia spp., 196
Brunfelsia americana, 153
Bursera simaruba, 176
Butia capitata, 178

C

Caladium x hortulanum, 44
Calathea spp., 204
Calendula officinalis, 23
Callicarpa americana, 147

Camellia japonica, 147
Campsis radicans, 220
Canna spp., 45
Capsicum annuum, 27, 85
Carica papaya, 66
Carissa macrocarpa, 154
Carya illinoinensis, 67
Catharanthus roseus, 133
Celosia argentea, 23
Cercis canadensis, 180
Cestrum nocturnum, 154
Chrysobalanus icaco, 148
Chrysophyllum oliviforme, 182
Citrullus lanatus, 87
Citrus spp., 58–61
Clematis spp., 216
Clerodendrum thomsoniae, 214
Clivia miniata, 47
Coccoloba diversifolia, 178
Coccoloba uvifera, 158
Coccothrinax argentata, 175
Cocculus laurifolius, 153
Cocos nucifera, 63
Codiaeum variegatum, 199
Coleus x hybridus, 23
Combretum indicum, 220
Cordia boissieri, 183
Cordia sebestena, 175
Cordyline fruticosa, 207
Coreopsis spp., 128
Cornus florida, 175
Cortaderia selloana, 115
Cosmos spp., 24
Costus spp., 206
Crinum spp., 45
Crossandra infundibuliformis, 131, 132
Cucumis melo, 81
Cucumis sativus, 82
Cucurbita spp., 86
Cuphea hyssopifolia, 113
Curcuma spp., 202
Cynodon spp., 100

D

Daucus carota, 81
Delonix regia, 181
Dendrobium spp., 200
Dianella tasmanica, 136
Dianthus spp., 28
Dietes spp., 42
Diospyros virginiana, 67
Dracaena spp., 201
Dypsis lutescens, 173

E

Echinacea purpurea, 128
Eragrostis spectabilis, 115
Eremochloa ophiuroides, 101
Eriobotrya japonica, 65
Eugenia confusa, 180
Euphorbia milii, 199
Euphorbia pulcherrima, 134
Euryops chrysanthemoides, 127
Evolvulus glomeratus, 110

F

Fatsia japonica, 153
Ficus carica, 64
Ficus pumila, 111
Ficus spp., 201
Forestiera segregate, 150
Fragaria × ananassa, 69

G

Gaillardia spp., 126
Galphimia gracilis, 158
Gardenia jasminoides, 150
Gazania spp., 110
Gelsemium sempervirens, 216
Gladiolus spp., 46
Gloriosa spp., 46
Gomphrena globosa, 25
Guaiacum sanctum, 177
Guzmania, 198
Gypsophila paniculata, 22

H

H. aculeatus, 151
H. coccineus, 151
Hedychium spp., 202
Helianthus spp., 29
Heliconia spp., 202
Hemerocallis spp., 45
H. grandifloras, 151
Hibiscus spp., 151
Hippeastrum spp., 42
H. moscheutos, 151
Hydrangea macrophylla, 152
Hydrangea quercifolia, 155
Hymenocallis latifolia, 49

I

Ilex spp., 176
Impatiens walleriana, 25
Ipomoea batatas, 85, 114
Iris spp., 47
Ixora coccinea, 152

J

Jacobaea maritima, 24
Juniperus conferta, 116
Juniperus virginiana, 180
Justicia brandegeeana, 205

L

Lactuca sativa, 83
Laelia spp., 198
Lagerstroemia indica, 174
Leucanthemum x superbum, 134
Leucojum aestivum, 48
Licuala grandis, 181
Liquidambar styraciflua, 183
Liriope muscari, 112
Litchi chinensis, 65
Livistona chinensis, 174
Lobelia erinus, 26
Lolium spp., 102
Lonicera sempervirens, 217
Loropetalum chinense, 148
Lycoris spp., 46

M

Macadamia spp., 66
Magnolia grandiflora, 182
Magnolia virginiana, 182
Malus domestica, 62
Mandevilla spp., 218
Mangifera indica, 66
Melampodium divaricatum, 22
Mimosa strigillosa, 117
Mirabilis jalapa, 131, 132
Monarda spp., 126
Monstera deliciosa, 200
Morella cerifera, 159
M. spicata, 84
M. suaveolens, 84
Muhlenbergia capillaris, 114
Musa spp., 62
Mussaenda philippica, 203

N

Neoregelia, 198
Nephrolepis biserrata, 130
Nerium oleander, 155
Nicotiana alata, 27

O

O. × africanum, 80
O. americanum, 80
Ocimum basilicum, 80
Odontonema cuspidatum, 131, 132

Oncidium spp., 200
Ophiopogon japonicas, 113
Origanum vulgare, 85
Osmunda regalis var. spectabilis, 130
Osmundastrum cinnamomeum, 129

P

Pandorea jasminoides, 215
Paspalum dissectum, 102
Paspalum notatum, 100
Passiflora spp., 219
Pelargonium x hortorum, 24
Pentas lanceolata, 133
Peperomia spp., 204
Persea Americana, 62
Petrea volubilis, 220
Petunia x atkinsiana, 28
Phalaenopsis spp., 202
Phaseolus spp., 80
Philodendron spp., 219
Phlox divaricate, 127
Phoenix roebelenii, 179
Phyla nodiflora, 112
Pilea microphylla, 110
Pinus spp., 178
Pittosporum tobira, 155
Platycerium spp., 206
Plinia cauliflora, 64
Plumbago auriculata, 134, 156
Plumeria spp., 179
Podocarpus macrophylla, 156
Portulaca grandiflora, 28
Prunus persica, 67
Prunus spp., 68
Psychotria nervosa, 159
Punica granatum, 68
Pyrostegia venusta, 217

Q

Quercus virginiana, 177

R

Ravenala madagascariensis, 207
Rhaphiolepis indica, 152
Rhapis spp., 176
Rhododendron spp., 147
Rosa spp., 157
Roystonea regia, 181
Rubus spp., 63
Rudbeckia spp., 126
Ruellia caroliniensis, 137
Russelia equisetiformis, 149

S

Sabal palmetto, 174
Salvia coccinea, 30
Salvia rosmarinus, 86
Salvia splendens, 29
Scadoxus multiflorus, 43
Selenicereus undatus, 203
Serenoa repens, 158
Solanum lycopersicum, 87
Solanum melongena, 83
Sophora tomentosa, 154
Sorghastrum secundum, 113
Spartina bakeri, 116
Spathiphyllum spp., 203
Sphaeropteris cooperi, 197
Spinacia oleracea, 86
Sprekelia formosissima, 43
Stenotaphrum secundatum, 103
Stephanotis floribunda, 215
Stokesia laevis, 135
Strelitzia reginae, 197
Strobilanthes dyerianus, 204
Strongylodon macrobotrys, 218
Swietenia mahagoni, 177

T

Tabebuia spp., 184
Tagetes erecta, 26
Tamarindus indica, 69
Taxodium distichum, 173
T. caraiba, 184
Tecoma capensis, 215
T. floridanum, 112
Thymus vulgaris, 87
Tillandsia spp., 198
Tithonia rotundifolia, 26
Torenia fournieri, 30
Trachelospermum jasminoides, 216
Trifolium spp., 101
Trimezia spp., 49
Tripsacum dactyloides, 112
T. rosea, 184
Tulbaghia violacea, 48

U

Ulmus alata, 184
Urceolina × grandiflora, 43

V

Vaccinium spp., 63
V. acerifolium, 159
V. dentatum, 159
Verbena x hybrida, 31
Veronica spicata, 136

Viburnum spp., 159
Viola x wittrockiana, 27
Vitis vinifera, 64
V. obovatum, 159

W

Watsonia spp., 44

Y

Yucca aloifolia, 135

Z

Zamia integrifolia, 149
Zantedeschia spp., 44
Zea mays, 82
Zephyranthes spp., 48
Zingiber spp., 202
Zinnia elegans, 31
Zoysia spp., 103

A

Abelia, 160
Achimenes, 50
African Daisy, 110
African Iris, 42, 138
African Lily, 42, 50
African Tuliptree, 186
Ageratum, 22, 32, 34
Allamanda, 160, 214, 221
Aloe, 196
Alstroemeria, 50
Alyssum, 32, 34
Amaranthus, 32, 34
Amaryllis, 42, 50
Amazon Lily, 43, 50
American Beautyberry, 147
American Holly, 186
Anemone, 50
Angelonia, 138
Angel's Trumpet, 196
Anise, 88, 160
Anthurium, 196
Apple, 62, 70
Areca, 185
Areca Palm, 173
Artillery Plant, 110
Asiatic Jasmine, 118
Asparagus, 90
Aster, 32, 34
Atemoya, 70
Attenuate Holly, 186
Aucuba, 160
Australian Fan, 185
Australian Tree Fern, 197
Avocado, 62, 70
Azalea, 147, 160
Aztec Lily, 43, 50

B

Baby's Breath, 22, 32
Bahia Grass, 100
Bald Cypress, 173, 186
Balsam, 32, 34
Banana, 62, 70
Banana Shrub, 160
Barbados Cherry, 70
Basil, 80, 88
Bay Laurel, 88
Beach Morning Glory, 118
Beach Sunflower, 118
Beans, 80, 91
Beautyberry, 160
Beebalm, 126, 138
Beets, 90

Bengal Clock Vine, 221
Bermudagrass, 100
Bird of Paradise, 138, 197
Bird's Nest Fern, 197
Bismarck, 185
Bismarck Palm, 173
Blackberry, 63, 70
Blackberry Lily, 50
Black-Eyed Susan, 126, 139
Black Olive, 186
Black Sapote, 70
Blanket Flower, 126, 138
Bleeding Heart, 221
Bleeding Heart Vine, 214
Blood Lily, 43, 50
Blueberry, 63, 70
Blue Daze, 110, 138
Blue Flag Iris, 50
Blue Ginger, 138
Blue Phlox, 127, 138
Blue Sage, 138
Borage, 88
Bottlebrush, 160
Bougainvillea, 214, 221
Bower Vine, 215, 221
Breath, 34
Bridal Wreath, 215, 221
Broccoli, 80, 90
Bromeliads, 118, 198
Browallia, 32, 34
Brunfelsia, 160
Brussels Sprouts, 90
Bugle Lily, 44
Bugle Weed, 111, 118
Bush, 160
Bush Daisy, 127, 138
Butia, 185
Butter Daisies, 22

C

Cabbage, 33, 35, 81, 90, 185
Cabbage Palm, 174
Caladium, 44, 50
Calendula, 23, 32, 34
California Poppy, 32, 34
California Washingtonia, 185
Calla Lily, 44, 50
Camellia, 147, 160
Canary Island Date, 185
Canistel, 70
Canna, 45, 50
Cantaloupe, 81, 91
Cape Honeysuckle, 215, 221
Cape Jasmine, 160
Carambola, 70

Caraway, 88
Cardamom, 88
Cardinal's Guard, 138
Carissa, 70
Carolina Yellow Jessamine, 216
Carpetgrass, 100
Carrot, 81, 90
Cassia, 160
Cast Iron Plant, 111, 118
Cat's Claw Vine, 221
Cat's Whiskers, 138
Cattleya, 198
Cattley Guava, 70
Cauliflower, 90
Celery, 90
Celosia, 23, 32, 34
Centipede Grass, 101
Century Plant, 127
Chalky Bluestem, 119
Chaste Tree, 160
Chenille Plant, 148
Cherry Laurel, 186
Chervil, 88
Chickasaw Plum, 186
Chinese Cabbage, 90
Chinese Elm, 186
Chinese Evergreen, 198
Chinese Fan, 185
Chinese Fan Palm, 174
Chinese Fringe Bush, 148
Chinese Pistache, 186
Chives, 82, 88
Cinnamon Fern, 129
Citrus, 58–61
Clematis, 216
Cleome, 32, 34
Cleyera, Japanese, 160
Clover, 101
Cocculus, 160
Coconut Palm, 63, 70
Cocoplum, 148, 160
Coleus, 23, 32, 34
Collards, 90
Coneflower, 128, 138
Confederate Jasmine, 118, 216, 221
Coontie, 118, 149
Copperleaf, 199
Coral Honeysuckle, 217
Coral Vine, 221
Coreopsis, 128, 138
Coriander, 88
Corn, 82, 91
Cosmos, 24, 32, 34
Costus, 50
Crape Myrtle, 160, 174, 186

Creeping Fig, 111, 118
Crinum, 50
Crinum Lily, 45
Crocosmia, 50
Crossandra, 138
Croton, 199
Crown of Thorns, 199
Cucumber, 82, 91
Cumin, 88
Cut-Leaf Philodendron, 200

D

Dahlberg Daisy, 32, 34
Dahlia, 50
Dahoon Holly, 186
Dancinglady Orchid, 200
Date, 185
Daylily, 45, 50, 118
Delphinium, 32, 34
Dendrobium, 200
Dianthus, 32, 34
Dichondra, 118
Dill, 83, 88
Dogwood, 175, 186
Dracaena, 201
Dusty Miller, 24, 32, 34
Dutchman's Pipe, 217, 221
Dwarf Gardenia, 118
Dwarf Palmetto, 185

E

Eggplant, 83, 91
Elephant Ear, 50, 201
Elliott Lovegrass, 119
Endive/Escarole, 90
European Fan, 185

F

Fakahatchee Grass, 112, 119
False Dragon Head, 138
Fatsia, 160
Feijoa, 70, 160
Fennel, 88
Ferns, 129–130
Fig, 64, 70, 201
Firebush, 149, 160
Firecracker Plant, 131, 149, 160
Firespike, 131, 138
Flame Vine, 217, 221
Florida Gammagrass, 119
Florida Privet, 150, 160
Florida Silver, 185
Florida Silver Palm, 175
Florida Yew, 160

Fogfruit, 112, 118
Fortune's Mahonia, 161
Fountain Grass, 119
Four O'Clock, 131, 138
Foxglove, 32, 34
Freedom Lawn, 101
Fringe Tree, 186

G

Gardenia, 150, 161
Garlic, 88
Garlic Vine, 218, 221
Gaura, 138
Gazania, 32, 34
Geiger Tree, 175, 186
Geranium, 24, 32, 34
Gerbera Daisy, 132, 138
Giant Plumegrass, 119
Ginger, 50, 88, 202
Ginger Lily, 50
Gladiolus, 46, 50
Globe Amaranth, 25, 32, 34
Gloriosa Lily, 46, 50
Goldenrod, 132, 138
Golden Shower Tree, 186
Grape, 64, 70
Grapefruit, 58, 60
Great Dame, 119
Gru-Gru, 185
Gumbo-Limbo, 176

H

Heliconia, 50, 139, 202
Hibiscus, 151, 161
Holly, 161, 176
Holly Fern, 118
Hollyhock, 25, 32, 34
Holly Malpighia, 161
Horehound, 88
Hosta, 132, 139
Hurricane Lily, 46, 50
Hydrangea, 152, 161

I

Impatiens, 25, 32, 34
Indian Hawthorn, 152, 161
Italian Cypress, 186
Ivy, Algerian, 118
Ixora, 152, 161

J

Jaboticaba, 64, 70
Jacaranda, 186
Jackfruit, 65, 70

Jacobinia, 139
Jade Vine, 218
Jamaica Thatch, 185
Japanese Aralia, 153
Japanese Boxwood, 161
Japanese Clematis, 221
Jasmine, Arabian, 161
Jasmine, Downy, 161
Jasmine, Primrose, 161
Jasmine, Shining, 161
Jerusalem Thorn, 186
Johnny-Jump-Up, 32, 34
Juniper, Chinese, 118, 161
Juniper, Shore, 118, 161
Juniper, Spreading, 161

K

Kaffir Lily, 47, 50
Kale, 90
King's Mantle, 161
Kohlrabi, 90
Kumquat, 58

L

Lady, 185
Lady-of-the-Night, 153
Lady Palm, 176
Lantana, 118, 139
Lapeirousia, 50
Laurel-Leaf Snailseed, 153
Laurel Oak, 186
Leather Fern, 130
Leatherleaf Fern, 118
Lemon, 58, 61
Lemon Balm, 88
Lettuce, 83, 90
Licuala, 185
Lignum Vitae, 177, 186
Lily, 50
Lilyturf, 112, 118
Lime, 58, 61
Lion's Ear, 139
Live Oak, 177, 186
Lobelia, 26, 32, 35
Loblolly Bay, 186
Longan, 70
Lopsided Indian Grass, 113, 119
Loquat, 65, 186
Loropetalum, 161
Louisiana Iris, 47, 51
Lovage, 88
Lychee, 65, 70

M

Macadamia, 66, 70
MacArthur, 185
Mahogany, 177, 186
Malayan Dwarf Coconut, 185
Mamey Sapote, 70
Mandevilla, 218, 221
Mango, 66, 71
Maple-Leaved Viburnum, 159
Marigold, 26, 32, 35
Marjoram, 88
Melampodium, 32, 35
Mexican Flame Vine, 221
Mexican Heather, 113, 139
Mexican Sunflower, 26, 32, 35
Mexican Washingtonia, 185
Milkweed, 133, 138
Mint, 84, 88
Miracle Fruit, 71
Mondo Grass, 113, 118
Monstera, 71, 221
Moraea, 51
Moss Rose, 33, 35
Moth Orchid, 202
Muhly Grass, 114, 119
Mussaenda, 203
Mustard Greens, 90

N

Narcissus, 51
Nasturtium, 33, 35, 88
Natal Plum, 154, 161
Necklace Pod, 154
Nectarine, 67, 71
Needle, 185
Nicotiana, 27, 33, 35
Nierembergia, 33, 35
Night-Blooming Cereus, 203
Night-Blooming Jessamine, 154

O

Oakleaf Hydrangea, 155
Okra, 84, 91
Oleander, 155, 161
Onion, 84, 90
Orange, 58, 60
Orange Jessamine, 161
Oregano, 85, 88
Ornamental Kale, 33, 35
Ornamental Pepper, 27, 33, 35
Ornamental Sweet Potato, 114, 221

P

Painted Trumpet, 219, 221
Pampas Grass, 115, 119
Pansy, 27, 33, 35
Papaya, 66, 71
Parsley, 90
Passion Flower, 221
Passion Fruit, 71
Passion Vine, 219
Paurotis, 185
Peace Lily, 203
Peach, 67, 71
Peacock Plant, 204
Peanut, 91
Pear, 71
Peas, 90, 91
Pecan, 67, 71
Pentas, 133, 139
Peperomia, 204
Pepper, 27, 33, 35, 85, 91
Periwinkle, 33, 35, 133
Persian Shield, 204
Persimmon, 67, 71
Peruvian Lily, 47
Petunia, 28, 33, 35
Philippine Violet, 139
Philodendron, 161, 219
Phlox (Annual), 33, 35
Pigeon Plum, 178, 186
Pindo Palm, 178
Pine, 178, 186
Pineapple, 68, 71
Pineapple Lily, 51
Pineland Dropseed, 119
Pinks, 28
Pittosporum, 155, 161
Plum, 68, 71
Plumbago, 134, 156, 162
Plumeria, 179, 186
Podocarpus, 156, 162
Poinsettia, 134, 139
Pomegranate, 68, 71
Ponytail Palm, 205
Portulaca, 28
Potato, 90
Potato, Sweet, 85, 91
Powder Puff, 162
Prickly Pear, 71
Pride of Burma, 51
Puerto Rico Hat, 185
Pumpkin, 91
Purple Lovegrass, 115, 119
Purslane, 33, 35
Pygmy Date, 185
Pygmy Date Palm, 179

Pyracantha, 162

Q

Queen's Crape Myrtle, 187
Queen's Wreath, 220, 221

R

Radishes, 90
Rain Lily, 48, 51
Rangoon Creeper, 220, 221
Redberry Stopper, 180
Redbud, 180, 187
Redcedar, 180, 187
Red Maple, 179, 187
Red-tip Photinia, 162
Reeves Spirea, 162
Rhubarb, 90
River Birch, 187
Rosemary, 86, 88
Rose of Sharon, 162
Roses, 157
Royal Fern, 130
Royal Palm, 181, 185
Royal Poinciana, 181, 187
Ruellia, 139
Ruffled Fan Palm, 181
Ryegrass, 102

S

Sage, 88
Salvia, 29, 139
Sand Cordgrass, 116, 119
Sapodilla, 71
Satinleaf, 182
Saucer Magnolia, 187
Savory, 88
Saw Palmetto, 158, 162, 185
Scarlet Sage, 33, 35
Sea Grape, 71, 158, 187
Seashore Paspalum, 102
Senegal Date, 185
Serissa, 162
Shasta Daisy, 134, 139
Shell Ginger, 51
Shore Juniper, 116
Short-spike Bluestem, 119
Showy Combretum, 221
Shrimp Plant, 139, 205
Shumard Oak, 187
Silk Flower, 33, 35
Silver Buttonwood, 187
Silverthorn, 162
Simpson Stopper, 162
Snapdragon, 29, 33, 35

Snowbush, 162
Snowflake, 48, 51
Society Garlic, 48, 51
Solitaire, 185
Southern Arrowwood, 159
Southern Juniper, 187
Southern Magnolia, 182, 187
Spanish Bayonet, 135
Spider Lily, 49, 51
Spinach, 86, 90
Spiral Ginger, 206
Spring-summer, 118
Squash, 86, 91
Staghorn Fern, 206
Star Apple, 71
Star Fruit, 69
St. Augustine Grass, 103
Stock, 33, 35
Stokes' Aster, 135, 139
Strawberry, 69, 90
Strawflower, 33, 35
Sugar Apple, 71
Sugarberry, 187
Sunflower, 29, 33, 35
Sunshine Mimosa, 117, 118
Surinam Cherry, 71
Sweet Acacia, 187
Sweetbay Magnolia, 182, 187
Sweet Gum, 183, 187
Sweet Osmanthus, 162
Sweet Pea, 33, 35
Swiss Chard, 90
Sword Ferns, 130
Sycamore, 187

T

Tamarind, 69, 71
Tangerine, 58
Tarragon, 88
Texas Sage, 162
Texas Wild Olive, 183
Thryallis, 158, 162
Thyme, 87, 88
Tibouchina, 162
Tiger Flower, 51
Ti Plant, 162, 207
Tomato, 87, 91
Torenia, 30, 33, 35
Traveler's Tree, 207
Tritonia, 51
Tropical Sage, 30
Trumpet Creeper, 220, 221
Trumpet Honeysuckle, 221
Trumpet Tree, 184, 187
Tuberose, 51

Tuberous Begonia, 51
Tuliptree, 187
Turnip, 90

V

Variegated Flax Lily, 136
Verbena, 31, 33, 35
Veronica, 136, 139
Viburnum, 159, 162
Violet, 139
Voodoo Lily, 51

W

Walking Iris, 49, 51
Walter's Viburnum, 159
Wampee, 71
Watercress, 88
Watermelon, 87, 91
Water Oak, 187
Watsonia, 51
Wax Myrtle, 159, 162, 187
Weeping Fig, 187
White Sapote, 71
Wild Coffee, 159
Wild Petunia, 137
Windmill, 185
Winged Elm, 184, 187
Wiregrass, 117, 119

Y

Yarrow, 137, 139
Yaupon Holly, 187
Yellow Alder, 139
Yellow Jessamine, 221
Yellow Poinciana, 187
Yew Podocarpus, 187

Z

Zinnia, 31, 33, 35
Zoysia Grass, 103